Nation-building and Identity Conflicts

Ariel Hernandez

Nation-building and Identity Conflicts

Facilitating the Mediation Process in Southern Philippines

Springer VS

Ariel Hernandez
Leipzig, Germany

ISBN 978-3-658-05214-0 ISBN 978-3-658-05215-7 (eBook)
DOI 10.1007/978-3-658-05215-7

The Deutsche Nationalbibliothek lists this publication in the Deutsche Nationalbibliografie; detailed bibliographic data are available in the Internet at http://dnb.d-nb.de.

Library of Congress Control Number: 2014933050

Springer VS

Printed on acid-free paper

Springer VS is a brand of Springer DE.
Springer DE is part of Springer Science+Business Media.
www.springer-vs.de

For my late father Angel Hernandez Penetrante.
Nasaan ka man ngayon, alam kong ako ay iyong ginagabayan sa aking pakikipagsapalaran.

Table of Contents

List of Acronyms and Abbreviations

ADB	Asian Development Bank
AFF	Arab Foundations Forum
AFP	Armed Forces of the Philippines
AIM	Asian Institute of Management
ARMM	Autonomous Region of Muslim Mindanao
ASEAN	Association of Southeast Asian Nations
ASG	Abu Sayaff Group
BATNA	Best Alternative to Negotiated Agreement
BDM	Barangay (Village) Defense Mechanism
CA	Consultative Assembly
CAFGU	Citizens Armed Forces Geographical Unit
CAR	Cordillera Autonomous Region (now: Cordillera Administrative Region)
CBA	Cordillera Bodong Administration
CCP	Communist Party of the Philippines
COHA	Cessation of Hostilities Agreement
CONCORD	Constitutional Correction for Development
CPC	Civilian Protection Component
CPLA	Cordillera People's Liberation Army
EDSA	Epifanio De Los Santos Avenue
EU	European Union
FPA	1996 Final Peace Agreement
GRP	Government of the Republic of the Philippines
HDC	Centre for Humanitarian Dialogue
HDN	Human Development Network
HUKBALAHAP	Hukbo ng Bayan Laban sa mga Hapon (People's Army Against the Japanese)
ICG	International Contact Group
ICM	International Civilian Monitor
IDB	Islamic Development Bank
IDMC	International Displacement Monitoring Center
IMT	International Monitoring Team
INGO	International Non-Governmental Organization
IPCC	Intergovernmental Panel on Climate Change
JSC	Joint Security Committee
KBMK	Joint Committee on Security Modalities
LGU	Local Government Units

MEO	Mutually Enticing Opportunity
MHS	Mutually Hurting Stalemate
MILF	Moro Islamic Liberation Front
MNLF	Moro National Liberation Front
MOA-AD	Memorandum of Agreement – Ancestral Domains
MoU	Memorandum of Understanding
MP-GAM	Free Aceh Movement Council
NATO	North Atlantic Treaty Organization
NCR	National Capital Region
NGOs	Non-Government Organizations
NICC	National Islamic Command Council
NUJP	National Union of Journalists of the Philippines
OIC	Organisation of Islamic Conference
PAGs	Partisan Armed Groups
PNP	Philippine National Police
PNSO	Philippine National Statistics Office
RBAF	Royal Brunei Armed Forces
SEC	Securities and Exchange Commission
SZOPAD	Special Zone of Peace and Development in the Southern Philippines
SPCPD	Southern Philippines Council for Peace and Development
UN	United Nations
UP	University of the Philippines
ZOPA	Zone of Possible Agreement

Preface

Asking why this book was written inevitably touches upon my life experience. Everything started when I was a child and it ends with the aspirations I have for a country that I left more than a decade ago. Very often I ask myself why I accepted such as huge challenge. Why should I look behind when looking forward promises more fulfillment? But I feel that there is no way I can move forward when one question remains unanswered - the question of "why".

This book seeks to answer a question I formulated when I was made to witness how human lives can be so cheap to certain people on the other side of the divide. This book does not seek to allocate blame, nor does it offer absolution for things that went wrong in the past. Ultimately, it is not the political that is at fault, but an incapacity of breaking the chain of violence. It is not our religion or ethnicity that brings pain, destruction, and anguish, but bigotry and a lack of compassion. It is violence that destroys the future of a whole nation.

My search started the night it was proven in front of an eight-year old boy that humans can be blinded by hatred and by narratives without thinking beyond what is told to them. Questions led to a yearning for knowledge and as the child grew up, he was no longer satisfied by simply posing questions. Now, he wants answers. This book originated from my PhD studies at the University of Vienna, under the supervision of Prof. Hannelore Kreisky and Prof. Ottmar Höll. At the beginning of my studies, it was highly contentious as to whether it was actually possible for someone in my position to write scientific or academic papers on issues that have personally affected me. My personal attachment to the issues may undermine my objectivity as a researcher. However, I believe that it isn't impossible to write on issues of violence and agony without becoming emotionally affected, regardless of personal involvement. As such, my personal attachment may provide additional insights and aid comprehension of the problem and its context.

Throughout my PhD studies, I had the privilege of meeting other scholars and peace activists who, like me, were looking for ways to end violence in the Philippines. Surprisingly, although the academic landscape in the country is not always conducive to rigorous discourse, dialogues among researchers still take place, although there are several lost opportunities that could have been exploited if the environment for researchers was different. In the later stages of my PhD studies, while being part of the Processes of International Negotiations (PIN) Program (now housed in Clingendael, the Hague) I was frequently invited into discussions with government negotiation panel members, and to suggest how impasses could be broken. The former head of the government negotiation panel, Undersecretary Rafael Seguis, was aware of how easily the negotiation process experiences impasses due to minor issues. Our personal talks influenced the focus of my research project by identifying various stumbling blocks that make the negotiation process intractable. This is the main purpose of this project. Looking from a negotiation (systems) analytical perspective, complemented by rudiments of the Viennese Critical School, I have looked for existing approaches that could be re-developed to support measures in the peace negotiation process. For example, it was highly inspiring the use the thoughts of Hannah Arendt, Otto Bauer and Karl Renner to understand the nation-building process in the Philippines.

Although the peace process seems a volatile one, several breakthroughs have been achieved. This gives me cause for optimism. Nevertheless, the biggest challenge for the peace process in the Philippines is how to prevent the indifference of Philippine society to the mediation process, and their resignation to the inevitability of violence. This project aims to make each Filipino understand that the Philippine nation can only be as strong as its weakest member.

1 Introduction – Closing the Unfinished Business

"*In hell there is no other punishment than to begin over and over again the tasks left unfinished in your lifetime.*" (Andre Gide, quoted in Think Exist 2010)

Cases of violent internal conflicts based on contestation are confronted by the intractability of achieving closure. In identity conflicts, 'closure' refers to effectively establishing structural arrangements of social interactions that empower parties to cope with their differences. Closing negotiations represents a research area less explored in the academic community, as closure is perceived as self-evident and self-imposing. A negotiation process that is legitimate and that involves conflicting parties with a genuine interest in resolving conflicts is seen as self-evidently and self-imposingly leading to a closure (see Dupont & Faure 2002; Kremenyuk 2002; Alfredson & Cungu 2008). However, agreements resulting from the negotiation process may eventually collapse, because new sets of conditions are required by closure, many of which have not been adequately confronted in the negotiation process.

Agreements, no matter how comprehensive, are still vulnerable to failure because of changing conditions. When an agreement has been reached, new dynamics will surface due to new sets of expectations or new power configurations directly or indirectly resulting from the implementation of this agreement. These require adaptation and acceptance on the part of both negotiation parties.

The primary goal of this project is to *identify and assess the reasons for the intractability of identity conflicts as indicated not by the difficulties in reaching agreements but rather by the difficulties in maintaining and implementing agreements and closing the whole negotiation process.* Agreements are achieved after several negotiation rounds by conflicting parties, both with and without the assistance of third-party mediation. Agreements are supported by various other agreements and will intentionally or unintentionally promote or inhibit future agreements. In several cases, agreements to resolve identity conflicts may eventually collapse due to coincidental events that cannot be fully anticipated. In other cases, the signed agreement may actually lead to large-scale warfare or violent confrontation within a group, for example when subgroups or factions of a particular negotiating group refuse to accept the agreement. In various cases, agreements may fail to achieve the ultimate goal of the peace process – reconciliation, multilateral prosperity and human well-being. With such complexity of consensus-building surrounding this process, how are agreements to be related to the closure of negotiations?

1.1 Mediation and Negotiation – Bridge or Drift?

Mediations and negotiations as conflict-management measures are usually considered to be complete once agreements (as output) have been reached. 'Closure' simply means signing an agreement. However, conflicts involving identity contestations are frequently conducive to a seemingly infinite number of unfinished issues. There are several cases where mediation has led to an agreement which has subsequently collapsed in the following few years, or has failed to bring sustainable peace and grass-root reconciliation, the ultimate goal of the peace process.

This project argues that the focus of attention should not be given only to a single agreement, but also to the impact of this single agreement on the whole peace process. Closing agreements are to be defined through a long-term process outlook. Mediation and negotiation are procedures chosen to forward the peace process. The 'transformative approach' to mediation does not seek resolution of the immediate problem but rather seeks the empowerment and mutual recognition of the conflict parties involved (Bush & Folger 1994). 'Mediation', that is, negotiation involving at least one third-party, enables the parties to define their own issues and to seek independent solutions. 'Mediation' also refers to any instrument used to reach a consensual decision. This approach passes all responsibilities (and accountability) to the conflict parties. Despite the advantages of mediation, why are conflicting parties in many cases still unable to find solutions for their problems during negotiation? It is worth exploring whether the negotiation process itself has become the problem.

For the purpose of analyzing the impact of mediation on the whole negotiation process, a working definition of 'mediation' is provided by this project:

> *Mediation is a process of conflict management that involves the strategic facilitation of contestation through acceptable actors or structures, transforming contestation into a legitimate phenomenon.*

Part 4 of this book project deals with mediation as the chosen method of intervention to resolve identity conflicts. After answering the question of whether identity conflicts such as that in the Southern Philippines are amenable to mediation through the comprehensive conceptualization of identity conflicts (see chapters 5 and 6), this project intends to analyze mediation and negotiation, and how these very processes sometimes paradoxically contribute to the intractability of identity conflicts (see chapter 8). Mediation and negotiation are often considered to be the "end" of intervention efforts, diverting the negotiators' attention from the real issues to the "side-effects." For example, conflicting parties may find it difficult to decide where the next talks should occur, and who should be represented on the negotiating panel. Mediators may unintentionally reproduce existing conflictual paradigms during negotiation, further aggravating the intractability of the conflict. The complexity of identity conflicts may be further exacerbated by the complexity of negotiation configurations. Therefore, a critical analysis of mediation is an important aspect of this project, leading to the identification and conceptualization of negotiation-related stumbling blocks (see chapter 9). Finally, methods of coping with these stumbling blocks are suggested by the concept of strategic facilitation (see chapter 10).

1.2 Intractability of Identity Conflicts – Dealing with Slippery Agreements in the Philippines

Understanding how a single agreement refers to the peace process (see chapter 8) implies that an agreement should not be the final intended outcome of a negotiation process, but rather the departure point for future social interactions with the aim of detering violence in all its forms. Differences and mistrust between groups will not be completely eliminated with the signing of an agreement. Instead, agreements manage group relations and allow at least an opportunity for peaceful coexistence. The agreement serves as the minimum expression of trust that determines the path of peaceful social relations. The agreement should therefore be seen as part of a long-term process. Agreements are forward-looking. They codify the decisions of the conflicting parties to regulate future relations when the status quo is no longer viable. Guarantees included in agreements intend to promote the principles of empowerment and mutual recognition that will sustainably resolve identity contestations.

Because the effects of an agreement are not measurable in the short-term, and it is almost impossible to determine whether a specific agreement is solely responsible for a specific impact, agreements are embedded in a complex, multidimensional and uncertain system of causes and effects. Some agreements may for example enhance or inhibit the favoring conditions for subsequent agreements. Furthermore, while some negotiation rounds may fail to produce an agreement, this failure does not always mean the breakdown of the whole peace process, as it may have established norms and valuable consensual knowledge to facilitate future talks. This implies that the negotiation process is a non-linear process.

An 'agreement' is an output of negotiation. This project uses the following working definition of an agreement:

> *An agreement is a formal or informal statement (oral, written or merely assumed) of an exchange of declared intentions that directly or indirectly result from a process of a cooperative and interdependent relationship-building following a specific course of conduct.*

No agreement stands alone. A single agreement is part of a complex web or puzzle with each agreement contributing a specific function. Moreover, as it is a part of a long-term process, its value can only be identified in the long-term. Agreements are complemented by other agreements to ensure implementation. The horizontal and vertical inter-linkages of agreements define the dynamic flow of the peace process. Hence, an analysis of agreements – and how they fulfill a specific function - may contribute important knowledge on how to deal with the complexity of the negotiation process. For example, a specific agreement may resolve a particular issue, but at the same time, it may be detrimental to other issues depending on the provisions of the initial agreement. Using the same logic, a positive outcome of the peace process is not retraceable to a single agreement.

Prior to the escalation of violence in Southern Philippines in 2000/2001 and 2008/2009, the 1996 Final Peace Agreement (FPA) between the Government of the Philippines (GRP) and the Moro National Liberation Front (MNLF) was signed through the mediation of the Committee of Four (headed by Libya) and the Committee of Six (headed by Indonesia) of the Organization of the Islamic Conference (OIC). The 1996 FPA was paradoxically followed by series of both sporadic and large-scale outbursts of violence after a break-away fraction, the Moro Islamic Liberation Front (MILF), continued the armed insurgency.

In 2001, the Memorandum on the Cessation of Violence was reached between the GRP and the MILF paving the way for further negotiations. However, it only survived seven years before the Supreme Court declared that the Malaysian-mediated 2008 Memorandum of Agreement on Ancestral Domains (MOA-AD) was unconstitutional, leading to some "rogue" MILF elements to attack Christian villages in Mindanao. These attacks spurred a new period of escalated violence when the Philippine military retaliated. The large-scale outburst of violence prompted the withdrawal of Malaysian-led International Monitoring Team (IMT), which was increasingly disappointed with the slow peace process. The formal GRP-

MILF negotiations that resumed in October 2012 have led to the signing of a preliminary peace agreement called the "Framework Agreement on the Bangsamoro (2012)", which calls for the replacement of the "failed" ARMM (Calonzo 2012).

The MILF refused to accept the provisions of the 1976 and the 1996 agreements, and a break-away faction - the MNLF - reverted to violence. The Autonomous Region of Muslim Mindanao (ARMM) government proved to be inefficient and too corrupt to govern, prompting some stakeholders to question the 1996 Final Peace Agreement, wrongfully blaming it for the ineffectiveness of the autonomous government of the ARMM. No agreement can guarantee good governance. As a process, good governance requires new norms that need to shift the structures of an armed struggle to structures of consensus-building.

Furthermore, in 2001 the MNLF founding chairman Professor Nur Misuari and his supporters reverted to violence following the loss of his leadership of the MNLF and of his governorship of the autonomous government. On September 9, 2013, Nur Misuari launched another series of attacks in several coastal villages in Zamboanga city leading to many fatalities, the hostage-taking of more than 200 civilians and the displacement of 67,000 residents. The city was paralysed for weeks (PDI 2013), and all this could have been averted if the new leadership did not ascribe the "personified politics" typical of the political landscape of the whole of the Philippines.

The Bangsamoro conflict seems to be continuously trapped in a complex web of dilemmas, with minor setbacks quickly leading to the collapse of the negotiation process and the delay of the peace process in general. The agreements seem to have failed to bring sustainable peace, reconciliation and economic development. After more than 18 years after the 1996 Final Peace Agreement (and 38 years after the 1976 Tripoli Agreement), the armed conflict still remains. The Bangsamoro conflict seems not only to be an "endless war" (Noble 1976), but also a conflict with "no face" as it has become a conflict about "everything". Currently, the armed insurgency of the Muslim population is defined through terrorism, political warlordship, private armies and private security, clan wars (*rido*) (see Torres 2007), proliferation of small arms and light weapons (see Greene & Penetrante 2011), organized crime and environmental deterioration.

1.3 Identity Violence in the Philippines – Between Misrecognition and Nation-building

Answering the question of whether the conflict in Mindanao is an ethnic conflict or a religious conflict remains a contested issue in academic research. This project argues that before intervention measures such as mediation can be analyzed, it is necessary to conceptualize the conflict involved, no matter how complex it is. The lack of vibrant, critical and comprehensive academic discourse about the nature of the conflict in Mindanao has led to misleading policies in the past.

Another aim of this project is to support the call of Kit Collier (2004) for a more contextualized theorization of the conflict in Southern Philippines (see chapters two and five). There is a need to re-evaluate current academic discourse on the conflict in the Southern Philippines. According to Collier, primordialist accounts dominate the understanding of ethnic conflicts, particularly of the "four-century old history of Muslim-Christian hostility" in the archipelago (see Tan 1977; George 1980; Aijiz 1982; Bauzon 1991; Gomez 2000), which lacks explanatory leverage in several crucial respects, leading to misleading assumptions and gaps in policy-making. For example, the popular notion that the hostilities in Mindanao are "Moro wars" frames the conflict as a zero-sum condition where the other groups are perceived to be the problem. This idea that "*the Moro problem can only be solved when Moros disappear*" conditions the mind-set of Filipinos. Furthermore, George (1980) sees the conflict as "fundamentally religious in character". However, he ignores the socio-economic dimensions of the conflict. Primordialist approaches, which tend to view the social bonds of religion, blood, race, language and custom as "given", "overpowering" and "ineffable" (see Hutchinson & Smith 1996) have dominated the discourse of the conflict in the Philippines.

Another popularly accepted belief is that the conflict in Mindanao refers to an ethnic conflict. This misleading understanding attempts to apply "Western" understanding of ethnicity to an analysis of the conflict in the Philippines. The Filipinos do not totally assume the primordialist concept of ethnicity. Ethnicity in the Philippines is based not on birth but on "life experiences" such as language, socialization and consciousness. The main criterion of ethnicity in the Philippines is language. Language is assumed after birth, and membership is rather fluid as a result. Ethnicity in this country is not a 'backward-looking phenomenon', which means that the ethnicity of the parents is not necessarily reproduced by the children if these children grew up in a different area, for example in the Tagalog-area. Ethnicity is connoted by the dialectic of center-periphery (or urban-rural) where it does not really matter which ethnicity one belongs to. The significant criterion for misrecognition is that they are from the "province." The main identifying factor for being a "promdi" (from the province) is the "accent" with its implied "inferior" socialization of backwardness (see Montalvan 2010). The accent is given a social meaning and determines perceived inferiority. The Bangsamoro conflict is just one of the manifestations of the center-periphery notion of superiority and inferiority in social relations. It is not the traditional features of ethnicity that causes misrecognition, but the perception that one is inferior.

McKenna (1998) and Abinales (2000) share the view that the Bangsamoro identity project lies in more recent patterns of state construction and transformation. This paper argues that conflict hides behind the subordination processes that groups experience in the "society at large", which were inherited from the colonial past. Primordial ties and kinship connections are indeed given; however, these attributes will not always lead to conflict. If the attributes of one group are not interpreted as inferior by the other, if claims for participation are not denied, and if mechanisms of cooperation are not missing, armed conflict is not likely to emerge.

Although religion plays a significant role in the mobilization of the Bangsamoro in its claim for self-determination, the conflict in Mindanao is not a religious conflict. Religion falls short of explaining political loyalty. It is an identity conflict that involves social domination (see chapters two and five). Religion is part of the identity of the Muslims; however, their identity is not solely determined by religion. Although religion has united the thirteen Muslim ethno-linguistic groups in Mindanao, the reference to the so-called "Bangsamoro" (the Muslim People) identity group does not encompass all domains of the loyalty of the members. Many Muslims identify themselves with the Bangsamoro to for protection, but in terms of trade or cultural affiliations the members of the Bangsamoro prefer to remain loyal to their ethno-linguistic groups (e.g., Maguindanaoan, Maranao, Tausug, etc.).

The Bangsamoro is not a homogeneous group because it does not encompass all domains of Muslim life. The conflict in Mindanao is about identity. It is about the identity of a marginalized group that resists the state policies and structures that prevent them from participating as social peers (Fraser 2003). The main function of Bangsamoro identity is to provide Muslims a platform through which they can express grievances and resist violence and other forms of misrecognition. Identity is therefore defined by its purpose. The armed resistance of the Bangsamoro aims to achieve a new social contract. The resistance is about adjusting or even finding a replacement to the normative order that was inherited by the hegemonic national group from the colonial past.

The relations between power and violence determine the concept of identity conflicts. The use of violence as a manifestation of power refers to the instruments chosen by the "hegemonic" national group to maintain power, legitimacy and authority. Chapter two discusses the elusive concept of identity conflict, and aims to describe and understand how conflict arises and how it relates to identity.

Misrecognition through state policies summarizes how violent subordination through the hegemon (see chapter five) becomes inherently connected to nation- and state-building. Chapter five aims to analyze how the nationalistic terms of state-building legitimize the use of violence towards minority groups. The connection between violence and nation-building leans on the notions of Hannah Arendt (2009b; 2009a) and Charles Tilly (Tilly 1985; Tilly 1990), who suggest that nation-building tends to legitimize violence (see chapter 6). If this is the case, then there is a need to find ways to shift paradigms on how the state is assessed. The features of nation-building that initiate and maintains violence should be identified and re-framed. Nation-building does not need to be violent. As nation-building occurs only in the minds it can be manipulated.

Furthermore, chapter three offers a more systematic study of the nation as the subject of scientific studies by introducing the "four streams" of the study of the nation:

1) Historicity and subjectivity/normativity
2) Historicity and objectivitiy/Methodism
3) Non-historicity and subjectivity/normativity
4) Non-historicity and objectivity/Methodism

The four different streams involve variations on how nationhood is understood in academic literature. All streams share a common denominator: that nations derive their meaning from social contexts. The understanding that there could be different perspectives of what a nation is motivates a conceptualization of nationhood that does not necessary initiate and maintain violence. A "non-Arendt" or a "non-Tilly" notion of nationhood should be found to enrich the current discourse on nationhood and nation-building. The concept of "non-competitive nation-building" (see chapter six) preconditions the identification of the features of nation-building that promote violence. Afterwards, strategies can be found to enable paradigm shifts. A shift in paradigms offers a change of worldview, or at least a change in how this worldview is framed when the use of violence becomes obsolete or too costly.

1.4 Stumbling Blocks and Strategic Facilitation – Assessing the Negotiation Process

'Stumbling blocks' refer to the complexities of the negotiation process that promote intractability in resolving identity conflicts. These are factors that contribute to the intractability of the conflict by negatively influencing the flow of the negotiation process. Stumbling blocks may either delay the achievement of an agreement, reduce the quality of outcomes or prevent the implementation of the negotiation outputs. By introducing the taxonomy (actor, issues, structures, processes and outcomes) of how stumbling blocks can be systematically categorized, a comprehensive evaluation of how negotiations are to be related to the whole peace process is possible.

The critical and systematic analysis of stumbling blocks enables the drawing of lessons from negotiations. The inherent implication of the identification of stumbling blocks is the formulation of prescriptions on how to cope with such impediments to strategically facilitate the negotiation process. Strategic facilitation involves the introduction of additional measures to cope with stumbling blocks. It therefore involves the strategic manipulation of the negotiation process by using strategies to turn the flow of the process in a more desirable direction. The following table offers a glimpse of the stumbling blocks identified, and the prescriptions suggested in this project:

Table 1.1: Strategic Facilitation of Stumbling Blocks

	Stumbling Blocks	Prescriptions (Strategic Facilitation)
Actors	Diversity of actors, professional cultures and communication skills; lack of information and lack of institutional memory; spoilers and negotiators for "side-effects"	Problem-solving by separating persons (relationships from problems); management of professional cultures and group cohesion in negotiation; capacity-building; dealing with spoilers by identifying structural weaknesses; dealing with "side-effects" and hardliners through engagement
Issues	Problem of ranges; horizontal and vertical linkages of issues; low-politics vs. high-politics; the zero-sum trap	Knowledge management; sequential agreements and amendment procedures to ensure flexibility
Structure	Power structures and asymmetries; lack of information and immeasurability of stakes; constituency accountability; multi-party setting	Integrative bargaining; dealing with constituency gaps through public spheres
Processes	Time-frame paradox; sectoral arrangements	Process management
Outcomes	Varying expectations; the "outcome-is-not-enough" dilemma	Expectation management; dealing with insufficient outcomes through evaluation and selection of alternatives

1.5 Research Objectives and Contributions

The ultimate objective of this project is to assist negotiators and mediators in order to ensure that the agreements they achieve may actually resolve the conflict and ultimately endure. This project is ambitious in its attempt to provide a comprehensive study of the conflict in Southern Philippines. This study involves the theorization of the conflict in Mindanao, and intends to initiate a theoretical discourse in the Philippines less limited in its scope and meaning than that which is presently dominant. The academic landscape in the Philippines lacks a vibrant "local discourse." A discourse may find new approaches for looking at the nature of the conflict which enables thecreation of new sets of alternative intervention measures to resolve the conflict. The armed conflict between the government and the Muslim insurgent groups started more than 40 years ago. Since then, attempts were made to resolve the conflict, however all agreements have collapsed, failing to bring peace and human well-being. Therefore, there may be something not only in the conflict, but in the negotiation procedure itself that prolongs the conflict. This project claims to have found at least one of the reasons for the intractability of the conflict in the Philippines: the negotiation process itself through the complexity of its configuration and the uncertainties of its outcomes.

References:

Abinales, P., 2000. Making Mindanao: Cotobato and Davao in the Formation of the Philippine Nation-State, Quezon City, Philippines: Ateneo de Manila Press.

Aijiz, A., 1982. Four Hundred Year War: Moro Struggle in the Philippines. Southeast Asia Chronicle, 82, pp.1–28.

Alfredson, T. & Cungu, A., 2008. Negotiation theory and practice. A review of the literature., Rome: Food and Agriculture Organization of the United Nations. Available at: http://www.fao.org/docs/up/easypol/550/45_negotiation_background_paper_179en.pdf.

Arendt, H., 2009a. Elemente und Ursprünge totaler Herrschaft. Antisemitismus, Imperialismus, totale Herrschaft 13. Auflage., München & Zürich: Piper Taschenbuch.

Arendt, H., 2009b. Macht und Gewalt, München & Zürich: Piper Taschenbuch.

Bauzon, K., 1991. Liberalism and the Quest for Islamic Identity in the Philippines, Durham, NC: Acorn Press.

Bush, R.A.B. & Folger, J., 1994. The Promise of Mediation: Responding to Conflict through Empowerment and Recognition, San Francisco, CA: Jossey-Bass Publishers.
Calonzo, A., 2012. Govt, MILF agree to create "Bangsamoro" to replace ARMM. GMA News Online. Available at: http://www.gmanetwork.com/news/story/277218/news/nation/govt-milf-agree-to-create-bangsamoro-to-replace-armm [Accessed July 31, 2013].
Collier, K., 2004. A Carnival of Crime: The Enigma of the Abu Sayaff. In 56th Annual Association for Asian Studies Conference. San Diego, CA.
Dupont, C. & Faure, G.O., 2002. The Negotiation Process. In V. Kremenyuk, ed. International Negotiation. Analysis, Approaches, Issues. San Francisco: Jossey-Bass, pp. 39–63.
Fraser, N., 2003. Rethinking Recognition: Overcoming Displacement and Reification in Cultural Politics". In B. Hobson, ed. Recognition Struggles and Social Movements. Contested Identities, Agency and Power. Cambridge: Cambridge Univeristy Press, pp. 21–34.
George, T.J.S., 1980. Revolt in Mindanao: The Rise of Islam in Philippine Politics, Kuala Lumpur: Oxford University Press.
Gomez, H., 2000. The Moro Rebellion and the Search for Peace: A Study on Christian-Muslim Relations in the Philippines, Zamboanga City: Silsilah Publications.
Greene, O. & Penetrante, A.M., 2011. Arms, Private Militias and Fragile State Dynamics. In O. Greene & N. Marsh, eds. Small Arms, Crime and Conflict. Global Governance and the Threat of Armed Violence. Berlin, Heidelberg & New York: Routledge.
Hutchinson, J. & Smith, A. eds., 1996. Ethnicity, Oxford: Oxford University Press.
Kremenyuk, V. ed., 2002. International Negotiation: Analysis, Approaches, Issues 2nd ed., San Francisco: Jossey-Bass Publishers.
McKenna, T., 1998. Muslim Rulers and Rebels: Everyday Politics and Armed Separatism in the Southern Philippines, Berkeley, CA: University of California Press.
Montalvan, A.I., 2010. The Man with the Sugbu-Anon Accent. Philippine Daily Inquirer. Available at: http://opinion.inquirer.net/inquireropinion/columns/view/20100201-250604/The-man-with-the-Sugbu-anon-accent [Accessed September 21, 2013].
Noble, L.G., 1976. The Moro National Liberation Front in the Philippines. Pacific Affairs, 49(3), pp.405–424.

PDI, 2013. Nearly 100 MNLF rebels killed or captured - officials. Philippine Daily Inquirer. Available at: http://newsinfo.inquirer.net/488043/nearly-100-mnlf-rebels-killed-or-captured [Accessed September 15, 2013].
Tan, S., 1977. The Filipino Muslim Armed Struggle, 1900-1972, Manila: Filipinas Foundation.
Tilly, C., 1990. Coercion, Capital and European States, AD 990-1990, Cambridge, MA: Blackwell.
Tilly, C., 1985. War Making and State Making as Organized Crime. In P. B. Evans, D. Rueschemeyer, & T. Skocpol, eds. Bridging the State Back In. Cambridge: Cambridge University Press, pp. 169–191.
Torres, W.M. ed., 2007. RIDO - Clan Feuding and Conflict Management in Mindanao, Makati City, Philippines: The Asia Foundation.

2 Catching the Slippery Fish – A Theorization of the Concept of Identity and Identity Conflicts

Managing identity conflicts requires the conceptualization of what identity is all about. The conceptualization of identity delivers insights into the nature of the conflict: how it is created, maintained and protracted, how conflicting actors formulate decisions and how structures determine behaviors. Relating power to violence uses identity as an analytical tool to understand social relations. This chapter briefly reviews some of the debate surrounding the elusive identity concept – the construction, nature and functionality of identity, how collective identity is determined by a group-building process and the point at which identity is translated into conflict cleavages. Such a conceptualization of identity conflict allows an analysis of thw factors that trigger the outburst of violent confrontations. Violence is not *per se* a necessary implication of identity conflicts.

A major endeavor of this research project is to contribute to the current debate in the Philippines around identity and what constitutes the "Philippine nation". The conceptualization of the "Bangsamoro identity" is inevitably a part of a larger discourse on Philippine nationhood. The dynamic construction and maintenance of Bangsamoro identity illustrates the identity-building process that is in part a reaction to the actions of the larger Filipino "society at large" in which a dominant group uses state authority mechanisms to pursue positively connoted principles such as republicanism, nationalism and centralism to maintain its dominance. These principles are translated into the subordination of deviating groups burdened with "distorted" and "inferior" identities. The construction of the identity of these deviating groups follows the maxim of establishing mechanisms of defense to a perceived threat. The Bangsamoro identity is however an identity that is emerging from an experience of violence and from its function to defend human well-being. It is an identity inextricably enmeshed in historical and contemporary struggle, and therefore it is to be explained and understood through its purpose ('utility').

Conflict researchers tend to distinguish communal (ethno-cultural) conflicts from class conflicts. Communal conflicts are about social cleavages in which parties define their conflict in cultural rather than economic terms (Hanf 1989). According to Hanf, one driver of communal conflicts is relative deprivation, where some groups see themselves as subordinated in the sense that they are prevented from having equal access to opportunities or rights, and from participating equally in social life. Another driver of communal conflicts is 'symbolic' deprivation, where a dominant group follows policies that elevate its own symbols, culture and language above others. Symbolic deprivation also encompasses the resignation of the state to protect the symbols, culture and language of minorities.

In contrast, class conflicts are about social stratification. Class conflicts refer to structural imbalances where there is the "actual or perceived inequality of control of resources, ownership or resource distribution" (Anstey 2006, p.17). As increasing wealth accumulates in the hands of a small group, their control over political, educational, public and legal institutions is consolidated, leading to social tensions. As Anstey and Zartman (2012) note, this distinction has validity, but in many instances, as the case in Southern Philippines would illustrate, they are conflated. The identity conflict in the Philippines involves both social cleavages and social stratification (see chapters five and six).

For the purpose of simplification, class conflicts will not be the focus of this research project, because the Philippines experiences a separate conflict with seventeen communist/Maoist insurgent groups for more than forty years. The communist insurgency in the country emerged at the same time as the contemporary armed Muslim insurgency is said to have been formally born. Nevertheless, the socio-economic dimension of the communal conflict will still be included in the conflict analysis, as it will be described later. Communal conflicts, like class conflicts, reflect a mechanism of playing with "identity cards" in which in- and out-groups are defined and are given meanings for mobilization purposes. Identity serves a function in power struggles between and within groups. Both conflicts involve the struggle of a weaker group against the hegemony of the stronger group.

Group identity is a multi-faceted and diffuse phenomenon, usually founded in social constructs such as territory, kinship circles, race, class, religion and language (Wiberg & Carlton 1996). Nevertheless, group identity-building processes do not always follow objective criteria to identify members. Furthermore, individuals are not clearly classified as belonging to coherent social groups, as they usually experience cross-memberships.

Identity can be conceptualized through its *utility* (Penetrante 2012). For which purpose was identity constructed? If there were no "identity", it would need to be invented. Identity is the "frame of reference" for the system that defines the motivations and actions of individuals within a collective group. In this sense, identity performs the organizational function of a guiding framework for the value system of a collective group through which sanctions and rewards for interactions are codified (*"what is right and what is wrong")* (see Penetrante 2012). Aside from being a guiding framework for actions, identity can also be regarded as an entrepreneur (seller) of social norms that determines processes of inclusion and exclusion (*"who is in and who is out")*.

Another way of conceptualizing identity is by examining why it was established. Group identity can be constructed through primordial ties and kinship connections (Geertz 1963; Khalaf 1968) focusing on categories resulting from the givens of birth such as "blood." This book project problematizes the "primordialist" definition of the givens of birth. Language, for instance, as the Philippine case shows, is socially ascribed, and is a product of socialization and of learning processes. Members of groups feel their connection with each other through commonalities in experience.

Huntington's (1997) concept of identity: "you only know who you are when you know who you are against" refers to those identity attributes of groups that are incompatible with the attributes of the others. As Huntington (1997) asserts, people, groups and civilizations often define their identities in terms of "what they are not" or by their "points of difference in a social milieu" (Anstey 2006, p.15). Coming back to the utilities of identity, value systems and processes of inclusion and exclusion are in their own right exclusionary, however, communal (ethno-cultural) difference is itself not generally the main driver of violence. It is how difference is related to inter-group relations that rather explains violence. For example, for Paul Collier (1999), violent conflict is about poverty and a lack of justice. Ethno-cultural differences are seldom the reason for escalation and outburst of violence. This confirms the idea that context matters in identity conflicts.

2.1 Conflict Defined

The term 'conflict' is derived from the Latin word *confligere* which means 'to strike together'. The term connotes a physical dimension in the sense that two or more bodies are moving against each other. Conflict is therefore explicable only in a social context. To "strike one together" can also mean "a struggle over values and claims to scarce status, power and resources in which the aims of the opponents are to neutralize, injure or eliminate their rivals" (Coser 1956, p.8).

While Himes (1980, p.14) understands conflict in terms of action, or "*purposeful struggles between collective actors who use social power to defeat or remove opponents and to gain status, power, resources and other scarce values*", Morton Deutsch (1973, p.10) refers to conflict as a situation which comes out whenever incompatible activities occur. Boulding (1962, p.5) suggests an additional definition that accommodates the psychological dimension of conflict. He states that conflict is a situation "in which the parties are aware of the incompatibility of potential future positions." His definition implies that parties can perceive goal incompatibility, but do not necessarily engage in behavior which is mutually incompatible. His suggestion that conflict refers to a cognitive rather than a behavioral state, which is supported by Stanger (1967) and Hammond (1965), enables the observation of differing attitudes in conflict situations.

Furthermore, Kriesberg (1973, p.17) argues that conflicts are rooted in the actors' belief that "they have incompatible goals". Building on this, Pruitt and Rubin (1986, p.14) define conflict as "*current aspirations cannot be achieved simultaneously*". Utilizing these contributions, the working definition of conflict in this project is as follows:

> *Conflict refers to the beliefs of actors about incompatibilities of goals (values, needs or interests) and behavior (actions to eliminate, defeat, neutralize the other as expression of how incompatibilities are intended to be handled) within a social context.*

This definition assumes that conflict does not automatically necessitate the outburst of violence; as such, conflict can be managed.

2.2 A Conflict Analysis – the Systematic Approach

The conflict in the Southern Philippines is complex, multi-dimensional and multi-level. It is complex, because it involves a diffuse system of almost untraceable interdependencies, dynamics and cause-effect relations. Complexity hinders any generic solution derived from other cases of conflict. The conflict is multi-dimensional, because it involves issues spanning security-based, socio-economic and cultural incompatibilities. It also involves contesting narratives and historical understanding that are highly contextual. For example, a resolution of religious tensions alone will not end conflict without comprehensive reforms in governance. Nevertheless, reforms in governance will not always be conducive to the peace process, particularly when reforms tend to reproduce existing hierarchies and power asymmetries. Furthermore, the conflict is multi-level, because it involves gaps in diverse relations – center vs. periphery, national vs. local, societal vs. personal. In each level, as the following table (Table 2.1) illustrates, different stakeholders follow different interests, maintain diverging priorities and pursue different strategies which require different outcomes in the negotiation process.

Table 2.1: Range of Scales of the Mindanao Conflict

	Scale 1	Scale 2	Scale 3	Scale 4
Conflict Parties	Government of the Philippines vs. MNLF, MILF	Center vs. Periphery (urban Manila vs. rural Mindanao)	Ethnic, religious and social communities, clans, warlords and political dynasties vs. each other	Interpersonal relationships (Mario vs. Pedro / Anita vs. Gloria)
Claims / Expected Outcomes	National sovereignty[1] vs. self-determination (independence or autonomy)	Centralization vs. Decentralization / Resource-sharing and empowerment of rural areas / Political Representation	Clan A vs. Clan B on local hegemony / empowerment of isolated communities Security	Individual Rights and Liberties (political, socio-economic) Empowerment Security
Issues	- Recognition of MILF / MNLF as negotiation partners; demobilization of MILF, MNLF; withdrawal of government troops in Mindanao (military) - banning the use of terrorism as a coercive strategy by the MILF (political) - national control of local resources in Mindanao or immediate economic aid to ARMM (economic) -autonomy in the educational system (culture) -adoption of sharia as law order (legal) - inclusion of ancestral domains now dominated by Christians to the Autonomous Region of Muslim Mindanao (ARMM) (territorial/ ancestral domains)	- distribution of income from concessions from foreign mining companies - allocation of development funds and international aid - Solidarity funds - Investment on Infrastructures -new forms of governance structures	- control of the local government units - the right of building mosques in Christian dominated communities -access to road and other infrastructures - access to water - Sharia courts in Christian dominated communities - Muslim holidays as public holidays	- access to health services - access to education - employment - personal security - enough food for the family - adequate income

[1] The government of the Philippines expects the adherence to the principles of national sovereignty in any outcome, whereas the Muslim minority groups strive for self-determination which is in itself a form of sovereignty. See Lingga (2008, p.61).

Procedural Measures	- mediation and negotiation - armed struggle - diplomatic, political, financial and military intervention of foreign countries	- public consultation - corporate partnerships - consultation with local and international investors, and other donor-givers	- collective rights and liberties protected by the constitution (legislation) - plebiscite - enhancing good governance and rule of law - enhancing public awareness	- communal conflict resolution methods such as mediation

Mark Anstey (Anstey 2006, p.77) identifies risks in conducting conflict analysis. First, the size of human casualties makes an "objective" analysis seem somehow inappropriate. An analysis implies allocating (often monetary) values to the ramifications of conflicts, a process based on normative judgement. Secondly, such an analysis tends to frame actors in subjective terms (as "good guys and bad guys,"), and focuses on conjunctures rather than on processes. However, in various conflicts such as in the Philippines, the escalated spiral of violence cannot be clearly attributed to perpetuators and victims. Thirdly, there is the risk of isolating responsibility and accountability for violence within one ethnic group and offering absolution for certain violent actions. This legitimizes violent actions, which is detrimental to any peace process.

The complex, multi-dimensional and multi-level nature of the conflict in Southern Philippines calls for a more systematic and integrative analytical approach. The 'scale of range' method (see Table 2.1) commonly used by the hierarchical theorists (such as Ahl & Allen 1996) states the significance of considering different levels of analysis in filtering information when observing phenomena. Upon doing this, different sets of priorities can be observed which require different sets of strategies when confronting localized conditions.

Socio-economic differences, socio-economic marginalization and isolation, political patronage, ethnic rivalry, competition from concessions from foreign mining companies, four decades of militarization, and conflicting land claims define what is perceived by the Filipinos as conflict in the Southern Philippines (Bück 2007, p.101). The complexity of the conflict in the Philippines undermines concrete resolution measures, which may not only be mutually complementing but also mutually excluding, promoting the intractability of the conflict.

To demonstrate how the range of scales model can contribute to a more comprehensive understanding of the conflict, a cross-cutting issue will be used as an example of how priorities pertaining to this specific issue change as it progresses through the different scales. For example, the way justice issues are handled in the mediation process affects the consolidation of peace in the long run.

As Albin (2001; 2009) describes, justice is a common cause of conflict, but is often neglected in research into durable peace agreements. One constraint to achieving justice in negotiations is finding a common understanding of what justice means. Each scale has its own justice issue that is prioritized. For example, in scale 4, the primary justice issue is fair access to welfare and resources for individual citizens regardless of their group membership. Muslims, for example, along with other peripheral ethno-linguistic minorities tend to have limited access to resources and are denied equal participation in social life.

However, granting the Muslim population privileged access to resources and opportunities is perceived as a deterioration of the socio-economic status of the Christian population in Mindanao. Such a measure is similarly seen as unfair and unjustified. Moreover, one of the main justice issues in scale 1 is "procedural justice." The government and the rebel group should find a fair procedure to enable meaningful talks in order to achieve a peace agreement. This includes shouldering expenses of trips and meetings, finding an appropriate place for the talks, securing safety for both sides, and ensuring the negotiators immunity from persecution. To conclude, justice issues in the different scales require different policies and different institutional settings.

There are several evaluations of the conflict in Southern Philippines both in academic literature and public discourse.

2.2.1 Conflict and Scarcity – Reduced Human Capital

At first glance, the conflict in the Philippines may illustrate a classical intra-state conflict with disrupted relations between ethnic groups contesting for scarce resources (see Collier 1999). This structural condition of scarcity leads to intense competition which inevitable legitimizes the use of violence to pursue their goals, particularly when survival is at stake. With existing power asymmetries determining access to scarce resources, weaker groups seek to modify access mechanisms. This is resisted by stronger groups seeking to maintain privileged access. This conflict confirms the notion suggested by Mack and Snyder (1957), that a situation of resource or position scarcity is a condition that creates conflict. Aggravating this conflict is the condition of dependency. While weaker groups already have limited access to resources, they are furthermore dependent on the "goodwill" of stronger groups to provide them with basic needs.

Aside from providing security, one of the most important functions of the state is to provide education to its constituents. Knowledge and advanced skills are critical determinants of institutional capacity (governance), income, economic growth and the public sector (civic society). Although the concept of human capital tends to reduce individuals to the status of "commodities," as Becker (1994) attests, qualifications (such as diplomas) function as signals that provide assurance to employers that employees can manage technologies (Chong 2005). The concept of 'human capital' differentiates individuals based on their educational attainment. Muslims tend not to be able to compete in this selection process, because of their disadvantages in the educational system, aggravated by their constant exposure to violence.

The national average of the proportion of high-school graduates among adults in 2003 was 52.1 per cent. Provinces in Mindanao are far below the national average. The most probable cause for Moros not completing secondary education is the regular violation of ceasefires which leads to internal displacement of more than five months. The 2008 and 2009 conflict has led to the disruption of the education of an estimated 70,000 children, with a tendency towards yet more school drop-outs as the length of displacement increases (Bell 2011). In a recent survey conducted by the Philippine National Statistics Office (2003), it was concluded that 39 per cent of the Muslim respondents failed to complete secondary education due to lack of personal interest, while 13.9 per cent because of employment and 13.8 per cent attributed it to the high cost of education. However, it was not mentioned in the study that the lack of personal interest does not reflect any backwardness in their culture. Simply, the unfavorable environment for education impedes the establishment of a healthy learning culture.

Furthermore, schools are regularly used as evacuation centers. Classes are often disrupted for weeks, if not for months, to accommodate refugees. Furthermore, in most cases, after months of usage as refugee centers, school materials such as tables, chairs, and books are destroyed. Schools are then combined with bad memories and these memories help to foster a lack of personal interest. The ARMM has the lowest literacy rate with seven out of 10 persons (65.5 per cent) aged 10 to 64 years considered to be basically literate. The functional literacy rate of the population of 10 to 64 year olds in the ARMM in 2003 is 62.9 per cent, compared to the national average of 84.1 per cent and to the National Capital Region of 94.6 per cent (PNSO 2003).

Muslims tend to be less educated. The human capital theory states the correlation between education and access to the employment market. Persons with a high level of education tend to have better access to higher paid jobs (Becker 1994). Economists regard expenditures on education, training, medical care, and so on as investments in human capital. The relatively low investment in human capital through the Philippine state correlates with the relatively low income of Moro residents in ARMM. Of the estimated 82 million Pesos (approximately 1.5 million Euro) family expenditure for education (tuition fees, books, etc.), only 0.9

per cent is spent for education in Mindanao compared to 28.3 per cent in the National Capital Region (Metro Manila).

The low investment in education in the ARMM is reflected by the income and unemployment rate. The ARMM registered the lowest annual income among regions with 47 billion pesos compared to 734 billion pesos earned in Metro Manila in 2006. The average annual income of ARMM families is 89 thousand pesos at current prices, compared to the annual average income of NCR families valued at 253 thousand pesos (PNSO 2006). The Labor Force Participation Rate for the ARMM in 2008 is the lowest in the country (57.1 percent, compared to 61.6 per cent in the NCR and 63.4 per cent national average). Although the unemployment rate in the ARMM is the lowest in the whole Philippines (4 percent) compared to the national average of 7.4 per cent (PNSO 2007), this development can be attributed to the low percentage of Muslims employed as wage workers. This anti-Muslim bias may have led to 78 per cent of Muslims engaging in entrepreneurial activities, with the remainder focusing on agriculture.

Lastly, the ARMM tends on average to have an incidence of poverty that is higher by 32 percentage points (UNDP & NZAID 2005, p.24) than the national poverty rate. The 2000 incidence of poverty in the ARMM was also 68.6 per cent compared to 34.2 per cent of the national poverty rate. Wages of Muslims are driven down, because of the intense competition among each other for jobs. Because 80 per cent of Muslims are landless, they are obliged to sell their labor to survive. In addition, Christian employers are usually distrustful of employing Muslims, further contributing to the high unemployment of Muslim wage workers.

Another entrance point for analyzing the underlying causes of poverty and the disparities in income between different societal sectors is the availability of more opportunities and assistance to settlers from the North. McKenna (2008) states that the assistance obtained by Muslims is not only meager compared to the assistance given to Christian settlers, but it is also less than the assistance received under the US colonial regime.

This “primordialist” approach evolving within the civilizational fault line by Huntington can be interpreted to reflect the report of the Philippine Congress (Congress of the Philippines, House of Representatives, 1955 quoted in Glang 1969, p.35): "*In their ignorance and in their trend toward religious fanaticism, the Muslims are sadly wanting in the advantages of normal health and social factors and functions.*" Such an assumption indicates the devaluation of Muslim culture in the sense that Muslims are not capable of participating in social life, because of inferior cultural attributes. This assumption then serves as vindication and relativization of the structural imbalances that marginalize Muslims.

2.2.2 *Conflict and Colonization - the Distorted State-building*

For Jamail Kamlian (2003), the conflict in the Southern Philippines refers to the incomplete integration of ethnic and religious minorities sustained by the lack of legitimacy of the Philippine state. The absence of any democratic consultation during the state-building process is regarded as a major problem that impedes integration. The United States bestowed political independence on the Philippines immediately after the Second World War in 1946. The incorporation of the two sultanates in Southern Philippines into the newly established Philippine Republic was decided without any democratic consultation as to whether the Muslim population wanted to join the new republic. The new Philippine republic inherited the Spanish and US American colonial administrative structures, implying that the conflict in the Philippines was an immediate implication of colonialism.

The US Congress ignored petitions from the Muslim elite to create a separate Muslim state entity in Mindanao. The perception that their incorporation into the new state was arbitrarily imposed upon them, and was a decision made without Muslim groups being given the privilege of deliberative choice, reflects the historical underpinnings of the conflict and undermines the legitimacy of the Philippine state. While Kamlian (2003) refers to the lack of integration due to a lack of legitimacy, Magdalena (Magdalena, 1977, p. 299) considers the social strain or tension to be "unfortunate circumstance of colonial history."

The social tension in the post-colonial Southern Philippines is further aggravated by institutionalized deprivation, continuous Muslim displacement, decreasing size of the Muslim population (minoritization), and a highly uneducated population. This is a result of the continuation of the state-sponsored settlement of Christian Filipinos in Muslim areas, which was initiated by the United States. Smith (2002) suggests that colonization has contributed to intra-group violence, where Christianity is viewed by Muslims as synonymous with colonization.

Abhoud Syed Lingga and other authors state that the Moro rebel groups consider the incorporation of their homeland into the Republic of the Philippines to be illegal and immoral, since it was performed without their plesbiscitary consent. Without their consent, the Moro movement is simply a continuation of the struggle for the decolonization of their homeland. They see the Philippine government as the successor-in-interest of the Spanish and American colonialists (see Aijiz 1982; Kreuzer & Werning 2007; Lingga 2008). The idea that the Philippine state is the continuation of Spanish and American colonization connotes prejudice, displacement and violence. The conflict in Southern Philippines may be therefore attributed to gaps in the state-building process in the post-colonial period.

During the almost 50 year-long American colonial rule in the Philippines, the US colonial government sponsored mass migration from the north and central parts of the country to Mindanao in order to create more Christian enclaves in the south and to compensate the Christian Filipinos for the loss of their lands to Americans. Unlike its predecessor Spain - which failed to to be successful when engaged in warfare with the Moros - the United States used violence to conquer the remaining Muslim sultanates (Rodil 1994). According to Kreuzer and Werning (Kreuzer & Werning 2007, p.x), at least 80 per cent of the Moros are now landless.

The application of the American land policy led to the loss of traditional land rights for the majority of the Muslims. The 1935 Philippine Commonwealth government which was the transitional government leading to the country's independence. This prioritized the economic development of Mindanao "for the benefit of the nation", by means of Christian migration into traditionally Muslim regions (McKenna 2008). This policy of minoritization continued and even intensified after the granting of independence, with internal migration reaching a high in the 1960s. For example, the number of Christian settlers in Central Mindanao soared from 0.7 million in 1948 to an estimated 2.3 million in 1970, representing a growth rate of 229 per cent (Burley 1973).

The influx of Christian settlers from the north created tension between the Christian and Muslim populations, further intensified by different conceptions of land ownership and leasehold arrangements (Gaspar et al. 2002, p.11). The landlessness of the Muslims is an implication of the introduction of land registration policies in Mindanao by the Americans. As McKenna (2008) states, due to unfamiliarity with the procedures, expensive processing fees, and the requirement to regularly pay taxes, many Muslims did not apply for land registration for the land they currently occupied (Thomas 1971). Christian settlers were regularly obtaining land ownership to lands occupied by Muslims since generations (McKenna 2008). Poor Muslims who have become "squatters" in their own lands were eventually forced to vacate their former homes. Violence was employed in the face of resistance, often with arms supplied by the Philippine Constabulary (McKenna 2008).

Mindanao's original Muslim inhabitants have been reduced from as much as 76 per cent of the population in 1903 to 18 per cent in 2000, creating discontent in Muslim minorities. The most contentious aspect of the peace negotiations between the Philippine government and the MILF is how to deal with the historical designation of Muslim homelands to Christian settlers, particularly the inclusion of areas now dominated by Christians under Muslim governance.

2.2.3 Conflict and the Civilizational Fault-lines

A more issue-related discourse on the conflict in the Southern Philippines refers to the role of religion in the politics of identity. Huntington (1997) identifies religion as a major factor in identity conflicts through "fault-line wars". As Anstey (2006, p.117) states, "to accept that a different religion has validity is to deny the 'exclusive' truth of one's own belief system." The affiliation in the *ummah* (Muslim community) is issue related, because positions are formulated from within this affiliation and expressed to the outside through claims of politically and culturally sensitive categories such as the introduction of Sharia, the introduction of Muslim holidays, etc.

Magdalena (1977) argues that the conflict in Southern Philippines originates from the ethnic and cultural differences in which Muslims see themselves as defending their faith and *ummah* against *kafir* (non-believers) who threaten Islam. Nevertheless, it is worth asking how Islam is threatened. Threat pertains to a subjective perception of anticipated pain. Will the armed conflict disappear when Muslims are able to practice their faith? The context of the conflict in Southern Philippines moves beyond the mere concept of practicing faith.

Christians are historically perceived as colonizers due to centuries of resistance to Christian "colonialism", and the current Philippine state is seen as the continuation of this colonialism. Nevertheless, analytically speaking, it is a logical error to attribute pain to religion when humans are the ones who actually inflict pain. To what extent it is logical to attribute 'threat' to Islam and Christianity when neither religion is actually competing with the other for space within a specific territory? Therefore, it can be concluded that although religion mobilizes people, the conflict in the Southern Philippines is not a religious conflict, because it does not involve contestation between Islam and Christianity.

2.2.4 Conflict and Misrecognition – Hegemonial Identity Politics and Social Relations

This chapter introduces another type of conflict that focuses on the dynamics influencing the social relations between societal actors. This concept of identity conflict may serve as a departure point in formulating policies. To apply the logic of Hannah Arendt (2009, p.55), "violence comes when power is lost", and identity conflicts are understood through reference to group relations, with one dominant group subordinating other groups under the banner of nation-building. Subordination is maintained by the organizational premises of the system-structure of the state.

As Hannah Arendt (2009, pp.55–57) states, the real or potential *Machtverlust* (loss of power), understood in terms of legitimacy and authority, leads to the use of violence, which is understood as an instrument for the re-establishment of power. 'Identity' cannot be separated from 'power', either in the process of identity formation or in the rectification of misrecognition.

'Misrecognition' is the political situation in which a specific minority group is not able to effectively participate equally in social life (Fraser 2003) due to existing state architecture that defines "conditions of advantages and disadvantages" (*Begünstigungs- und Benachteiligungsverhältnisse*) through legal and political instruments such as the legal system, bureaucracy and the social system (Kreisky 1979, p.1). The perceived inferiority of the subgroup in relation to the dominant norms leads to the minority group becoming associated with denigrating images, and perceptions of the minority group becoming distorted (Hobson 2003). Equal participation is not envisaged, because the dominant group defines the minority as inferior or/and as a threat. Therefore, the minority group is not accepted as equal peers in societal life.

To understand misrecognition, the conflict framework by Thomas (1976) has been modified. The following model (Figure 2.1) follows the logic "conflict antecedents-conflict moderators-conflict behaviour" that Thomas (1976) suggested. It serves as the framework for an analysis of misrecognition, icluding the sources, the moderators and the behavior.

As the following model suggests, the main source of misrecognition is the state-building process through nationalist terms of reference. Nation-building legitimizes policies such as the use of violence to ensure internal coherence. In this regard, social coherence is understood as a variable ensuring stability, implying that a collectivity can only be stable when there are common denominators among actors which define social trust. The dominant group believes it is threatened by groups considered to be either inferior or culturally distorted. Misrecognition is therefore moderated and maintained by notions of centralism, republicanism and universalism, and these are reflected in narratives, institutions, the mechanisms for the distribution of resources and opportunities, and for the provisions of welfare. Misrecognition is therefore the legitimizing force behind various state policies.

Figure 2.1: Understanding Misrecognition

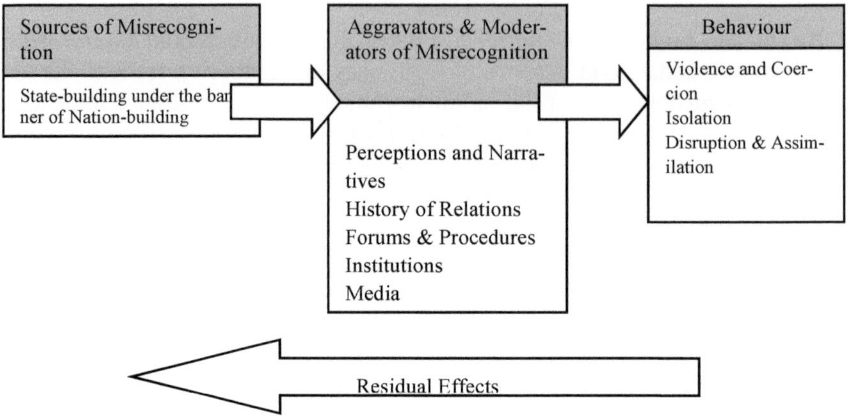

2.2.4.1 Deficient and Distorted Political Representation

Education does not only determine income, it also transforms individuals into citizens (Lipset 1981). Education provides individuals the resources to resist state repression, and to participate in deliberative processes of decision-making and bargaining at a political level. Education is nevertheless seen by the state as an instrument of ensuring social unity. However, when specific individuals are considered to be outside the community, the state tends not to feel obliged to provide education to these individuals. In this sense, the poor performance of the Philippine state in providing quality education to the Muslim population follows this logic of exclusion from the society at large, because the state feels neither responsible for them, nor obliged to provide individuals with education to prevent problems in the future.

The relative lack of education of the Muslim population is an indicator of misrecognition, as well as a factor that maintains misrecognition. Furthermore, education plays an important role in framing demands in various stages of the bargaining process. The work of Hannah Pitkin (1967) on the concept of representation refers to political representation as the activity of making citizen's voices, opinions, and perspectives present in the public policy-making process.

'Political representation' (Pitkin 1967; Pennock & Chapman 1968) refers to a bargaining relationship between formal representatives and their constituents.

Citizens define the rewards and sanctions of their representatives. Political representation is deficient when the constituents do not have the resources to formally sanction their representatives when they cease to represent the will of their constituents. In evaluating the quality of the representation of the Muslim population, the four different views of representation proposed by Pitkin (1967) offer an appropriate analytical framework: 1) formalistic representation, 2) descriptive representation, 3) symbolic representation, 4) substantive representation.

Formalistic Representation

'Formalistic representation' (Warren & Castiglione 2004; Grant & Keohane 2005) refers to the institutional arrangements that precede and initiate representation. The institutional position of a representative is the focus of this view. The application of this view in the context of the Philippines requires two distinctions of representation: *the representation of the Muslim constituents in the government of the ARMM, and the representation of the Muslim population in the overall national political framework of the Philippine state.* Importantly for constituents, formal sanctioning mechanisms must be available to serve as instruments for the authorization and accountability of representatives. In the first type of representation, Filipino Muslim constituents have rather poor sanctioning mechanisms, particularly because the leaders of the ARMM have yet to transform themselves into political bureaucrats. In addition, the lack of a robust political party system provides an environment conducive to armed clans and political warlords, where the interests of the constituents are subordinated by personal interests of armed groups.

The absence of a functioning parliamentary political party system in the ARMM, and the resistance of the MNLF to accept non-MNLF members in the autonomous government, limit the recruitment of new "political blood". The main implication of this patriarchal landscape in the ARMM is the personalization of politics in which representatives are elected based on their names and clan membership, rather than their socio-political programs and qualified experience. Furthermore, the formalistic representation of the Muslim population in the state-wide political framework has improved very slowly in the last decades. Under President Gloria Macapagal-Arroyo, one cabinet member was usually drawn from Muslim Mindanao such as Datu Nasser C. Pangandaman to serve as secretary of the Department of Agrarian Reform. However, none of the 23 members of the Philippine Senate is Muslim, as senators are directly elected by a national constituency wherein Muslim candidates are usually unable to garner enough electoral votes to win a seat in the senate. Muslims are formally represented in the Philippine House of Representatives both by district representatives and by the party-list organization *Anak ng Mindanao* (Children of Mindanao), who are quite constrained in their influence on national politics in general.

While the formal criteria of representation are clearly provided, a critical observation of the situation suggests more space for improvement. It should be asked whether the acceptance and therefore the legitimization of the representatives from violent agents such as the MNLF, MILF or political warlords solely depend on their capacity to create violence. The basis for representation should move beyond the 'entrepreneurship' of violence and include welfare and socio-economic development. How can agents of violence such as the MILF, MNLF and prominent political clans (with their own private armies) be accepted as political representatives and respond to the preferences of their constituents, particularly when they are not genuinely held accountable to their constituents by formal measures such as impeachment?

Descriptive Representation

'Descriptive representation' (Pitkin 1967; Young 1986; Young 2000; Mansbridge 2003) refers to the extent a representative resembles those being represented. In Southern Philippines, the assessment of the descriptive representation of the Muslim population answers the question of how the interests and experiences of the Muslim political elite resemble the interests and experiences of the Muslim constituents. As there are huge gaps between the interests of the agents of violence and the interests of the Muslim population, a "bridging process" is necessary to facilitate the transition of armed groups to political parties. The absence of a political arm in the insurgency limits the initiation of the deliberative process necessary to enhance social capital. Furthermore, when alternatives to the rebel groups are themselves agents of violence (political warlords) instead of political parties such as the case in Southern Philippines, deliberation becomes impossible. Gaps are then filled by local NGOs. Local NGOs however are usually confronted by violence both from the Philippine military and Muslim rebel groups, and also lack the financial capacity to voice the interests of the Muslim population. Furthermore, some NGOs are merely used by agents of violence to pursue vested interests.

The limitation of the descriptive representation of the Bangsamoro in the Philippines is defined by insurgent groups and political warlords who do not always pursue the interests of the Bangsamoro. The motivations of these representatives are not always transparent, and they are not always held accountable for their actions, which promotes graft and corruption. In several cases, their positions are incompatible with the positions of the Bangsamoro. The culture of impunity in the context of deficient accountability aggravates the lack of descriptive representation of the Bangsamoro.

Symbolic Representation

The 'symbolic representation' (Pitkin 1967) of the Bangsamoro pertains to the ways that a representative stands for the represented in front of other represented groups in an integrated political system. The degree of legitimacy that the representative enjoys depends on how this representative is able to project their interests to the other groups. In Muslim Mindanao, because representatives are considered to be agents of violence, the symbols projected to the others deter acceptance. Furthermore, it should be noted that within the Muslim population, internal coherence has been challenged by the fragmentation of the group into several ethno-linguistic and religious subgroups (e.g., secular, Islamist) , blurring the boundaries constituting Bangsamoro interest.

While the secular MNLF is mainly supported by the Sulu-based Tausug group, the secular MNLF-Reformed Bangsa Moro Liberation Organization is supported by the Maranaos, and the Islamist MILF has gained support from the Maguindanaos. As discussed above, the symbolic representation of the Muslims in the state-wide framework determines their degree of participation in the society at large. Furthermore, symbolic representation also refers to the use of symbols, pictures, images, signs and ceremonies to imply the 'belongingness' of the constituents to the state. However, when symbols are solely determined by armed groups, the represented group will most likely not enjoy acceptance from the society at large.

Only lately were symbolic actions introduced in the country, such as the signing of the Republic Act No. 9177 in 2002 that created the Eid ul-Fitr (Feast of Breaking the Fast), as public holiday which was enacted in deference to the Muslim community in the Philippines. Furthermore, discussion about the inclusion of the ninth ray of the sun of the Philippine flag (representing the ARMM), implies the recognition of the Muslim resistance to the Spanish colonial rule. The rays of the sun in the flag represent the 8 provinces that led to the uprising against Spain. The representation of the Muslim population in societal symbols such as these is a precondition for their integration. However, such symbolic representations of Muslims in the Philippines remain limited.

Substantive Representation

Finally, the 'substantive representation' (Pitkin 1967; Sabl 2002; Hardin 2004) refers to the policies advanced by the representatives that are allegedly in the best interests of the constituents. Substantive representation implies that representatives advocating for specific groups can reconcile their personal background with the interests of the represented. The landscape of the Moro elite is not conducive to substantive representation. Powerful warlord clans produce a political landscape for the Moro elite to create policies that bring huge revenues and state-of-the art weaponry through violence and electoral fraud (Torres 2007; Lara 2010). Political offices are often awarded to perpetrators of violent activity. Political offices are appealing to warlord because seats in the Philippine congress and senate, as well as in local offices, offer access to the so-called "pork barrel" (officially termed as the Priority Development Assistance Fund) which allocates millions of pesos to legislators. Through the recent "Napoles Pork Barrel Scam", where various senators and congressmen were found diverting funds to 82 ghost NGOs between 2006 and 2011, totalling an amountingof 10 billion Pesos (approximately 172 million Euro), it becomes obvious how vulnerable political offices are to corruption (Ubac 2013; Carvajal 2013). Furthermore, substantive representation of Muslim Mindanao is undermined by the new type of civil war economy (*Bürgerkriegsökonomie*), where warlords hold power through their control of a vast, illegal and secretive economy.

As Lara (2010) concludes, political legitimacy in Muslim Mindanao is given to entrepreneurs of violence whose main interest is not to protect people's rights or to provide basic welfare services. Generally, people in Mindanao, as well as in the whole of the Philippines, rarely depend on the government for welfare services such as health and education. Legitimacy is drawn from their capacity to provide protection and revenue to fellow clan members. In this political environment, potential political alternatives to these agents of violence are impeded in their assumption of political roles. Over the last decade, peaceful and moderate Muslims are leaving the ARMM. Some of them have established communities outside Muslim Mindanao or have left the country. It is estimated that over a million Muslims live outside Mindanao (Rasul-Bernardo 2006), inhibiting political transition in the area.

The political representation of the Muslim population, both within the ARMM and within the state-wide framework, is distorted by system-structural imbalances and conditions preventing political transformation. Identity conflicts have protracted violence and produced new agents of violence who demand and attain legitimacy, dislodging moderate elite Muslims from positions of political power. While the Bangsamoro insurgency aims to reach a new social contract, the lack of a socio-political arm of the insurgency means that the Bangsamoro insurgency fails to achieve effective political representation.

2.2.4.2 Anti-Muslim Bias

Pulse Asia was commissioned in March 2005 by the Human Development Network (HDN) to conduct a survey on anti-Muslim bias in the Philippines. The organization published the Philippine Human Development Report analyzing the perception of adult Filipinos towards Muslims. Pulse Asia interviewed 1,200 Filipino adults asking 16 questions. Four dealt with "proximity", that is, whether a respondent was willing to have a male Muslim for a boarder (tenant) in his or her home, hire a female Muslim domestic help, hire a male Muslim as a worker, or live near a Muslim community. Five questions focused on stereotypical images of Muslims. Specifically, the respondents were asked if they agreed with statements suggesting that Muslims are oppressive to women, prone to run amok, hate non-Muslims, are terrorists or extremists, or do not consider themselves as Filipinos. The 15th question was about the respondents' sources of information on Muslims, and the last question asked the respondent to name a group that he or she associates with the word "terrorism".

The findings of the survey suggest that testimonies of anti-Muslim bias are not imagined or isolated. Only 10 per cent of the respondents surveyed would employ or hire someone with a Muslim-sounding name (male border 3 per cent, female domestic helper 7 per cent, male worker 4 per cent). The majority of Filipinos think that Muslims are probably more prone to run amok (55 per cent). Around 47 per cent believe Muslims are probably terrorists or extremists and 44 per cent believe that Muslims secretly hate non-Muslims.

This negative image of Muslims is possibly due to the fact that less than 15 per cent of the respondents had direct dealings with Muslims. An identity cleavage functions as a separating line between public spheres. When asked about their sources of information about Muslims, only 14 per cent could cite their own personal experiences of Muslims. Television was the main source of information (78 per cent), followed by radio (44 per cent) and newspapers (29 per cent).

2.3 The Construction of the Bangsamoro Identity – The Collective Memory of Misrecognition

The Philippine case offers an interesting insight into how "identity markers" are used to mobilize people in a self-sustaining conflict cycle. Identity provides armed groups the resources (e.g., legitimacy) to assume the role of "entrepreneur" selling inclusion (operationalized as security and protection) in exchange for loyalty and participation in the "occupying" Philippine state. Although categories such as religion and ethnicity are not the only sources of conflict, the political instrumentalization of differences leads to *"mutually incompatible behaviors"* (Boulding 1962, p.5).

The politicization of differences implies the logic of marginalization at a cultural level. The culture of "otherness" is perceived as an imminent threat to the integrity of one's own collective culture (*Lebenskultur*), and the foundation of common weal on one's own terms (Meyer 2002, pp.35–38). Differences are then perceived as threats leading to their securitization. Peaceful diversity depends very much on the behavior of the dominant group, and this group defines the threshold of tolerable differences. On one hand, identities are constructed through primordial ties and kinship connections in which members themselves are responsible for shaping group perceptions and actions. On the other, identities are also constructed through experiences of violence and marginalization manifested to a significant degree in reduced individual responsibility for determining the group's perceptions and actions because these perceptions are already predetermined by those on the outside. Identity therefore is to a significant degree exogenous.

Interestingly, as Friedrich Hegel (1941, p.182) notes, it is not only the emerging nation that undergoes a process of self-consciousness. The dominant group also experiences the same process of self-consciousness. Hence, the process that establishes self-consciousness is self-enforcing. A perception is established where the identity of complete self-consciousness must be achieved through the negation of an equivalent identity in the other to justify its own cause. At its most extreme, this suggests that the only way to ensure self-preservation is the destruction of the other. This is the point where identity is securitized.

The securitization of identity leads to the promulgation of the Hegelian 'master-slave' dialectic in the power relations between the dominant group and the minority. This dialectic entails a relation of domination and subordination. It is within this master-slave dialectic that misrecognition is legitimized through the assumed inferiority of the "slave" within the predominant norms of identity as determined by the "master." As the identity-building process of the emerging minority unfolds, the group eventually gains the understanding of itself as an independent subject, but is still subordinated by an oppressive power. The consciousness of being deprived of its autonomy leads to the claims of recognition either in form of independence or full participation.

Following the development of self-consciousness, the mobilization of the "*Bangsamoro*" led to its political organization. Since then, it is able to pose a legitimate and efficient defence mechanism to the violence posed by the Philippine state, and Philippine society at large. It is worth asking whether the construction of the Bangsamoro identity, which led to the mobilization of its members, was also the main factor preventing a full-scale genocide in the Philippines (Penetrante 2012). Genocide cases such as those in Rwanda and Armenia may have occurred due to the lack of armed opposition capable of resisting the coercive force of the perpetuators. Thus, the mobilization of the Bangsamoro may have effectively offered a defense from violence.

The hypothetical identity narratives of the Bangsamoro (Moslem people) in Southern Philippines can be summarized as the following:

> *I am a Bangsamoro*[2]*, deprived of our rights in our own homelands by the occupying Philippine state.*

The hypothetical identity narratives of the Muslim population in Southern Philippines are expressed in academic literature about their culture, including contemporary art, music and film (Kreuzer & Werning 2007; Bara 2013). This self-representation offers a personal ("I am") narrative exploring the contemporary experience of marginalization as well as their demand for recognition ("deprived of our rights"). The narratives involve modalities of self-awareness ("own homelands"), implying the perceived disassociation from the "society at large", and the historical event representing the cultural trauma ("occupying the Philippine state"). For instance, the MILF states that the Moro history is a history of struggle (Hashim 1998). Memory plays an important role in the way in which the relationship to the "soil" is conceptualized ("own homelands") (Roudometof 2008, p.189).

The consciousness of group identity is in cognitive terms maintained by cultural trauma (Alexander 2004). Cultural trauma occurs when members of the collectivity feel that they have been "subjected to a horrendous event that leaves indelible marks upon their group consciousness, marking their memories forever and changing their future identity in fundamental and irrevocable ways" (Alexander

---

[2] The name "Bangsamoro" was actually first used by Muslim leaders to differentiate themselves from the Christian Filipinos and denote the citizens of the "new" nation in the course of the popular mobilization. However, though Bangsamoro is generally made up of Muslims, there are Christian Bangsamoro as well as Christian armed members of the MNLF or Muslim paramilitary forces affiliated with the Armed Forces of the Philippines (AFP) (Bück 2007, p.101).

2004, p.1). Cultural trauma is the manifestation of a 'tipping point' that permanently shifts self-perception. Relations between groups are now incapable of returning to the conditions that existed previously.

The experience of trauma can be understood as a socio-psychological process that defines a painful injury to the collectivity, establishes a victim, attributes responsibility, and distributes the ideal and material consequences (Alexander 2004, p.24). Cultural trauma, therefore, is the basis on which a new understanding of how social groups interact is developed, to create new and binding understandings of social responsibility (Alexander 2004).

Cultural trauma presupposes a previously existing group with a stable sense of identity. This is not problematic in cases of identity groups established through primordial ties and kinship connections. The Bangsamoro as a group is a complicated entity. Prior to the violence of the 1960s, the term "Bangsamoro" was not existent in the sense that there was no united group with coherent attributes in the Muslim population. Loyalty was given rather to groups based on language lines and not to groups based on religion. Instead, language was the main motor of identity.

The event that triggered the group-building process was the so-called *Jabidah* massacre on the night of March 18, 1968. The Philippine dictator Ferdinand Marcos ordered soldiers to infiltrate Sabah in his quest to occupy the Malaysian territory claimed by the Philippines. When 28 Muslim soldiers refused, they were massacred. This event is regarded as the causal event behind the modern Moro insurgencies in the Southern Philippines.

The mass violence in the Southern Philippines does not accord with any state ideology or express intention to destroy Muslims as a group, but it was successful in marginalizing them, reducing them to a minority status in their own homelands and ignoring their claims to participation in the larger political system. There were no measures to preserve the homelands of the Muslims who did not have concepts of land titles, because they regarded land as "*God's property*".

Cultural trauma implies the importance of history, because it permits the justification of some forms of resistance (Honneth 1995) to the status quo. Muslim separatist movements in the Philippines seek to justify their armed struggle more by reference to the past than by religion. Muslims tend to refer to present and past injustices as legitimisation of their pursuit of independence rather than claiming that the struggle as a "religious duty".. Past and present injustices maintain nostalgia for an embryonic state, suggesting a 'golden age' attracts popular support (Gilquin 2005, p.63). The romanticism of the ancient sultanate of Sulu and Maguindanao reminds Muslims of a happier past which should be re-established.

From the perspective of broader society, such groups are minorities that need to be assimilated or integrated. Subgroups, however, see themselves as "emerging nations" and demand equal political participation. The principle of national sovereignty and territorial integrity is paradoxically blocking the emergence of "new nations." Historical memory has provided the production and reproduction of these newly formed identities (Lowenthal 1985), suggesting the political use of history. However, not all will eventually use violence as a means of gaining independence. An outburst of violence can be prevented, for example, when the society at large does not see bargaining as threat.

The demonization (Faure 1995) of the minority group impedes bargaining, because the minority group is then perceived as a threat by society at large. When the other party is assumed to be the problem, negotiation will not be integrative enough for a mutually acceptable decision to be reached. In the Philippines, other minority groups experiencing forms of marginalization and isolation were able to achieve some power-sharing mechanisms through autonomous regulation of their areas. For instance, more than twelve ethno-linguistic groups of indigenous people in the Cordillera region, comprised of the five landlocked provinces of Abra, Benguet, Mountain, Kalinga-Apayao, and Ifugao, successfully achieved self-determination as a form of recognition.

Violence was about to erupt in 1986 with the creation of the Cordillera People's Liberation Army (CPLA), when the former dictator was removed through a popular revolt. The newly elected democratic government of President Corazon Aquino promised more "democratic space", and pushed for the Cordillera autonomy through the creation of the Cordillera Autonomous Region (now Cordillera Administrative Region) (CAR) (Malanes 2007). The re-establishment of peaceful relations between the ruling national group and the ethno-linguistic groups from the Cordillera region promoted deescalation and management of the conflict. The goal (self-determination) was framed in "positive-sum" terms. The CPLA, unlike other armed groups, immediately joined the Cordillera Bodong Administration (CBA) and made peace with the government through the *Mt. Data Peace Accord* of 1986. Ultimately, the CPLA was able to effectively transform itself into a political entity in the region.

As implied by the definition of conflict by Boulding (1962), Stanger (1967), and Hammond (1965), goals may be "perceived" as being incompatible, but are not always mutually exclusive. Goals as perceptions that can be "manipulated" through a detailed understanding of the interests and needs behind such goals (Bartos & Wehr 2002). However, behavior such as violence is negative-sum, because one either experiences violence or not. For the other actor, the use of violence is the preferred instrument in the elimination of threats. Particularly when combined with securitization, violence becomes a moral imperative. Although threats are also explicable in cognitive terms, the implications of such instruments have become *ends*, therefore, the main challenge for resolving violent identity conflicts is how to eliminate the sense of threat.

Subordination and recognition are at first glance incompatible. The incompatibility of identity politics is determined by the contestation of imagined and/or real narratives (histories), and the contestation of contemporary issues. The contemporary political, cultural, and diplomatic struggle for recognition in the form of power-sharing mechanisms and autonomy is a "struggle within the premises of particular national narratives" (Roudometof 2006, p.7).

The direct comparison between competing national narratives is inevitable, and may lead to violence when the dominant group sees its existence and privileges threatened. In Southern Philippines, Muslims mythologize their forceful incorporation into the Philippine state that occurred during the state-building process. Such a narrative legitimizes claims for independence on the basis of the principle of self-determination. The society at large, on the other hand, claims sees Muslims as responsible for bombings both in Manila and in the Southern Philippines, and mythologises their pronounced gun culture, their dishonesty in trade, and their aggressive way of life (Penetrante 2012). Interestingly, such narratives found acceptance during and after the outburst of violence in the 60s, as well as during the series of bombings in Manila between 2000 and 2004.

Lowenthal (1985) pinpoints the relationship between memory and history. He argues that a process of selection from the pool of past experiences occurs for specific reasons, including the legitimization of strategic measures such as claims for independence. Complementing the contestation of narratives is the contestation of contemporary issues. At a societal level, the "dysfunctional identity" of the minority groups as defined by the narratives of the dominant group, is reaffirmed by contemporary issues of dominance. The society at large does not acknowledge the marginalization of the members of the subgroup as such, but as necessities behind the notions of nationalism, universalism, centralism and republicanism (Sidanius & Pratto 1999).

Policies and institutional structures reflect the notion that deviation from uniformity and the accepted value system is a threat to national sovereignty and the integrity of the state. Broader society dissuades others from challenging established norms through real and symbolic sanctions. Sanctions become necessary to ensure "unity" by leveling differences. This practice is likely to be intensified if such minority groups are identified with rival neighboring states (e.g. Malaysia vs. Philippines, Georgia vs. Russia).

From the perspective of the subgroup, contemporary issues of marginalization are manifested by social comparison (Penetrante 2012). The subgroup perceives the current society at large not as a source of protection, but rather of deprivation. While law is perceived by broader society as a vehicle for order and justice, for the emerging nation, it is merely an instrument of oppression and indifference (*Gleichgültigkeit*). As Anstey (2006) argues, perceptions of "relative deprivation" or "unfair discrimination" create fertile ground for mobilization. In light of the long history of oppression and marginalization, the emerging nation wants to address grievances, and considers this their moral right. The society at large sees this very same process as a threat to their own identity, and hence the state as a whole.

The struggle for recognition is accurately conceptualized by the social and political thought of Hegel, who stresses that recognition is defined as the circumstance where full participation is not only assumed, but actually implemented (Hegel 1977). As Hegel argues, the process of identity-formation always lacks the kind of equality and transparency that would facilitate guiding. Nancy Fraser (2003) asserts that in such a circumstance of misrecognition, certain subject groups will be devalued and prevented from becoming full members of the society.

2.4 Conclusion – Initiating a Theoretical Debate in the Philippines

The Philippines needs a more vibrant theoretical discourse around the conflict in the Southern Philippines. This claim does not mean that there is no academic community in the country addressing the issues surrounding Mindanao. This project however claims that regular communication between academic scholars should be institutionalized in order to establish an academic discourse around the conflict in Mindanao. Current research on the nature of the conflict is dominated by descriptive works that mainly refer to the particulars of the conflict but fails to address how and why the conflict developed. Moreover, these works do not really acknowledge each other and therefore discourse is not promoted.

The historical experience and academic tradition of the Philippines impedes such a discourse. For example, the independence of universities and other institutions of higher learning in the Philippines cannot always be guaranteed by the state. The majority of universities in the Philippines are run by the Catholic Church. Without claiming that church-run universities are incapable of participating in robust discourse, these universities tend to merely reproduce well-established knowledge and not really explore new dialogues. A provocative claim that the author of this project makes is that church-run universities and other institutions of higher learning in the country are not really interested in engaging in independent academic research. Furthermore, these universities exercise latent bias against provocative theoretical claims which are perceived as being incompatible with the teachings of the Church.

In addition, academic scholars from non-religious universities are impeded from participating in academic discourse, because of a lack of an institutionalized communication platform. Furthermore, the focus of public universities in the Philippines tends to be on teaching rather than researching. This is indicated by the scarcity of local journals and academic/university publishers in the country, as well as the heavy teaching load of professors, preventing them from conducting research. Textbooks used in Philippine universities are usually imported from abroad. The Philippine state should furthermore refrain from intervening in discourse. Academic scholars representing provocative theoretical notions are quickly branded as "anarchists" or "communists." They tend to become targets of extra-judicial killings and intimidation. The high level of politicization and securitization of academic discourse in the country impedes its development.

This chapter poses a challenge to the local academic community in the country: to initiate independent and tolerant academic discourse. This is necessary to identify underlying causes of the identity conflict in the Philippines and to find measures to resolve it.

References:

Ahl, V. & Allen, T., 1996. *Hierarchy Theory. A Vision, Vocabulary, and Epistemology*, New York: Columbia University Press.

Aijiz, A., 1982. Four Hundred Year War: Moro Struggle in the Philippines. *Southeast Asia Chronicle*, 82, pp.1–28.

Albin, C., 2001. *Justice and Fairness in International Negotiation*, Cambridge: Cambridge Univeristy Press.

Albin, C., 2009. Peace vs. Justice - and Beyond. In J. Bercovitch, V. Kremenyuk, & I. W. Zartman, eds. *The SAGE Handbook of Conflict Resolution*. Los Angeles & London: SAGE Publications, pp. 580–594.

Alexander, J., 2004. Toward a Theory of Cultural Trauma. In J. Alexander et al., eds. *Cultural Trauma and Collective Identity*. Berkeley, CA: University of California Press, pp. 1–30.

Anstey, M., 2006. *Managing Change: Negotiating Conflict*, Lanadowne: Juta Legal and Academic Publishing.

Anstey, M. & Zartman, I.W. eds., 2012. *To Block the Slippery Slope: Reducing Identity Conflicts and Preventing Genocide*, New York: Oxford University Press.

Arendt, H., 2009. *Macht und Gewalt*, München & Zürich: Piper Taschenbuch.

Bara, H., 2013. *The History of the Muslim in the Philippines*, National Commission for Culture and the Arts. Available at: http://www.ncca.gov.ph/about-culture-and-arts/articles-on-c-n-a/article.php?igm=4&i=232 [Accessed September 23, 2013].
Bartos, O. & Wehr, P., 2002. *Development of Incompatible Goals, Using Conflict Theory*, New York: Cambridge University Press.
Becker, G., 1994. *Human Capital: A Theoretical and Empirical Analysis with Special Reference to Education,* 3rd Edition., Chicago: The University of Chicago Press.
Bell, E., 2011. *Violent Conflicts and Displacement in Central Mindanao. Challenges to Recovery and Development. Key Findings*, Washington D.C.: World Bank. Available at: http://www.internal-displacement.org/8025708F004CE90B/%28httpDocuments%29/A170CB649E7992A2C12579B10030A4D8/$file/Full_Report_3547+feb+2012.pdf [Accessed August 29, 2013].
Boulding, K., 1962. *Conflict and Defense*, New York: Horper & Row.
Bück, P., 2007. Civil Society and Conflict in Mindanao. In P. Kreuzer & R. Werning, eds. *Voices from Moro Land. Perspectives from Stakeholders and Observers on the Conflict in the Southern Philippines*. Petaling Jaya, Malaysia: Strategic Information and Research Development Center & Vinlin Press Sdn. Bhd, pp. 99–124.
Burley, T.M., 1973. *The Philippines: An Economic and Social Geography*, London: G. Bell and Sons Ltd.
Carvajal, N., 2013. Napoles, 3 senators face day of reckoning. *Philippine Daily Inquirer*.
Chong, T., 2005. *Modernization Trends in Southeast Asia*, Singapore: Institute of Southeast Asian Studies.
Collier, P., 1999. On the Economic Consequences of Civil War. *Oxford Economic Papers*, 51, pp.168–183.
Coser, L., 1956. *The Functions of Social Conflict*, London: Routledge and Kegan Paul.
Deutsch, M., 1973. *The Resolution of Conflict*, Princeton, NJ: Princeton University Press.
Faure, G.O., 1995. Conflict Formation: Going Beyond Culture-Bound Views of Conflict. In M. Deutsch, ed. *Conflict, Cooperation, and Justice: Essays Inspired by the Work of Morton Deutsch.* San Francisco: Jossey-Bass Publishers.
Fraser, N., 2003. Rethinking Recognition: Overcoming Displacement and Reification in Cultural Politics". In B. Hobson, ed. *Recognition Struggles*

and Social Movements. Contested Identities, Agency and Power. Cambridge: Cambridge Univeristy Press, pp. 21–34.
Gaspar, K., Lapad, E. & Maravillas, A., 2002. *Mapagpakamalinawon: A Reader for the Mindanawon Peace Advocate*, Davao: Alternate Forum for Research in Mindanao.
Geertz, C., 1963. Primordial Ties. In J. Hutchinson & J. Smith, eds. *Ethnicity*. New York: Oxford University Press, pp. 40–45.
Gilquin, M., 2005. *The Muslims of Thailand*, Chiang Mai: Silkworm Books.
Glang, A.C.O., 1969. *Muslim Secession or Integration?*, Quezon City: Alunan Glang.
Grant, R. & Keohane, R., 2005. Accountability and Abuses of Power in World Politics. *American Political Science Review*, 99, pp.29–44.
Hammond, T., 1965. New Directions in Research on Conflict Resolution. *Journal of Social Issues*, 21, pp.44–66.
Hanf, T., 1989. The Prospects of Accommodation in Communal Conflicts. In H. Giliomee & L. Schlemmer, eds. *Negotiating South Africa's Future*. Johannesburg: Southern Book Publishers.
Hardin, R., 2004. Representing Ignorance. *Social Philosophy and Policy*, 21, pp.76–99.
Hashim, S., 1998. Perhaps the Moro struggle for freedom and self-determination is the longest and bloodiest in the entire history of mankind. Available at: http://www.fas.org/irp/world/para/docs/ph2.htm [Accessed September 23, 2013].
Hegel, F., 1941. *La Phénoménologie de l'Esprit*, Paris: Aubier, Éditions Montaigne.
Hegel, F., 1977. *Phenomenology of Spirit*, Oxford: Oxford University Press.
Himes, J., 1980. *Conflict and Conflict Management*, Athens: University of Georgia Press.
Hobson, B. ed., 2003. *Recognition Struggles and Social Movements. Contested Identities, Agency and Power*, Cambridge, UK: Cambridge University Press.
Honneth, A., 1995. *The Struggle for Recognition: The Moral Grammar of Social Conflicts*, Cambridge, UK: Polity Press.
Huntington, S., 1997. *The Clash of Civilization and the Remaking of World Order*, New York: Touchstone.
Kamlian, J., 2003. Ethnic and Religious Conflict in Southern Philippines: A Discourse on Self-Determination, Political Autonomous and Conflict Resolution. In Islam and Human Rights Lecture. School of Law, Emory University, Atlanta, GA. Available at:

http://www.law.emory.edu/ihr/worddocs/jamail1.doc [Accessed September 21, 2013].

Khalaf, S., 1968. Primordial Ties and Politics in Lebanon. *Middle Eastern Studies*, 4(3), pp.243–269.

Kreisky, E., 1979. *Alternative Strategien der Organisation staatlichen Handelns*, Vienna: Institute for Advanced Studies.

Kreuzer, P. & Werning, R. eds., 2007. *Voices from Moro Land. Perspectives from Stakeholders and Observers on the Conflict in the Southern Philippines*, Petaling Jaya, Malaysia: Strategic Information and Research Development Center & Vinlin Press Sdn. Bhd.

Kriesberg, L., 1973. *The Sociology of Social Conflicts*, Englewood Cliffs, NJ: Prentice-Hall.

Lara, F., 2010. The Ruthless Political Entrepreneurs of Muslim Mindanao. *Planet Philippines*. Available at: http://planetphilippines.com/politics/the-ruthless-political-entrepreneurs-of-muslim-mindanao/ [Accessed September 21, 2013].

Lingga, A.S., 2008. Negotiating Peace in Mindanao. In I. Narongraksakhet, A. Kaba, & Y. Talek, eds. *Peace Building from Various Experiences*. Pattani: Saudara Press.

Lipset, S.M., 1981. *Political Man: The Social Bases of Politics*, Baltimore: John Hopkins University Press.

Lowenthal, D., 1985. *The Past is a Foreign Country*, Cambridge, UK: Cambridge University Press.

Mack, R. & Snyder, R., 1957. The Analysis of Social Conflict. Toward an Overview and Synthesis. *Journal of Conflict Resolution*, 1, pp.212–248.

Magdalena, F., 1977. ntergroup Conflict in the Southern Philippines: An Empirical Analysis. *Journal of Peace Research*, 4(14), pp.299–313.

Malanes, M., 2007. Elusive Cordillera Autonomy. *Philippine Daily Inquirer*. Available at: http://newsinfo.inquirer.net/inquirerheadlines/regions/view/20070919-89373/Elusive_Cordillera_autonomy [Accessed September 21, 2013].

Mansbridge, J., 2003. Rethinking Representation. *American Political Science Review*, 97(4), pp.515–528.

McKenna, T., 2008. The Origins of the Muslim Separatist Movement in the Philippines. *Asia Society*. Available at: http://asiasociety.org/countries/conflicts/origins-muslim-separatist-movement-philippines [Accessed September 23, 2013].

Meyer, T., 2002. *Identitätspolitik. Vom Missbrauch kultureller Unterschiede*, Frankfurt am Main: Suhrkamp Verlag.

Penetrante, A.M., 2012. Mass-Violence and Struggle for Recognition in Identity Conflicts - Negotiating Memories and Justice in the Philippines. In M. Anstey & I. W. Zartman, eds. *To Block the Slippery Slope: Reducing Identity Conflicts and Preventing Genocide*. New York: Oxford University Press, pp. 85–109.

Pennock, R. & Chapman, J. eds., 1968. *Representation*, New York: Rebenstorf.

Pitkin, H., 1967. *The Concept of Representation*, Berkeley and Los Angeles, CA: University of California Press.

PNSO, 2006. *Family Income and Expenditure Survey*, Philippine National Statistics Office. Available at: http://www.census.gov.ph/data/sectordata/2006/fies0608r.htm [Accessed September 21, 2013].

PNSO, 2003. *Index of Education and Mass Media Statistics*, Philippine National Statistics Office. Available at: http://www.census.gov.ph/data/sectordata/2003/fl03tabA.htm [Accessed September 21, 2013].

PNSO, 2007. *Population and Annual Growth Rates for Region, Provinces and Highly Urbanized Cities. Based on Censuses 1995, 2000 and 2007*, Philippine National Statistics Office. Available at: http://www.census.gov.ph/data/census2007/index.html [Accessed September 21, 2013].

Pruitt, D. & Rubin, J., 1986. *Social Conflict: Escalation, Stalemate, and Settlement*, New York: Random House.

Rasul-Bernardo, A., 2006. *Young Muslims Face an Uncertain Future*, Common Ground News Service, World Press Organization. Available at: http://www.worldpress.org/Asia/2519.cfm [Accessed September 21, 2013].

Rodil, R., 1994. *The Minoritization of the Indigenous Communities of Mindanao and the Sulu Archipelago*, Davao City: Alternate Forum for Research in Mindanao.

Roudometof, V., 2006. *Collective Memory, National Identity, and Ethnic Conflict. Greece, Bulgaria, and the Macedonian Question*, Westport, Connecticut: Praeger.

Roudometof, V., 2008. Greek-Orthodoxy, Territoriality and Globality: Religious Responses and Institutional Disputes. *Sociology of Religion*, 68(1), pp.67–91.

Sabl, A., 2002. *Ruling Passions: Political Offices and Democratic Ethics*, Princeton, NJ: Princeton University Press.

Sidanius, J. & Pratto, F., 1999. *Social Dominance: An Intergroup Theory of Social Hierarchy and Oppression*, Cambridge: Cambridge Univeristy Press.

Smith, A., 2002. The Southern Philippines: Conflict and Co-operation Anthony Smith Backgrounds the Separatist Conflict That Has Wracked the

Southern Philippines and Discusses the US Military Involvement in the Area. *New Zealand International Review*, 27(66), pp.24–29.
Stanger, R. ed., 1967. Essays on Intervention. *Journal of Conflict Resolution*, 13(2).
Thomas, R.B., 1976. Conflict and Conflict Management. In M. Dunnette, ed. *Handbook of Industrial and Organisational Psychology*. Chicago: Rand McNally, pp. 889–935.
Thomas, R.B., 1971. *Muslim but Filipino: The Integration of Philippine Muslims, 1917-1946*. PhD Thesis. Department of History, University of Pennsylvannia.
Torres, W.M. ed., 2007. *RIDO - Clan Feuding and Conflict Management in Mindanao*, Makati City, Philippines: The Asia Foundation.
Ubac, M.L., 2013. Palace: "Three Furies" will prosecute people in non-Napoles NGO scandal. *Inquirer News*. Available at: http://newsinfo.inquirer.net/481885/palace-three-furies-will-prosecute-people-in-non-napoles-ngo-scandal [Accessed September 6, 2013].
UNDP & NZAID, 2005. *Philippine Human Development Report 2005. Peace, Human Security and Human Development in the Philippines*, United Nations Development Programme (UNDP) & New Zealand Agency for International Development (NZAID). Available at: http://www.hdn.org.ph/phdr2005.html.
Warren, M. & Castiglione, D., 2004. The Transformation of Democratic Representation. *Democracy and Society*, 2(1), pp.20–22.
Wiberg, H. & Carlton, D., 1996. Identity, Ethnicity, Conflict. In S. Bekker, ed. *Racism, Xenophobia and Ethnic Conflict*. Durban: Indicator Press, pp. 1–20.
Young, I.M., 1986. Deferring Group Representation. In W. Kymlicka & I. Saphiro, eds. *Nomos: Group Rights*. New York: New York University Press, pp. 349–376.
Young, I.M., 2000. *Inclusion and Democracy*, Oxford: Oxford University Press.

3 The Nation as a Subject of Scientific Studies

The study of nationhood has produced different terms such as 'nation-building', 'nationalism', 'nation-state' and 'nationality'. Furthermore, it seems that when studying the term 'nation', it is inevitably concomitant with 'society', 'state', and 'ethnicity' leading to the impression that the focus of a study of the nation is not at its core characteristic, but is rather context-specific. Moreover, the study of nationhood involves interdisciplinary communication that inhibits consensus-building, for example when finding the definition of the nation. It is precisely this interdisciplinarity that exacerbates the complexity posed of the term 'nation'. The combination of perspectives from the fields of history, sociology, political science, psychology, philosophy and legal studies enables a comprehensive analysis of the nation and its implication in the social interactions, social communication, decision-making and dynamics of conflict.

3.1 The Nation and Postcolonial Studies

Chernilo (2007, p.1) depicts nationhood as "complicated for social sciences at large." Although deified, demonized, and even declared obsolete, as Chernillo (2007, p.1) continues, "the nation-state succeeded (...) in presenting itself as a solid, stable and ultimately the necessary form of social and political organization in modernity." This "success" as institutionalized by the Peace of Westphalia in 1648 is, paradoxically, attributed to the stagnancy of the production of new nations. The current understanding of sovereignty as rewarded to nation-states delimitates the emergence of new nation-states, because such an emergence is redolent of a threat to the survival of existing nations. On one hand, those states seeking to alter existing boundaries are quickly branded as rogue states and threats to international stability. On the other, those states that are incapable of maintaining these boundaries are then branded as failed states.

In former colonies, the boundaries of nations were not determined through consultation but were imposed, disregarding "nationalistic membership". The majority of African and Asian countries can attribute their political boundaries to territorial demarcations drawn by European colonial powers. The European colonizers were not sensitized to ethnicity, nationality or any form of group membership of the local inhabitants, but rather followed vested geostrategic interests. In some cases, the Europeans such as the Belgians in Rwanda artificially constructed ethnicity that was subsequently inherited and maintained. Exposed to real and imagined ethnic heterogeneity, these newly independent states had to build a base for political cohesion within their territory, while addressing power vacuums and shouldering the costs of transition periods in the first years of independence.

In the context of "fixed" state boundaries with modifications perceived antithetical to international norms, violence is legitimized and used to protect national integrity. Mark Levene (2008) argues that in the construction of a "nation", violence occurs to homogenize groups internally and to destroy all potential alternate sources of power within the territory. For instance, the United States as a pursued the active elimination of the majority of its indigenous inhabitants. David Cesarani (2004, p.381) states that "in terms of the sheer numbers killed, the Native American Genocide exceeds that of the Holocaust." Australia has reduced its Aborigines to only 2.5 per cent of the total Australian population today. It is estimated that prior to the arrival of British settlers, the population of indigenous Australians was approximately 318,000 – 750,000 (Australian Bureau of Statistics 2002). Around 200 of over 250 Aborigine nations are now extinct or on the verge of extinction.

3.2 The Four Streams of the Study of the Nation

The literature on nationhood, nation-states, and nation-building involves variations that seem to be irreconcilable. The inter-linkage of the term 'nation' with other terms such as 'society' and 'state', as well as variations in the terminologies such as 'nation', 'nation-building', 'nationhood', 'nationalism' and 'nationality' contribute to the disingenuous nature of the term "nation". To cope with this, this chapter offers a functional overview of the literature, a framework that shows a red line. For this purpose the following figure enables the positioning of relevant literature contributions on the study of the nation.

Figure 3.1: A Systemic Study of the Nation

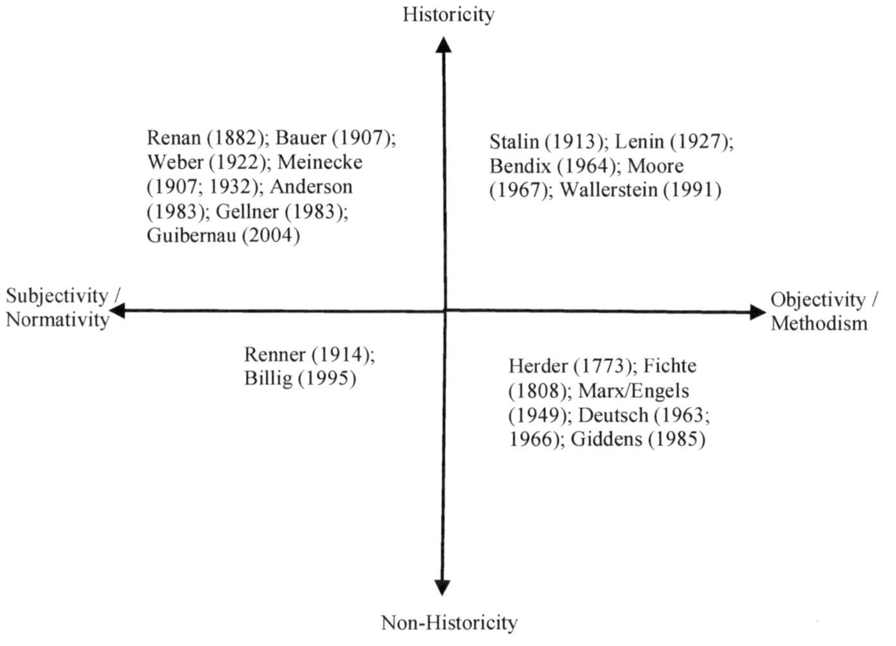

It should, however, be noted that the selection of the authors does not claim a complete listing of all authors that have attempted to define the nation. The collection is a mere representation of the four different streams on the study of nation. This chapter classifies the different authors into four streams:

1) historicity and subjectivity/normativity,
2) historicity and objectivity/methodism,
3) non-historicity and subjectivity/normativity,
4) non-historicity and objectivity/methodism

To show the "red line" among the different definitions and conceptualizations of the "nation", two questions are formulated:

> *How "nation-states" acquire, maintain and retain legitimacy* **(historicity or non-historicity)***?*

By what means are nations entitled to demand political loyalty and configure political organization **(subjectivity/normativity or objectivity/methodism).**

3.2.1 Historicity and Subjectivity/Normativity

According to this stream, the nation-state acquires and retains legitimacy through a learning process that occurs over time. Legitimacy is not a given condition but is amalgamated through a bargaining process. The constituents were persuaded that the nation-state is the most effective social organization to meet their needs. Legitimacy is therefore defined by its functionality. The bargaining process has a very dynamic setting with regards to the actors, the issues, the structure and the outcomes of negotiation.

Ernest Renan (1947) [1882] identified the past, the present, and the future as the factors that constitute the principal spirit of the nation. He argued that the 'nation' is established not through the same race, language or religion, not even through the same interest or geography, but rather through the same memories of the past, and the wish to live together in the present and in the future. The memories of the past forms perceptions of how the present and the future should be lived; hence, memories configure the political organization that is deemed to best achieve the normative expectations of the nation. The wish of the nation to maintain itself serves as the means to demand political loyalty.

Otto Bauer (1907) in his book "*Nationalitätfrage und die Sozialdemokratie*" (Nationality Questions and Social Democracy) defines 'nation', in the context of the Austro-Hungarian Empire as *"Charakter- und Schicksalsgemeinschaft"* (Communities of Destiny). Bauer argues that the multiplicity of historical determination leads to the formation of the "national character", which illuminates the will of the people. The origin of the will of the people is to be found in the diversity of historical experiences, historical conditions and forms of social organization as well as in the diverse geographical and physical conditions. The will of the people that defines the national character of the community is the product of the social process among the people and inherently illuminates political loyalty. Being a product of a social process, the nation is a historical phenomenon.

Otto Bauer's notion of "destiny" complements Friedrich Meinecke's (1962) [1907] notion that the nation acquires, maintains and retains legitimacy through collective experiences. Meinecke's thoughts can be summarized by his quote that Germans became "nationalists" through their experiences under the Napoleonic occupation. The bond established by that specific historical experience served as a source of political loyalty.

Max Weber (1985) [1922] recognized in his work "*Wirtschaft und Gesellschaft*" (Economics and Society) that the community based on the "common" feeling of roots (*Abstammungsgemeinschaft*) should be the normal determinant of a nation. Having worked on "ideal types," Weber, argued that in reality, roots are not enough to illuminate the construction of a nation. He suggested that common language is the normal basis for a political community. However, language alone is not sufficient for establishing a "national feeling." Differences along linguistic lines do not reflect absolute impediments to the development of a national feeling. Therefore, there are other considerations when explaining how nationhood is maintained.

Like Otto Bauer and Friedich Meinecke, Max Weber referred to experiences and memories. These are predicated on the significant role of common customs and morals (*Sitten*) that have been maintained over the course of time and which are expressed through political memories. Hence, the legitimacy of the political community occurs through the various stages of qualitative definitude of the national collective belief. Political loyalty is demanded by bureaucratic structures that have been established over the course of time, which concomitantly reflect the ruling customs and morals of the nation.

After more than 70 years, the historical materialism of the nation has been the focus of the analysis by authors such as Anderson (1983), Gellner (1983), and Guibernau (2004). Benedict Anderson (1983) follows the social constructivist approaches of sociology (Berger & Luckmann 1967; Best 1989). He defines nation as a historically interpreted "imagined political community that is imagined as both inherently limited and sovereign" (1983, p.7). From this definition, political loyalty can be derived from the formal universality of nationality. Anderson mentions that each person has a nationality. However, nationality is not enough to derive political loyalty. Instead, political loyalty is achieved through the "anthropological spirit" (1983, p.4) which is reflected by the "script-language" (1983, p.4). The anthropological spirit that encompasses the nation is a product of the industrial revolution and the development of capitalism and secularism, which led to bureaucratic and cultural centralization. Hence, legitimacy is the outcome of a learning process.

Ernest Gellner (1983), however, argues that a community is imagined through mutual recognition. In his 1983 work *Nations and Nationalism,* which has become the "lodestar exposition of the `modernist´ conception of nationalism" (Schlesinger 1999, p.4), he identified "entropy-resistant" traits that a society habitually invented (Gellner 1983, p.3). These stubbornly existing traits are maintained by sanctions to persuade citizens to conform and internalize societal norms. Such traits became socially and politically important, because they frame social interaction through the definition of communication modes. For instance, religious and cultural habits are virtually equal to those in the genetic constitutions of the group, because values and attitudes are illuminated by such habits. Gellner suggests that values and attitudes that are per se created through cognitive processes become “diacritical markers” (1983, p.6) for the population. However, one interesting point of Gellner's refers to the principle role of mutual recognition. According to him, “a mere category of persons…[e.g. language] becomes a nation if and when the members of the category firmly recognize certain mutual rights and duties to each other” (1983, pp.6–7). Reciprocity therefore leads to legitimacy of the nation-state. The interest of each member in being mutually recognized motivates each member to express political loyalty in exchange for recognition.

Another interesting author is Montserrat Guibernau. In her book “The Identity of Nations” (2004), she turned the focus away from nation towards “national identity”, indicating that her conception of nationhood was inherently behind the consciousness of the nation’s members. For her, “national identity is a collective sentiment based upon the belief of belonging to the same nation and sharing most of the attributes that make it distinct from other nations” (2004, p.11). She continues by suggesting that while political loyalty is encompassed in the consciousness of those expressing the national identity to the outside, the nation acquires legitimacy through its continuity over time. The conception of the nation as a “historically rooted entity that projects into the future” (2004, p.11) requires a set of common experiences in the past and a common meaning for the future.

3.2.2 Historicity and Objectivity/Methodism

Authors classified to this stream explain that legitimacy is acquired overs the course of time. They differ from those belonging to the first stream in that they consider the means of demanding political loyalty to be objective and methodical, therefore universal. In the conception of nationhood, objective categories such as institutions or primordial traits are seen as the self-evident means that entitle the nation-state to demand political loyalty or to configure the form of the political organization.

Vladimir Lenin (1927) viewed nations as representations of national cultures which he defined as a divisible unit. Lenin equated national culture with the ruling class, and employed the economic paradigm to understand nations. Contestation is the basic principle of social interaction between the democratic culture of the oppressed and the hegemonic “national” culture of the ruling class. From this assumption, Lenin drew his definition of ‘self-determination’, defined as the right to political separation of individual nations from alien national bodies, and to the formation of independent national states.

Interestingly, Lenin equated classes with cultural groups which implies that he understood culture to be not primarily extracted from religion and language, but from virtues, living conditions, and interests. His understanding of national culture as a divisible unit indirectly posits the existence of objective categories that enable such a division. Legitimacy is drawn from the historical contestation between groups (national cultures), and the environment of contestation practically demands political loyalty through mechanism of control.

The conceptions of Reinhard Bendix (1964) and Barrington Moore (1967) are to a significant extent mutually complementary. Bendix in his work "*Citizenship and Nation-Building*" understands nation-state as a form of political transition from traditional to modern forms of political authority. This understanding implies that the nation-state is a necessity in achieving any modern form of political authority. The legitimacy of the nation-state is therefore comprised of any form of political authority through its functionality.

The role of the nation-state is depicted by the reconfiguration of social life in relation to popular sovereignty and to the exercise of political policies. Nation-building is therefore the exercising of the bureaucratized public authority that demands political loyalty, because it dictates how social life should look. Political loyalty is ensured through the claim that the nation can "provide an adequate framework within which the required reconstitution of social relations could take place" (1964, p.23). Moore (1967), supporting the idea of the historical route of modernity, assumes that the nation-state is the result of bourgeois revolutions achieving their aim. Moore argues that the landed gentry and peasantry are important forces in determining the social and political order in the transformation from agrarian to industrial nation-states.

While Bendix takes the nation-state as a condition of transition, Moore assumes the nation-state is the final and necessary moment of modernity. Bendix connotes that "the rise of the nation-state challenges religious and patrimonial sources of social solidarity and both class and national identities were to try to fill that gap" (1964, pp.61–62). Finally, Bendix assumes that comparative sociological studies represent an attempt to develop concepts and generalizations at the level between what is objectively valid in all societies and what is objectively valid in one society at one point in time. This statement clearly confirms that he argues for objective and universally valid categories of nationhood, which further determine the configuration of any political organization.

Two authors that stridently illuminate the acquiring of legitimacy of the nation-state through historical contestation are Etienne Balibar and Immanuel Wallerstein (1991). For them, the nation-state takes the place of the hegemon by controlling industries, the financial sector and the value system. Without mentioning who the other competitors were, against whom the winning nation is prevalent, he assumed that the nation-state is not self-evident. Balibar and Wallerstein mention in the book "*Race, Nation, Class: Ambiguous Identities*" (1991), the concept of 'peoplehood' which mixes elements of ethnicity, race, and class. For them, the legitimacy of the nation-state is acquired through the "temporal dimension of pastness" (1991, p.78). According to Balibar and Wallerstein, "pastness is a mode by which persons are persuaded to act in the present in ways they might not otherwise act. *Pastness* is a central element in the socialization of individuals in the maintenance of group solidarity, [and] in the establishment of or challenge to social legitimization" (1991, p.78). Balibar and Wallerstein confirm the functionality of the past in the future in drawing legitimacy for the contemporary social organization, and this legitimized political organization serves as a means to demand solidarity in the future.

3.2.3 Non-historicity and Subjectivity/Normativity

This stream in the literature represents a minority in the discourse. Finding authors who do not follow the common conception of the nation as being historically determined seems to be impossible. The authors Karl Renner (1914) and Michael Billig (1995) recognize the significance of historical processes; however, it can be interpreted through some passages of their works that they have alternative thoughts which can potentially contest historical determinism. Karl Renner (1914), who relied heavily on the conceptions of Otto Bauer (1907) conceives of the nation as a "*Rechtsidee*" (idea of law). He introduces an interesting analytical point of view according to which the nation can be defined through various perspectives. From the physio- and anthropological perspective, the nation is a "*Abstammungsgemeinschaft*" (community based on ancestry). From the anthropological and geographical point of view, the nation is a "*Siedlungsgemeinschaft*" (community based on settlement). Renner states that another possible perspective in the conception of the nation is from the point of view of law. From this legal point of view, he derives the idea of moving from the territorial to a more person-based principle in the determination of nationality.

Michael Billig (1995) in his book "*Banal Nationalism*" refers to nationhood as providing a "continual background for […] political discourses, for cultural products, and even for the structuring of newspapers" (1995, p.8). He continues that national identity is to be "found in the embodied habits of social life" (1995, p.8), illustrated in the use of language and symbols. He is less interested in questions of nation-formation. He does not directly talk about the imminent role of history in acquiring legitimacy, but rather that "nationhood is still being reproduced" (1995, p.9). This implies that legitimacy is not an end product resulting from historical events, but is rather a self-reproducing phenomenon created through "ideological habits" (1995, p.6). The nation is not to be understood as the outcome of a historical process. Instead it serves as a point of departure for further analysis. Political loyalty is achieved through the regular "flagging" of the nation through symbols such as flags and national songs. A process of customization follows where such an activity will be accepted and its significance will no longer be interrogated. Acquiring legitimacy is in this sense a manipulative act. As he further states, "established nations are those states that have confidence in their own continuity" (1995, p.8). Political organizations are established for the purpose of reproducing the nation.

3.2.4 Non-Historicity and Objectivity/Methodism

The fourth stream refers to authors that recognize the role of objective criteria in demanding political loyalty and configuring political organization. Furthermore authors such as Herder (2002) [1773], Fichte (1808), Marx and Engels (1949), Deutsch (1953; 1966), Geertz (1963), and Giddens (1985) draw the conclusion that legitimacy is not acquired, but is maintained and retained in historical terms. It is either existent or non-existent. Johann Gottfried von Herder (2002) [1773] and Johann Gottlieb Fichte (1808) are exponents of the 'romanticism' of the nation. According to Herder in his work *"Stimmen der Völker in ihren Liedern"* (Voices of the People in their Songs) (2002) [1773], every group has its own distinct traits which define it and serve to differentiate them from others. Herder noted taht this distinctive cultural personality is summed up in the *"Volksgeist"* (people's spirit). This spirit, according to Herder, allows people to identify the political subject and legitimately constitute the nation-state.

Meanwhile, Fichte (1808) understood a rather static process of acquiring legitimacy. The "substance" or the "essence" of a nation is unchangeable. This essence is responsible for the disposition and behavior of the people and there is no other possible type of behavior. This essence refers to the core identity that is timeless. Similar to Herder's *Volksgeist*, Fichte argues that the nation-state is the expression of the absolute will of the people. Understanding that only the nation-state can provide law and order leads to the conclusion, as the Idealist tendency of Fichte confirms, that modes of national education (*Nationalerziehung*) are needed to demand political loyalty.

What differs from the claims of the authors on the first two streams is Herder's assertion that this cultural identity should be seen as the mere expression of the will of the group at a given moment. Cultural identity is something more transcendent, particularly given that the groups of people at the heart of the romanticist nation are seen as a living and persisting organism, and a moral entity greater than the sum of its parts. For Herder, the *Volksgeist* is objective, and for Fichte this "national essence" is unchangeable, hence similarly objective. The *Volksgeist* serves as a guardian of political loyalty. Because, as Herder has argued, the whole (*Volksgeist*) is greater than individual the members of the group, it is assumed to be legitimate.

The 1949 publication of the letters exchanged between Karl Marxs and Friedrich Engels between 1844 until 1883 offers an insight into how the two authors conceptualized the nation. They both agreed that nationhood is situated at the point of intersection between politics, technology and social transformation. This assumption seems to give the impression of a very dynamic process of nation-building. It is dynamic; however, looking closely at the means through which the nation should be analyzed – in terms of political, technical, administrative, economic and other conditions and requirements - the nation-state is empirically, hence objectively identifiable. Furthermore, even though Marx and Engels talked about historical materialism, the assumption was that the nation-state is the starting point for the subsequent evolution towards socialism. As such, it can be interpreted that the historical events leading to the creation of the nation-state does not play a role in the functionality of the nation-state in future social interactions. The nation-state is itself the point of departure for the future.

Coming from a different point of view is Karl Deutsch (1953; 1966). In his work "*Nation-Building and National Development*", he focused on modes of communication and how it determines societal conditions institutions. He argues that the so-called "communication space" serves as the "essential aspect to ensure unity of a people" (Deutsch 1966, p.4). Necessary for this thesis is the assumption that a group of people may become a "nation" when political space is redrawn amid changing geopolitics, leading to changing loyalties. Similar to the ideas of Otto Bauer and Karl Renner, Deutsch with his allegedly "deep post-Habsburgian sensibility" (Schlesinger 1999, p.2) suggested that it is the people who provide a notion of nationality. The nation-state is the principle that ensures political loyalty; hence, the group's cohesion and the continuity of its identity are ensured through a national educational system. The nation-state determines social communication that "sustains a mode of being that integrates a given people and provides it with singularity (Deutsch 1966, pp.96–87). The nation-state is therefore compulsorily understood as a means to an end.

The nation-state provides the means to demand political loyalty of the community. Legitimacy is not acquired from history, but from the self-reproducing "information channels for […] [the] dissemination and interaction, and facilities for deriving further information" (Deutsch 1966, p.75). The culture of the nation is therefore identified with the communication space that ensures its "self-containedness" (Schlesinger 1999, p.2). Significantly, Deutsch differentiates 'nation' from 'national identity'; whereas the nation-state is defined as the "communication space" and produces nationality which itself becomes an objective function of communication mechanisms. Nationality or national identity is the outcome of the structural cohesion measures that come about through social communication.

3.3 Conclusion – The Nation Defined

The systematic illustration of the different streams of the concepts of the nation provides a holistic overview of how nationhood can be understood. The comparison of these different streams pertains to the process of how political legitimacy is derived, and how the established nation demands political loyalty as well as how it configures political organization. The classification of the most important concepts of the nation into four streams leads to the observation that the nation does not pertain to the physical entity of the group. It rather pertains to the meanings given to the social interactions in a collectivity. The nation pertains furthermore to the utility such a collectivity may provide to its members – security, survival, human well-being etc.

The systematic review of existing literature on nationhood confirms the assertion that the nation is explicable only through a specific context. The nation is linked with other entities – identity, territories, culture, society and the state. It is perhaps these horizontal linkages with other concepts that impede more focused research the concept of nationhood.

An important limitation of this exploration is the lack of concepts of nationhood by non-Western authors. This poses the question of whether the concept of the "nation" is trapped in the historical development that occurred in Europe. Is the nation a "European invention" that ceases to be valid in Africa, Latin America and Asia? If this is true, is the application of this concept outside of Europe actually prolonging violent conflicts? Is there any alternative concepts to the nation-state?

References:

Anderson, B., 1983. *Imagined Communities: Reflections on the Origin and Spread of Nationalism* Second Edition., London: Verso Editions.

Australian Bureau of Statistics, 2002. *Year Book Australia, 2002*, Available at: http://www.abs.gov.au/ausstats/abs@.nsf/94713ad445ff1425ca25682000192af2/bfc28642d31c215cca256b350010b3f4!OpenDocument.
Balibar, E. & Wallerstein, I., 1991. *Race, Nation, Class : Ambiguous Identities*, London: Verso.
Bauer, O., 1907. *Die Nationalitätenfrage und die Sozaldemokratie*, Wien: Verlag der Wiener Volksbuchhandlung Ignaz Brand.
Bendix, R., 1964. *Nation Building and Citizenship*, New York: John Wiley.
Berger, P. & Luckmann, T., 1967. *The Social Construction of Reality: A Treatise in the Sociology of Knowledge*, Garden City, NY: Anchor.
Best, J. ed., 1989. *Images of Issues: Typifying Contemporary Social Problems*, New York: Aldine de Gruytet.
Billig, M., 1995. *Banal Nationalism*, London: SAGE Publications.
Cesarani, D., 2004. *Holocaust: Critical Concepts in Historical Studies*, London & New York: Routledge.
Chernillo, D., 2007. *A Social Theory of the Nation-State. The Political Forms of Modernity beyong Methodological Nationalism*, London & New York: Routledge.
Deutsch, K., 1966. *Nationalism and Social Communication* 2nd Edition., Cambridge, MA: The MIT Press.
Deutsch, K., 1953. *Nationalism and Social Communication: An Inquiry into the Foundations of Nationalism*, Cambrige, MA & London: The MIT Press.
Fichte, J.G., 1808. *Reden an die deutsche Nation*, Berlin: In der Realschulbuchhandlung.
Geertz, C., 1963. The Integrative Revolution: Primordial Sentiments and Civil Politics in the New States. In C. Geertz, ed. *Old Societies and New States: The Quest for Modernity in Asia and Africa*. New York: The Free Press of Glencoe, pp. 105–157.
Gellner, E., 1983. *Nations and Nationalism*, Oxford: Basil Blackwell.
Giddens, A., 1985. *The Nation State and Violence*, Cambridge: Polity Press.
Guibernau, M., 2004. *The Identity of Nations*, Cambridge: Polity Press.
Herder, J.G., 2002. Auszug aus einem Briefwechsel über Ossian und die Lieder alter Völker (Extract from a correspondence about Ossian and the Songs of Ancient Peoples) [1773]. In M. Forster, ed. *J.G. Herder: Philosophical Writings*. Cambridge: Cambridge University Press.
Lenin, V., 1927. *The Right of Nations to Self-Determination*, Moscow: Progress Publishers.
Levene, M., 2008. *Genocide in the Age of the Nation State vol. 1: The Meaning of Genocide*, London and New York: I.B. Tauris.

Marx, K. & Engels, F., 1949. *Briefwechsel von 1844 – 1883*, Berlin: Dietz.
Meinecke, F., 1962. *Weltbürgertum und Nationalstaat*, Stuttgart: Die Werkausgabe.
Moore, B., jr., 1967. *Social Origins of Dictatorship and Democracy: Lord and Peasant in the Making of the Modern World*, Boston: Beacon Press.
Renan, E., 1947. Qu´est-ce Qu´une nation? Conference Fait en Sorbonne. Le 11 Mars 1882. In H. Psichari, ed. *Oevres Complètes de Ernest Regan*. Paris: s.n., pp. 895–905.
Renner, K., 1914. *Die Nation als Rechtsidee und die Internationale*, Wien: Verlag des Vereines - in Komission bei der Wiener Volksbuchhandlung Ignaz Brand & Co.
Schlesinger, P., 1999. Changing Spaces of Political Communication. The Case of the European Union. *Political Communication*, 16, pp.263–269.
Weber, M., 1985. *Wirtschaft und Gesellschaft*, Tübingen: Mohr Siebeck Verlag.

4 The Hegemonic Nation – How Minorities are Invented

Analyzing how a specific group achieves political dominance or hegemony as the state-building process unfolds requires understanding the structural imbalance that promotes marginalization of national minorities. 'Structural imbalance' illustrates what Hannah Arendt (2009, p.560) meant when she said that following the triumvirate *citizens-territory-state,* which is promulgated as the 'nation', statelessness emerges. This triumvirate, based on nationhood, is considered to perpetrate the production of "minorities without nations", who now see themselves as dependent on the goodwill of the host nation (2009, p.563).

Minorities are produced when the goal of the nation is to acquire and express "national sovereignty" within the state (Renner 1914, p.16). When the status of a specific group is dependent on the goodwill of the host, measures to "denaturalize or to remove citizenship [become] the most effective weapons of totalitarian regimes in international politics" (Arendt 2009, p.563), particularly because these minorities will have no other means to demand human rights in the international arena. The minorities, although somewhat tolerated (*Duldung*) in the state territory, will find themselves regularly treated as second class citizens based on givens of birth. Individuals of other nationalities now defined as 'minorities' can refer only to "exceptional law" (*Ausnahmerecht*) (Arendt 2009, pp.574–575) within the legal framework of the "hosting nation". Hence, the completed transformation of the state from a legal to a national institution, as Arendt (2009, p.574) summarizes, leads to the "occupation of the state through the nation". The realization of the state through nation(al) institutions will inevitable reduce those who are perceived not to fit into the status of minorities.

The purpose of this chapter is to conceptualize this "hostage-taking" of the state through the nation. How is it possible that a specific identity group that came to define itself as a nation is able to reduce the state to its property? How effective is the control of state structures when these are instrumentalized to maintain privileges? With what means can a nation legitimize the hierarchical bureaucratic order that it chose to establish? Theoretical explanations will be derived from hegemonic theories and Charles Tilly's theory of "criminal states" (1985; 1990) to explain the processes leading to the formation of the state through the nation. Furthermore, referring to the points made in this chapter allows the evaluation of the current state structures in the Philippines and how a nationalistic mind-set of state-building led to violence and eventually to the mobilization of the Bangsamoro. Formulating strategies to resolve identity conflicts requires a shift in the several paradigms that caused violent escalation of conflict in the first place. These paradigms will be identified throughout this chapter.

4.1 The Hegemon vs. the Leader – Identifying the Fundament of Bureaucracy

Assessing the state-building process in the Philippines offers an answer to the question of how pluralistic societies develop political and normative orientations. Pluralistic societies encompass a territory with several nation-groups historically incorporated into each other. In pluralistic societies, a specific group emerges as the hegemon which is capable of providing cultural and political resources to ensure social cohesion. The hegemonic stability theory suggests some very interesting approaches to understanding the processes leading to the domination of an identity group in state-building. It should be noted that the hegemonic stability theory has been used thus far in analyzing processes in the international system. However, it is assumed that the same theory can be applicable to understand the political process in a national context. The main argument of the hegemonic stability theory is that the international system is more likely to remain stable when there is a single state that is the dominant world power or hegemon. In analogy, the "national system" requires a hegemonic group that will fill up the security vacuum in the state-society, particularly in the post-colonial period. In both the international and national system, the hegemon essentially exercises leadership, either through diplomacy, coercion, or persuasion. As Goldstein (1987; 2005) summarizes, the hegemon is actually deploying its "preponderance of power" (Goldstein 2005, p.107). The hegemon maintains the representation of its worldview – also called "normative order" through bureaucratization. The hegemon becomes a hegemon, because it has the capability to behave as one.

The absence of a hegemon is assumed in the hegemonic stability theory to be detrimental to ensuring stability and cohesion in the system. For instance, Kindleberger (1973) argued in his book "*The World of Depressions: 1929-1933*", that the Great Depression between the two World Wars could be blamed in part on the lack of a world leader with a dominant economy. He concludes that the stability of the global system is dependent on the hegemon to develop and enforce the rules of the status quo. 'Stability' is assumed to be the situation where predictability is perceived, and when a specific normative order remains unchallenged. Furthermore, it is assumed that stability can be achieved with both low and high legitimacy of the bureaucratic normative order through which the hegemon has established. The hegemon is therefore to be understood as the "fundament of bureaucracy", as it ensures compliance to the rules after it has established mechanisms of verification and sanctions.

The role as the guarantor of the normative bureaucratic order, however, requires the hegemon to have the capacity in terms of resources and legitimacy to lead and to enforce the rules of the status quo. Its ability to set the political and legal configuration of the state enables the hegemon to legitimize its behavior. 'Hegemony' is not to be equated with leadership. Conceptually speaking, 'leadership' connotes a situation where the leader accommodates the interest of their followers. As implied by the word follower, the leader enjoys legitimacy based on charm, formality/legality and tradition (Weber 1985).

Legitimate authority is enjoyed only in a social context. There exists a communication channel between the leader and the followers, whereas the leader is held accountable for his or her actions. The hegemon on the other hand, does not necessarily enjoy the same legitimacy of a leader. The hegemon's authority is rather reified by the lack of a challenger. The authority of the hegemon can be unilateral. The hegemon will prefer to use coercive means to secure loyalty. Furthermore, the hegemon is accountable only to itself and follows the dictates of self-interest. Although a hegemon provides stability and the secure the implementation of rules, this stability mainly serves a vested interest.

A society is stable when the status quo is favorable towards the hegemon. The rules are established by the hegemon mainly without a genuine consultation process with the others, and with the mind-set that the state belongs to the members of the hegemonic group. A normative order established by the hegemon can however be legitimized through customization. An order is seen as legitimate not because of its functionality or rationality, but because of habits that occurred over the course of time.

The hegemon's normative order can only remain stable as long as no potential contender emerges. However, it should be noted that the emergence of a credible contender does not necessary mean the instability of the system. Those who were excluded from the establishment process tend to be disadvantaged by the order. They comply with the norms and bureaucracy because of expected sanctions for non-conformity (Walker et al. 1988). When these groups stop fearing these sanctions, this order will eventually be publicly rejected. The hegemon can either accommodate calls for revision or confront these claims with violence. Instability arises when the hegemon does not recognize that it is to its own interest to accommodate the claims of the contender. It will then eventually be costly for the hegemon to maintain the order while defending it.

Instead of accommodation, the hegemon tends to follow the strategy of containment through violence and social engineering, primarily because it can do so within a culture of impunity. The hegemon sees the contender as a threat to social cohesion, therefore, a threat to securite relations. The paradigm behind this is the perception of threat to one's status when a contending group emerges. Contestation is taken as a threat to the status quo. This conceptual difference between hegemony and leadership leads to the assumption that it is hegemony and not leadership that has determined the state-building process in the Philippines.

4.2 The Hegemonic Nation – Profiling the Philippine Nation

Looking at the state-building process in the Philippines through the perspective of hegemonic stability theory is possible through a brief historical illustration of how the "*Tagalog*" (the inhabitants of the National Capital Region, or NCR) dominated the state-building process. Was this small group, consisting of only 28.1 per cent of the total population, really responsible for the events leading to the state-building process? How did their struggle for independence lead to the monopolization of the state-building process? Is the bureaucratic order that the Tagalog group established exclusive in nature? What resources are available for the hegemonic group to enable it to configure the political structure in a way that favors its own members? How does this group maintain legitimacy up to this point?

The systemic school of thought of the hegemonic stability theory (McCormick 1990) offers an interesting description of the hegemon as the possessor of sole power and control of economic production, trade and finance. Furthermore, the hegemon considers its role as the logical consequence of favorable geography, technological innovation, ideology, resources and other factors.

To find a profile of the hegemon in the Philippines, a historical analysis of the state-building process that mirrors the processes leading to the emergence of the hegemon seems to be inevitable. The following assumptions will be examined:

- The dominance of the role of the "Tagalog" as the hegemonic ethno-linguistic group in the Philippines can be traced from its position during the colonial period to the struggle of independence from Spanish, American and Japanese colonial rule *(a question of functionality)*
- The dominant role of the Tagalog in configuring the socio-political and constitutional system has formally legitimized and consolidated its hegemonic role through the bureaucracy system that the group has erected *(a question of legitimacy)*

- The Tagalog ethno-linguistic group is to a significant degree able to maintain its hegemonic status through its lack of competitors able to challenge the current hegemon, through diverging coalitions with local political entrepreneurs, and through the maintenance of the dependency of the other groups *(a question of rivals and resources).*

4.2.1 The Tagalog as Freedom Fighters – The Role of Independence Entrepreneurs

The emergence of the *Tagalog* (which literally means "those living at the river bank") as the hegemonic group is traceable from the country's colonial past. It can be argued that the Tagalog inherited hegemonial structures from the colonial regimes. With the colonial strategy of divide and rule, local elite groups, which tend to concentrate themselves in the capital, were created to supply human resources to the colonial bureaucratic system. Manila became the center of the Spanish colonial administration, including military, religious, and commercial activities. While local Filipinos were usually treated as second class citizens, the Tagalog elite had more privileges compared to their peers in other areas by hosting the colonial administration in the region.

The opening of the Suez Canal in 1869 cut travel time to Spain. This prompted the rise of the *ilustrados*, a Filipino upper class mostly coming from the Tagalog region and who could avail themselves of education in Spain. The current elite structure of the Philippines mainly represents this group of *ilustrados*. Furthermore, being the political and economic center of the Philippines that was consolidated during the colonial period, the Tagalog region dictates the political culture in the country. The role of the political elite from the Tagalog region in toppling the "Ilocano" dictator through the so-called "people powers revolution" in 1986 confirms the enormous political resources this group has. This mobilization of millions of people (now called EDSA 1) in the streets of Manila led to the change of the regime and demonstrated that power was concentrated in this region. This was later confirmed by EDSA 2 in 2001, the group that ousted President Joseph "Erap" Estrada. This role of "guardian of the constitution" will be discussed later in this chapter.

Although there were resistance movements all over the archipelago during the more than 300 years of Spanish colonial regime, only the resistance initiated by Andres Bonifacio through the armed revolutionary group "*Katipunan*" posed credible resistance against the colonial regime. Bonifacio, born in Manila, was one of the most influential leaders of the Philippine Revolution against Spain. The first eight provinces[3] that declared state of war against Spain are from the Tagalog region, as symbolically represented in the current Philippine flag through the eight primary rays of the sun spelling out the important role of these Tagalog areas in gaining independence.

On June 12, 1898, Emilio Aguinaldo declared in Cavite the independence of the Philippines. Although it was never recognized by Spain, this act finally separated the Philippines from Spain. The United States intervened in the Philippines following the outburst of war between the United States and Spain. In the battle of Manila in August 14, 1898, the United States captured Manila from Spain. However, independence was not formally granted to the Philippines. Instead the Philippines was handed over to the United States. The Philippine-American war eventually broke out in 1899. Aguinaldo was captured at Palanan, Isabela on March 23, 1901 leading to the official end to the war (Dolan 1991).

The United States passed the Tydings-McDuffie Act in March 24, 1934, and this allowed for the establishment of the Commonwealth of the Philippines, which enjoyed a ten-year period of peaceful transition to full independence (Dolan 1991). A constitution was framed and approved by US President Franklin D. Roosevelt in March 1935. This was followed by the formation of a Filipino government. Manuel L. Quezon, a Spanish mestizo from the Tagalog part of Baler, Tayabas (now Aurora), was elected president (Agoncillo 1990, p.392). Quezon, also known as the "Father of the National Language", approved the selection of Tagalog as the basis of the national language in the 1937 constitution, which was strongly opposed by the Cebuanos (Gonzales 1998). This selection followed a recommendation by the Institute of the National Language (established in 1936) to adopt Tagalog as the national language with the intention of gradually integrating all other Philippine languages into the Tagalog language, now called "*Pilipino*". With presidential approval, the institute started to work on a grammar and dictionary of the new national language (Molino 1961).

The Japanese occupation of the Philippines in 1941 was followed by the 1943 establishment of the Japanese-sponsored government of the Philippines headed by President Jose P. Laurel (born 1891 in Batangas). An estimated 1 million Filipinos were killed, and Manila was extensively damaged during the occupation (Dolan 1991). Japan formally surrendered on September 2, 1945. The United States decided to continue with the plan of granting independence to the Philippines. Elections were held in April 1946 with Manuel Roxas becoming the first president of the independent Republic of the Philippines. Although born in Capiz he spent long years in Manila developing his education and professional career. The United States ceded its sovereignty over the Philippines three months after the elections.

---

[3] Manila, Bulacan, Cavite, Pampanga, Nueva Ecijia, Tarlac, Laguna and Batangas

4.2.2 Language and Constitution – Consolidating the Hegemonic Bureaucracy

Through this brief analysis of the history of the Philippines, it can be assumed that the Tagalog group was able to initiate its hegemonic position through its role as the "entrepreneur" of independence. This role provided the opportunity to monopolize the configuration of the political and constitutional system within the nation-state. As this chapter argues, language played the most important role in consolidating the hegemony of the Tagalog, although it was understood as a necessity to unify the newly established state. Norms are reproduced by mechanisms of social communication. Language becomes the allocating scheme of sanctions and rewards, because it determines membership to the nation-state. Social communication is therefore the variable that maintains hegemonic bureaucracy.

The underground newspaper of the *Katipunan*, the *Kalayaan*, used the Tagalog language when writing about resistance and revolution (David 2004, p.27). The Kalayaan stands out as a "testimony to the revolutionary recuperation" (David 2004, p.27), as Tagalog was the first native language ever used to communicate the message of the revolutionaries to the mass population. With this, Tagalog became "the vehicle of autonomy and self-esteem" (David 2004, p.27). Nevertheless, it is not clear whether the Kalayaan reached the population outside of the capital region.

The hegemonic role of the Tagalog group was consolidated through its language, as a medium in the different constitutions of the new republic. The first constitution of the Philippines called the "*constitution of the biak-na-bato*" (constitution of the broken stone) was drafted by Isabelo Artacho and Felix Ferrer in 1897, known as the *Constitución Provisional de la República de Filipinas.* This constitution was written and promulgated in Spanish and Tagalog (Gonzales 1998). It was the (Tagalog) Katipunan revolution that led to the Tejeros convention at San Francisco de Malabon, Cavite on March 22, 1897, again in the Tagalog region. This convention was however exclusive to the members of the Katipunan.

Language functions as the primary "socializing mechanism" (*Vergesellschaftungsmechanismus*) (Demirovic 2002). It defines the scope of the validity of the "objective world." Humans interpret reality and pass on this interpretation, which is eventually institutionalized and defined in the normative order. With this process, those who do not use the same language are isolated and prevented from discursively contributing their own interpretation to the public discourse building process.

The present constitution (enacted in 1987) was drafted by a constitutional commission called by President Corazon Cojuanco Aquino through Proclamation

No. 9 following the "People Power Revolution" (EDSA 1) to frame a new constitution and to replace the 1973 constitution of President Ferdinand Edralin Marcos. The 1973 constitution took effect during the Marcos' martial law regime. Looking at the 50 members of the commission, the Tagalog region was over-represented. With more than 75 per cent of the members coming from the Tagalog region (being only 25 per cent of the total population), and almost all of the non-Tagalog members having had their education in Manila and practicing their profession in the National Capital Region, the previously established status of the Tagalog has been self-evidently reproduced.

The current constitution of the Philippines fails to recognize the ethnic diversity of the state through the containment of any discourse of diversity. The constitution as an institution should provide methods to resolve future social conflicts to ensure cohesion. However, the Philippine constitution merely expresses "permissive connivance" to minorities. The constitution does recognize individual human rights; however, it lacks measures to recognize collective rights. The declaration of Filipino as the official language in the past and current constitution and its usage as the medium of the media and medium of instruction in schools and universities inevitably alienated more than 75 per cent of the total Philippine population. Tagalog has been constructed as "Filipino" not because of its attributes as a language (semantic or grammatical), but simply because of its political meaning.

Pilipino (also written as Filipino) is based on Tagalog. Although it was mentioned that Tagalog should only be the point of departure for Filipino as language, the inclusion of elements of other Philippine languages is reduced to theory, particularly because there is no existing plan as to how to realize this promise. Although Tagalog is now spoken by approximately 64.3 million Filipinos or 96.4 per cent of the household population compared to the 22 million native speakers or 29 per cent (PNSO 2000; Lewis 2009), it is questionable whether the assimilative process of reducing other languages to mere dialects of Tagalog could lead to the recognition of other ethnic groups as social peers. Furthermore, it should be examined whether the functional literacy of non-Tagalog natives now speaking Tagalog matches the conversational proficiency of Tagalogs, particularly when they tend to speak their mother tongue at home. In this regard, further discussion is needed as to whether this language assimilation is merely the expression of "Tagalog imperialism" (Tan 2013).

The usage of Tagalog as the official language and medium of instruction poses questions about the educational performance of non-Tagalog students. Demirovic (2002) confirms that hegemony is practiced in the education system, particularly in the disciplines of literature, language and poetry. Without the chance of improving a learner's mastery of her or his native language, it is doubtful that there can be an effective second language (Tagalog) acquisition. The so-called "language immersion method" in school contexts delivers academic content through the medium of a foreign language (in the Philippine case Tagalog). For example, because the 776,000 Muslim Maranao speakers are dispersed throughout the Philippines, either as traders or due to the Mindanao conflict, their children end up speaking Tagalog, Cebuano or Ilocano, and it should be discussed whether social unity can only be achieved through language assimilation and the language extinction.

Several studies suggest that mastery of the language immersion method requires a particular level of proficiency in the native language (see Caroll 1964; Albert & Obler 1978; Dulay et al. 1982; Krashen 1985). Due to the "automatic transfer of the surface structure of the first language onto the surface of the target language" (Lott 1983, p.256), when there is a non-mastery of the first language, learners demonstrate difficulty in organizing knowledge into appropriate, coherent structures. Intellectual growth is thus impeded, and there appears to be a significant gap between the accumulation and the organization of the language.

Similarly to the introduction of Hindi as the official language in India, the notion that Tagalog ensures coherence among all Filipinos continues to dominate the discourse. The function of Tagalog as "the uniting factor" in the Philippine society is a myth. It may have given the impression of uniting the society, but only by taking away language proficiency and fluency from other groups. Citizens who are not functionally fluent of the official language are practically considered to be second class citizens. This policy leads to further structural imbalances, particularly in the social interactions between Tagalogs and non-Tagalogs, due to the perception that other languages are merely "inferior" and "funny" dialects of Tagalog (Pinoy Press 2007). These assumptions arise because dialects are grammatical and phonetic deviations from a language. Montalvan (2010) asserts in his article "*The Man with the Sugbu-Anon Accent*" that Filipinos with a "provincial accent" are seen as objects of laughter. The "culture of denigrating the promdi[4]" uses language as indicator of inferiority.

4.2.3 System Stability through the Absence of Challengers

Another assumption that should be analyzed is that the lack of a potential challenger to the hegemon consolidates the status of the Tagalog group. A group can only dominate as long as the other groups allow them to do so. Legitimacy is

[4] *Promdi* is the colloquial term referring to Filipinos coming from the province. A promdi is expected to be backward and ignorant. Because the promdi usually speaks another language, when he or she speaks Tagalog, a "funny" accent is to be heard.

maintained when no other group challenges the status quo. In terms of percentage of population and economic resources, the Cebuano group is perceived as the potential challenger of the Tagalog hegemony. Consisting of 13.1 per cent of the total population, the Cebuano as a group has however no real strategy to challenge the political and legal configuration that has been established. Although the Cebuano group has been empowered by the so-called "local government code", through which it gained partial autonomy and significant development in the region, the group is not capable of balancing the hegemon.

While there is an increasingly informal practice of including one cabinet member of the government from Muslim Mindanao as a consequence of the the ongoing conflict in Mindanao, the Cebuano, like the other groups, lacks effective political representation in the capital. For example, in the newly established government of the Philippines in June 2010, there is only one cabinet member from Mindanao, Socioeconomic Planning Secretary Cayetano Paderanga. Interestingly, he mainly resides in Manila and is not Muslim, and although the remaining three of 26 cabinet members are non-Tagalog, they also acquired their education, have resided and have worked in Manila (ABSCBN News 2010; Alvares 2010). The composition of the cabinet of the current President Benigno Aquino III shows an attitude that fails to reflect the diversity of Filipinos.

Although it is not true that Cebuanos are actively prevented from assuming high level political offices simply because they are Cebuanos, exposing the group and other ethnic groups to the same procedures that are valid for the Tagalog group inevitably leads to structural imbalances. Noting that almost all high quality institutions of higher learning are in Manila, non-Tagalog students are coerced into moving their residence to the capital region.

For instance, the Cebuano senator John Osmeña protested in 2000 that high school graduates from the Visayan region are under-represented in the University of the Philippines' (UP) annual intake of freshmen, compared to graduates from the Tagalog region (David 2004, p.123). But while the state university does make allowance for under-represented regions and ethnic minorities, it does not treat admission into the UP as a matter of regional representation and instead bases these decisions on test scores and high school grades. Furthermore, high level jobs are concentrated in Manila so that highly educated non-Tagalogs are essentially impelled to stay in the capital.

The Muslim ethno-linguistic groups comprise 4 per cent of the total population of the Philippines. While the Bangsamoro could challenge the military capacity of the central government, its financial dependence on the central government hinders the Bangsamoro's challenges to the hegemonic group. Challenging the hegemonic group implies that the challenger has the intention of taking the place of the hegemon. This is however not intended by the Bangsamoro. Furthermore, the lack of coherence within the Bangsamoro, due to the limitations of this identity group in the security domain, means that the Bangsamoro requires more processes to facilitate internal group cohesion.

4.2.4 People Power or Tagalog Power? – The Role of the Elites from the Capital

The political configuration of the Philippines is an evolving process. Narratives in the public discourse should not be left unquestioned. For instance, similar to President Ferdinand Edralin Marcos, President Joseph Estrada was ousted from the presidency by the "direct action of the Filipino people" (David 2004, p.154). Marcos and Estrada were removed from office extra-legally through these "people power revolutions" that brought millions of people to the Epifanio De los Santos Avenue (EDSA) in Metro Manila. Both presidents were neither impeached though a process defined by the constitution nor did they resign. They were not dead, mentally ill nor physically incapacitated. These two events, popularly called "EDSA I" (1986) and "EDSA II" (2001) led to the formation of a new government that were instantly recognized by the international community. The Chief Justice of the Philippine Supreme Court Hilario Davide Jr. elevated the ousting of President Joseph Estrada as an act of "judicial wisdom" following hearing the "voice of millions of Filipinos expressing their legitimate grievance and asserting their sovereign will" (David 2004, p.154).

Elevating the will of these millions of people to the sovereign will of the people remains problematic. The two EDSA revolutions are narrated as the vindication of the strength of the Philippine democracy. They are evaluated as the civic-democratic solution to the political crises. However, it should be questioned whether the sovereign Filipino people have really defined the two EDSAs. Or were these two revolutions carried out by the political elite from the capital? Narratives should be critically assessed. Months after EDSA II, the supporters of the ousted president launched the so-called "EDSA III." The supporters of Estrada, mainly from disadvantaged groups in both urban and rural areas, were almost able to occupy the presidential palace.

This "unpopular" revolt was however reduced to banditry, and was confronted with violence by the newly installed government. The media, which is controlled by a few families, was quick to degrade the revolt as 'criminal' and 'illegal'. Arguing that this EDSA III does not represent the will of the people leaves several questions open. By which means were the first EDSAs to be classified as the "will of the people"? Why was the third not representing the will of the people? Where is the threshold between "the will of the people" and "banditry"?

A more important question however still remains. Does it make a difference that the two EDSAs were conducted in Manila and not in other cities like Cebu? Can it be therefore argued that these two events represented the "will of the people" because they represented the will of the political elite of the national capital region? Would similar uprisings in cities aside from the capital region reach the same political effect as the two EDSAs in Manila did?

4.2.5 The Hegemon following the colonialist divide and rule strategy – the role of Political Warlords in Maintaining Hegemony

The dependency of the non-Tagalogs on the Tagalogs raises an interesting question about the ability of the Tagalogs to demand political loyalty from other groups. A group of less than 30 percent of the population cannot effectively rule the whole country. What occurs is more or less the collaboration between the statis quo and the political entrepreneurs – also called *'political warlords'* in the periphery. As Conde (2007) recognizes, national candidates seeking victories in national elections remain dependent on the vote-mobilizing capacities of their local allies.

The Philippine context of warlordism shows dynasties of local political (family) clans maintaining private armies or so-called "Partisan Armed Groups" (PAGs) to deter their rivals and to provide security in the area. The electoral victory of former President Gloria Macapagal Arroyo was only possible through the wide support she received from local political warlords particularly in Southern provinces in exchange for concessions from the capital. What happens is that the Philippine state enters into an informal agreement with local political warlords such as the Ampatuan clan in Maguindanao to ensure electoral victory and to provide security in those areas the government cannot reach. Political loyalty to the center is therefore assured through local political warlords that have sworn allegiance to the central government.

Furthermore, for instance, former President Gloria Macapagal Arroyo revived civilian militias - or the "force multipliers" as she calls them - to weaken the power of the communist and Muslim insurgents. In addition, the military conducted recruitment and assignment of local residents to the paramilitary group called "Citizens Armed Forces Geographical Unit" (CAFGU). This group worked closely with the military, and was subordinate to its command-and-control structure (Alston 2007, p.10). They patrolled the streets and enforced military checkpoints. The tolerated (and indirectly induced) militarization of local political warlords that were loyal to the central government functioned as leverage for the dominant national group to rule the whole state. Interestingly, the incapability of the nation-state to monopolize the legitimate use of violence was substituted by favored loyal political entrepreneurs that balanced the influence of separatist rebel groups and other insurgents (such as the 17 communist rebel groups in the local area). These political entrepreneurs, with their partisan armed groups, were complemented by civilian paramilitary groups sponsored by the military.

It could be argued that political violence was not mainly instigated by the national government. "Unlike Manila elites who operated within a culture of metropolitan civility, provincial families were forced to engage in systematic political violence either as agents or opponents" (McCoy 1994, pp.20–21). With the local ethnic elite groups mainly engaged in competition against their rivals, the elite in the Tagalog areas could sit back and rule the state. Franchising violence to local political warlords seemed to be an effective strategy of maintaining its hegemony within the state.

4.3 Interim Conclusion – Reframing Hegemony to Leadership

Political dominance leads to structural imbalances when the dominant actors perceive that a hierarchical bureaucracy promises more pay-off than an inclusive society. Hegemony is a state of mind which is determined by the role the dominant actor plays in the society. If the dominant actor sees itself as the guarantor of social cohesion to ensure stability and order, violence is legitimized. An armed conflict is therefore inevitable. If the dominant actor perceives diversity and social cohesion as non-mutually exclusive, conflict is manageable.

Dominance is a reality in all societies. It is not a question of whether or not there is a dominant group in the society, but rather how this dominance relates to the fibers of social interactions. Dominance does not need to marginalize minorities to reproduce itself. Dominance is not always to be equated with hegemony. With appropriate measures to strategically facilitate dominance, it can be transformed into healthy leadership.

The conflict in Mindanao is a direct implication of dominance understood as hegemony. The self-perception of the Tagalog group as the founder of the nation reduces other groups to minorities. The conflict in Mindanao is just one of many conflicts in the country that involves claims for recognition of marginalized groups. The Mindanao conflict is interlinked with other societal cleavages that produce conflicts. While some cleavages involve armed conflict (e.g. the insurgency of 17 communist groups), others are armed conflicts in the making. Therefore, there is a need to rethink the normative order in the country. The academic community should be motivated to initiate a comprehensive discourse on the structural deficiencies of the country. There is a need to rethink the political culture in the country. There is a need for a new social contract.

References:

ABSCBN News, 2010. Mix of old, new faces in Aquino Cabinet. *ABSCBN News*. Available at: http://www.abs-cbnnews.com/nation/06/29/10/mix-old-new-faces-aquino-cabinet [Accessed September 20, 2013].

Agoncillo, T., 1990. *History of the Filipino People* Eight Edition., Quezon City, Philippines: University of the Philippines Press.

Albert, M. & Obler, L., 1978. *The Bilingual Brain: Neuropsychological and Neurolinguistic Aspects of Bilingualism*, New York: Academic Press.

Alston, P., 2007. *Promotion and Protection of All Human Rights, Civil, Political, Economic, Social and Cultural Rights, Including the Right to Development*, Available at: http://www.inquirer.net/verbatim/A-HRC8-Philippines_Advance.pdf [Accessed September 20, 2013].

Alvares, K., 2010. Profile of Aquino's Cabinet Members. *Sunstar Online*. Available at: http://www.sunstar.com.ph/manila/profile-aquino-s-cabinet-members [Accessed September 20, 2013].

Arendt, H., 2009. *Elemente und Ursprünge totaler Herrschaft. Antisemitismus, Imperialismus, totale Herrschaft* 13. Auflage., München & Zürich: Piper Taschenbuch.

Caroll, J., 1964. *Language and Thought*, Englewood Cliffs: Prentice Hall.

Conde, C., 2007. Election violence escalating in Philippines. *International Herald Tribune*. Available at: http://www.iht.com/articles/2007/05/06/news/phils.php [Accessed September 20, 2013].

David, R., 2004. *Nation, Self and Citizenship: An Invitation to Philippine Sociology*, Pasig City: Anvil Publishing Inc.

Demirovic, A., 2002. Rekrutierung von Intellektuellen im Fordismus. Vergleichende Bemerkungen zu Horkheimers und Adornos Analyse der Kulturindustrie und Gramscis Analyse der Zivilgesellschaft. In *Zwischen Herrschaft und Befreiung kulturelle, politische und wissenschaftliche Strategien*. Münster: Westfällisches Dampfboot, pp. 55–69.

Dolan, R., 1991. *War of Resistance. Philippines: a Country Study*, Washington, D.C.: GPO for the Library Congress.

Dulay, H., Burt, M. & Krashen, S., 1982. *Language Two*, New York: Oxford University Press.

Goldstein, J., 2005. *International Relations*, New York: Pearson-Longmann.
Goldstein, J., 1987. *Long Cycles: Prosperity and War in the Modern Age*, New Haven: Yale University Press.
Gonzales, A., 1998. The Language Planning Situation in the Philippines. *Journal of Multilingual and Multicultural Development*, 19, pp.487–525.
Kindleberger, C., 1973. *The World in Depression: 1929-1939*, Berkeley and Los Angeles, CA: University of California Press.
Krashen, S., 1985. *Language Acquisition and Language Education*, Hayward, CA: Alemany Press.
Lewis, P. ed., 2009. *2009. Ethnologue: Languages of the World* Sixteenth Edition., Dallas, TX: SIL International.
Lott, D., 1983. Analysing and Counteracting Interference Errors. *ELT Journal*, 37(3), pp.256–261.
McCormick, T., 1990. World Systems. *Journal of American History*, pp.125–132.
McCoy, A. ed., 1994. *An Anarchy of Families: The Historiography of State and Family in the Philippines*, Quezon City, Philippines: Ateneo de Manila Press.
Molino, A., 1961. *The Philippines through the Centuries* Volume 2., Quezon City: University of the Philippines Press.
Montalvan, A.I., 2010. The Man with the Sugbu-Anon Accent. *Philippine Daily Inquirer*. Available at: http://opinion.inquirer.net/inquireropinion/columns/view/20100201-250604/The-man-with-the-Sugbu-anon-accent [Accessed September 21, 2013].
Pinoy Press, 2007. Visayans Unite! (Or Why They Should Boycott "Sakal Sakali Saklolo"). *Pinoy Press*. Available at: http://www.pinoypress.net/2007/12/27/visayans-unite-or-why-they-should-boycott-sakal-sakali-saklolo/ [Accessed September 21, 2013].
PNSO, 2000. *Philippine Census, 2000. Table 11. Household Population by Ethnicity, Sex and Region: 2000*, Philippine National Statistics Office.
Renner, K., 1914. *Die Nation als Rechtsidee und die Internationale*, Wien: Verlag des Vereines - in Komission bei der Wiener Volksbuchhandlung Ignaz Brand & Co.
Tan, M., 2013. 181 languages. *Inquirer*. Available at: http://opinion.inquirer.net/59901/181-languages [Accessed August 30, 2013].
Tilly, C., 1990. *Coercion, Capital and European States, AD 990-1990*, Cambridge, MA: Blackwell.
Tilly, C., 1985. War Making and State Making as Organized Crime. In P. B. Evans, D. Rueschemeyer, & T. Skocpol, eds. *Bridging the State Back In.* Cambridge: Cambridge University Press, pp. 169–191.

Walker, H., Rogers, L. & Zelditch, M., 1988. Legitimacy and Collective Action: A Research Note. *Social Forces*, 67(1), pp.216–228.
Weber, M., 1985. *Wirtschaft und Gesellschaft*, Tübingen: Mohr Siebeck Verlag.

5 The Nation and the Legitimacy of Violence –The Need for the Concept of "Non-Competitive Nation-Building

Understanding the connection between state-building (equated with nation-building) and violence promises to identify existing paradigms that need to be altered if a resolution of the "longest rebellion in Asia" (Damazo 2003) is intended. Several authors such as Hannah Arendt (Arendt 2009b; Arendt 2009a) and Charles Tilly (Tilly 1985) link nation-building with the legitimization of violence either to subdue threats from the outside or to ensure internal group coherence by eliminating potential competitors. Under the banner of nationhood, violence is used as an instrument of ensuring cohesion in a context where the universality of the nation applies. Universality however means that existing norms and actual practices should fit into the worldview of the national group. Cohesion is perceived to be important because it ensures a system's stability. Understanding violence as an instrument for cohesion, however, requires the analysis of what is meant by 'violence'. Is violence simply the application of force, e.g. weapons to achieve something? Violence requires an analysis of the notion of legitimacy.

Paradoxically, the situation in the Philippines illustrates the dependence of the nation-state on the existence of loyal political warlords in order to govern the whole territory. Violence is here not monopolized but rather contracted as a "franchise" to local actors. Can the Philippines to be considered a "failed state" when the central government is not capable and/or is not willing to monopolize the use of violence? Is its resignation and incapability to monopolize violence an indicator of failed nation-building?

Furthermore, the Philippines illustrate the "paradox of democracy" wherein the democratic institutional setting of the state actually nurtures high levels of violence. How can this be explained? Can democracy really be considered the antidote to violence? Violence itself is not always primarily the implication of state structures (e.g. institutionalization of discrimination). Violence may also refer to a power preponderance extracted from established hierarchical group relations. Democratic designs that fail to substantially delimit hierarchical relations will eventually witness high levels of collective violence. Violence is therefore the reification of hierarchical relations.

5.1 Nation-hood and State-hood – the Functionality of Violence

Exploring the antecedents of the destabilization of the system, this subsection intends to analyze the functionality of violence in the nation-building process in the context of national unity, in so far as it is seen as a necessary condition for successful statehood. Social cohesion is assumed to be the situation where the interrelated parts of society properly work together through (both formal and informal) rules and regulations. The need for cohesion in the societal system (Giddens 1984; Durkheim 1996) follows the perspective of structural functionalism that addresses society as a whole with interrelated parts.

Maintaining social order and creating equilibrium in society is necessary, because of societal segmentation (Durkheim, 1996[1893]). Scholars such as Maggee & Galinsky (2008) and Tiedens & Frigale (2003) have identified the functional benefits of stable systems for task coordination, cooperation and satisfaction of members. Hence, stability leads to efficiency and legitimacy. The hegemonic group has established the societal system (referred to as "society at large") according to its worldview. The group will ensure stability in this system by any means available.

The multi-nationalistic features of society are framed by the hegemonic group as a segmentation of a society that needs to be bonded together. Therefore, as Gramsci argues, stability in a heterogeneous society requires hegemony. Modern forms of governance (Herrschaft) are ensured through social institutions. Nevertheless, governance needs a balance between consensus and coercion. Particularly in times of social crises, as Buckel and Fischer-Lescano (2007, p.11) argue, "the repressive power of political institutions stabilizes social consensus." However, the definition of hegemony by Buckel and Fischer-Lescano fail to distinguish between leadership and hegemony, because these two authors see hegemony as the existing normative order, and not as the action of a dominant actor group. Hegemony is a status.

In the context of a hegemonic group that decides how cohesion can be ensured, national unity is inevitably politicized and securitized, because of the existing hierarchical nature of the society. Hierarchy is founded within the premise of power relations; therefore, claims that question the existing power structures are easily perceived as a challenge. The higher the degree of hierarchy, the higher the degree of securitization in society. The higher the degree of securitization in the society, the higher the likelihood of violence. As Kreuzer & Weiberg (2005, p.9) note, the necessity of unifying the nation-state leads to either assimilation of minorities or "ethnic cleansing". An outburst of violence is frequently the predictive outcome of nation-building. Hence, the functionality of violence lies in its role in ensuring social cohesion.

Charles Tilly (1985) introduces an interesting argument that tries to identify the link between state-building and violence. He makes the analogy of war-making and state-making with organized crime as observed from a few hundred years of European experience. He argues that the current experience of Third World countries is comparable with the experience of European countries. The "future of the Third World countries can be read from the past of European countries" (Tilly 1985, p.169). He adds, "war makes states, I shall claim. Banditry, piracy, gangland rivalry, policing, and war-making all belong to the same continuum – that I shall as well," (Tilly 1985, p.170).

Organized violence is therefore fundamental to the establishment of national states. As the state becomes relatively centralized, bureaucratization of the means of violence follows the formation of the military and police as well as the demilitarization of potential rival agents of violence such as landlords. The government that represents the state claims that it provides protection. The agents of the state, as summarized by Tilly (1985, p.181), characteristically carry on four different activities. First, they conduct war-making with the intention of eliminating or neutralizing their rivals outside the territories. Secondly, they conduct state-making in which rivals inside those territories are eliminated or neutralized. State-making therefore involves monopolizing the use of violence. Thirdly, these agents protect their "clients" through the elimination or neutralization of the enemies. However, the term "enemy" is a vague word that could encompass every threat to their "citizens". Lastly, these agents of the state conduct extraction through which the means of carrying out the first three activities are acquired.

State-making as Tilly (1985, p.171) argues often qualifies as racketeering given the fact that the threats against which a given government protects its citizens are imaginary or are consequences of its own activities. State-making creates the bureaucracy that includes the army, police, and later on the representative institutions and courts. This bureaucracy regulates the use of public violence to maximize efficiency. Some elements of this bureaucracy such as the guarantee of rights, representation and courts are to be considered as concessions following an organized resistance from citizens. Nevertheless, the successfully conducted demilitarization of the society is necessary to enable a state to monopolization on violence. This is then claimed as the 'protection of the citizens', although it guarantees de facto power for the rulers. National states therefore emerge from war-making, extraction and capital accumulation (Tilly 1985, p.172). Violence, as Karl Renner (Renner 1952, p.272) suggests, is historically speaking the first founder of the nation-state. "Public violence", he continues, was established before the rule of law: the state is the conqueror. Violence is therefore to be considered as the "glue" that binds the nation-state.

5.2 Defining Violence – What Lies Behind by this Elusive Concept?

The word 'violence'' covers a broad spectrum. The elusive term violence' can encompass physical altercations between individuals where minor injuries may be the outcome of actions taken. It can also mean the application of a wide variety of weapons to collective groups of people during war and genocide. How is violence to be conceptualized in a manner that enables analysts to understand its processes in civil war contexts such as in the Philippines? The context of violence in the Philippines seems to include other forms of violence that are not directly related to the application of modern weaponary. The conceptualization of violence inevitably requires addressing different types of violence: direct violence, structural violence, and symbolic violence. Although these different types of violence are intertwined and to a significant degree come together as a package, differentiations for the purpose of analysis are possible as indicated by the *agents pursuing direct violence* (actors), *structural settings that produce violence* (structures) and *the embedding of physical violence in the cognition of individuals* (processes).

5.2.1 Direct Violence

The expression of physical force through one or more actors to (an)other actor(s) is an obvious occurrence. It is more likely that the agents of violence are known (and therefore can be held accountable for their actions). Violence is intentionally conducted by agents such as the military, militias, rebel soldiers, terrorists, gangs, vigilant groups, private security guards and police. These agents conduct violence to reach a desired outcome – obedience, punishment or concession. Violence is therefore to be primarily conceptualized as means to an end.

Violence involves the actual or anticipated application of any form of weaponry to cause physical injury to compel action against one's will. It is the infliction of physical pain to sanction non-adherence to the will of the agent of violence. Although the measurability of direct violence can be conducted through an analysis of the number and degree of actual casualties, direct violence is framed as a matter of perception in the social context. Direct violence moves within cognitive processes in which memories of past infliction enable individuals to anticipate future violence. However, it should also be noted that fear can also be generated without any experience of inflicted pain. The unknown can generate as much fear as the known.

5.2.2 Structural Violence

The term *structural violence* was often used in the 1960s, and is ascribed to Johan Galtung (1990) in his work "*Cultural Violence*". It is a form of violence that prevents people from meeting their basic needs such as food, water, education and employment. Individuals or collective groups are systematically harmed by a given social structure or social institution that the state has established or has failed to correct. The agent of violence is in this case the given structural setting in the society. Violence is not to be understood only as the use of weaponry. While direct violence can be illegitimate, structural violence can be justified or legitimized through aspects of culture such as religion, language, history and tradition and thus made acceptable (Galtung 1990, p.291). Another form of structural violence is the actual absence of institutions or mechanisms that actively protect citizens from violence and from structural discrimination.

In the Philippines, the marginalization of the Muslim population and other ethnic minorities is party caused by the lack of retributive and compensatory mechanisms for the structural weaknesses of minorities brought on by historical processes. This has been discussed comprehensively in chapter 2 of this project. Furthermore, as David (2004, p.133) argues, the culture of pluralism and tolerance that already define the Philippine constitution is still in the process of institutionalization in the country. The realization of cultural pluralism in the country needs "experience."

The measurability of structural violence is more complex, because negative social structures can be both actively manipulated or merely tolerated. The quality or degree of harm inflicted on the people can be measured only in terms of perceptions. Structural violence can be manifest or latent, and it can be measured in the perceived outcome.

5.2.3 Symbolic Violence

Another form of violence is the so-called symbolic violence as introduced by the French sociologist Pierre Bourdieu (1991). From the sociological perspective, symbolic violence refers to the legitimate system of meanings called culture. It is to be distinguished from structural violence. While structural violence is not necessarily legitimate and justified in the eyes of the harmed, symbolic violence refers to dominated social agents who accept the social order unconsciously as 'just'. Symbolic violence requires asymmetry in symbolic capital such as prestige and honor in consolidating hierarchical relationships. Furthermore, symbolic violence can be caused by asymmetry in cultural capital such as in competencies, skills and qualifications.

Bourdieu refers to symbolic violence as the exercise of power that seeks to alter actions through holding more symbolic capital against an agent who holds less. Measurability is therefore problematic because symbolic violence accounts for unconscious modes of social domination occurring within the daily social habits. The incorporation of unconscious structures tends to determine the structure of actions of the dominant party. Perceiving their actions to be right, the weaker agents (who hold less symbolic capital) tend to be misrecognized in the social matrix.

In the Philippines, the Muslim minorities are seen to hold less symbolic (e.g. prestige) and cultural capital (e.g. education) within the Philippine state. The latent anti-Muslim bias is deeply embedded in Philippine society. Demonization and the insistance upon the supposed 'inferiority' of Muslims have constantly determined societal norms, and affected individuals in countless ways, such as in the granting bank loans or the selecting of employees. Muslims tend to be less educated and therefore tend to have less income than their Christian Tagalog peers. For instance, the lack of educational success of Muslim citzens, as Bourdieu would argue, entails a whole range of cultural behaviors that include attire, assertiveness and vocabulary.

The lack of educational opportunities available to Muslims further reproduces the economic position of their parents in the wider social system. Interestingly, there is a tendency to assume the disposition, manner, skills and qualifications of Muslim individuals based on the status as Muslims, rather than actually investigating their real skills and qualifications. For instance, a highly educated Muslim is often classified at first impression as less qualified than their Tagalog peers with the same qualification. The lack of educational success of Muslims eventually impedes them in entering networks that are important in accessing higher incomes.

The latent anti-Muslim bias in Philippine society leads to more competition among Muslim professionals, who then compete for the remaining employment opportunities or are forced to seek employment abroad. The "uneducated" Muslims are not seen as social peers (misrecognition), and the "educated" Muslims are less qualified than their peers with the same qualification. Symbolic violence means that the distribution of income according to qualification is considered a legitimate social mechanism.

The perceived legitimate social mechanism of selection however fails to consider the preexisting structural imbalances in the society. Although access to education is not equal, and is in fact biased against minority groups, this selection mechanism is accepted as legitimate, both by the dominant group and the minorities. In this sense, symbolic violence can be more powerful than direct violence because it is embedded in the very modes of action and structures of cognition of individuals. It imposes the specter of legitimacy on the social order (Bourdieu 1991). Symbolic violence moves with the latent and subconscious channels of societal interactions.

5.3 The Bureaucracy of Violence – Acquiring and Maintaining Legitimacy

The legitimacy of the use of violence in the nation-building process presupposes the legitimacy of the hierarchical system, or 'bureaucracy'. The bureaucratization of violence serves as a precondition for the maintenance of legitimacy. While assuming that 'legitimacy' is interchangeable with the term 'justifiability', Hannah Arendt (2009b) argues that violence can never be objectively legitimate and can only, at most. be justified. In the context of a hegemonic group establishing the normative order in a specific state, violence will tend to be justifiable, particularly under the banner of a cohesive nation. The history of a nation has always been entangled with the story of war and destruction through nationalism (Dionisio 2004, p.11).

The Philippine-American war resulted in the deaths of several thousands of Filipinos and Americans. After several years of sporadic violence, independence was negotiated and continued for 10 years after the signing of the Philippine constitution of 1935. However, the Japanese occupation descended shortly afterwards. The Japanese occupation was ended by war that resulted in an estimated one million casualties, and the destruction of properties in the country. In the first years of its independence, the Republic of the Philippines had to deal with the remnants of the *Hukbalahap* (*Hukbo ng Bayan Laban sa mga Hapon* or People's Army Against the Japanese), a rebellion that was the military arm of the Communist Party of the Philippines. Hukbalahap continued its fight against the pro-Western leaders of the government until 1954. The insurgency was ended through a series of reforms and military victories by President Ramon Magsaysay (Goodwin 2001, p.119).

After almost two decades of independence, the young republic had to deal with both communist insurgents and Muslim separatist groups. There is a consensus that the "Filipino nation is unfinished business" (David 2004, p.xii), and that this nation still aspires to grow into full modern nationhood. The government sees the use of violence against several rebel groups as existentially important. This necessity confers legitimacy as claimed by the government.

Assuming that the armed rebel confrontation was nothing other than an attempt to protect the integrity of the Philippines and its citizens, the maintenance of the legitimacy of the use of direct violence seems to be taken as self-evident and necessary. Furthermore, this legitimacy is rigorously maintained not only by the functionality of violence but also by the habits of violence. Functionality is substituted by the perception of efficiency brought by routines, hence, leading to legitimization. As Kreisky (Kreisky 2008, pp.58–59) argues, through the inclusion of the "Kalaschnikow life standard" in the "way of life", a dynamic is triggered. Social norms that limit the use of violence which exists in all societies are effectively abrogated.

Weber (1968) argued that hierarchical legitimization occurs over time through a collective construction of social reality in which the elements of a social order become consonant with norms that are perceived to be widely shared. In this regard, it should be noted that from day one the legitimacy of the hierarchy is claimed by the hegemon. Hierarchy is established in order to consolidate its own advantageous position. The hegemonic group maintains legitimacy not only through the bureaucratization of violence through the army and police, but also through the bureaucratization of its normative order.

As the case of the Philippines illustrates, the legitimacy of bureaucracy is reproduced by the educational system. The standardized educational curriculum instills values and confirms narratives that are positive in the eyes of the Tagalogs and their elite allies. Stories about local heroes such as the Dagohoy of Bohol, who initiated revolts against the Spanish colonizers, are denigrated and replaced by "national heroes" from the Tagalog region. Furthermore, while there are many legitimizing forces that tend to stabilize status-based hierarchies, some hierarchies are never legitimized (Ridgeway & Berger 1986) and others still lose legitimacy over time (Berger 1998; Goar & Sell 2005). However, in spite of the lack of legitimacy of some hierarchies, there are practically no measures that can be taken to remove these hierarchies. The lack of credible challengers to the hegemon eventually leads to these illegitimate hierarchies remaining unchanged. When dissent about a hierarchy is expressed, the dominant group works to restore the normative order (Zelditch 2001). This can be accomplished in different ways, depending on the perceived legitimacy of the hierarchy. Unlike a leader, a hegemon tends to be non-accommodative and would find ways to justify the use of violence to restore the normative order it supports. A leader might be open for change. Of course, the hegemon might calculate the use of violence to be too costly (politically and financially speaking), and may accommodate demands to change the hierarchical bureaucracy. However, if the dissent is widely securitized, the perception of cost will eventually be distorted.

5.4 Failure to Monopolize Violence as State Failure? - Franchising Violence to Political Warlords

Charles Tilly (1985, p.173) writes that the distinction between legitimate and illegitimate force came only very slowly. This distinction followed the process through which the armed forces of the states became relatively unified and permanent. For example, the English nation-state was only able to monopolize violence when the Tudors were successful in demilitarizing the great lords (Tilly 1985, p.174). In France, the monopoly of violence was achieved through policies of disarmament pursued by Cardinal Richelieu in the 1620s. For example, the prohibition of duels and sanctioning of private armies led to the consolidation of the French army leading to the concentration of power to the center. These two examples prove that the monopoly of violence has been achieved through the elimination of rivals. The monopolization of power was not an inherent outcome of a single deliberation on efficiency, but rather of a long process.

The Philippine government is to date unsuccessful in monopolizing violence. Kreisky (Kreisky 2008, p.151) warns that where a minimum degree of state monopoly is not realized, social zones emerge where criminal groups can operate without impediments. However, it can be argued that this failure to monopolize violence does not necessarily indicate failure of nation- and state-building. The failure to monopolize violence can be an outcome of the political deliberation of the newly independent nation-state. Political realities dominate the calculation of the state, disregarding imposed standards of nationhood from the outside.

Franchising violence to political warlords and private security firms is perceived to be more appropriate, because of the limited capacity of the national group to monopolize violence. The Philippine context of warlordism involves local political dynasties maintaining private armies for their own protection and for the containment of emerging rivals. Franchising violence therefore involves the invalidation of the Westphalian state through the decentralization of violence.

The government of the Philippines is not aiming for the disarmament of private armies, particularly those of local political allies. This resignation of the state creates the so-called "areas open to violence" (*gewaltoffene Räume*) (Elwert 1997, p.86) that offer favorable conditions for the rise of warlordism (Mair 2003, p.2), also referred to as gang warfare (Kreisky 2008, p.155).

Franchising violence to local political warlords serves the interests of the state, as this deters possible challengers to the national group. With loyal local elite groups concentrating their resources on their own security, the dominant national group can consolidate their status from the center. Violence is then limited to the local level. This practice however has legitimated private armies of political warlords in the political landscape of the Philippines, particularly in the areas outside Manila. The Philippine National Police (PNP) in its 1999 reports on partisan armed groups identified 93 Partisan Armed Groups (PAGs) with 2,129 members and 1,072 firearms (see Percy 2007). Partisan Armed Groups (PAGs) are private armies that are formed to protect the local political elite that strives to consolidate governance mechanisms in their area. Political warlords serve as the "arms" of the central government to counter-balance communist and Muslim rebel groups; without, however, the intention to overtake the state. They reach an informal agreement with the state not for altruistic reasons, but to profit from the "economy of violence" that they establish in their own areas. In several cases, the economies of these warlords are based on looting and smuggling (Jean & Rufin 1999).

According to Jovencito Puno, the Philippines top prosecutor, "Philippine politicians can't afford to be gun shy, and few it seems are. They don't take any chances with their opponents" (Percy 2007). Moreover, local political warlords use their security resources to intimidate local voters, assassinating political rivals, journalists and activists. The Alston Report of the Human Rights Council confirms the alarming increase of extrajudicial executions of leftist activists, civil society leaders, trade unionists, and land reform advocates (Alston 2007). Between 2001 and 2006, more than 800 activists were victims of extrajudicial killings. Alston identifies a lack of political will to put an end to the culture of impunity in the country,and a deficiency of constitutionally mandated accountability arrangements. Franchising violence to local political warlords can be likened to as the kinds of "new wars" that Kaldor (2000) describes. These new wars dissolve the boundaries between war, organized crime and massive human rights violations (Kaldor 2000, p.8).

5.5 Democracy Nurturing Violence – Between Power and Hierarchy

Assuming that peace means the absence of violence, the popular term "democratic peace" offers an analytical framework for answering the question of whether democracy can actually nurture violence. Machiavelli and Montesquieu among others suggested the correlation between governance structures and peace. According to them, violence does not emanate from republics (Czempiel 1996, p.320), due to the equal distribution of values. However, it should be questioned whether republics are always democratic. Immanuel Kant's *Zum ewigen Frieden* (Perpetual Peace) (1983) [1795] is considered as the primary philosophical foundation of the theory of democratic peace. He argues that democratic states are peaceful, because the citizens decide whether war is to be pursued or not. Citizens tend to be skeptical of starting a dangerous game (1983, pp.12–13 [1795]).

Although Kant and the other proponents of the theory of democratic peace refer to the behavior of democratic states toward other states, both democratic and non-democratic, it may still be relevant to the case of Southern Philippines. First, there should be no difference between the perception of the legitimate use of violence when expressed outside and the perception of the use of violence when expressed inside. It is illogical that the same republican constitution that prohibits war with other states and the same structural-institutional setting of democratic states that deescalate violent conflicts suddenly legitimize the use of violence against dissenting groups within its territory. It should not be the case that the same politically participating citizens who decide against war will decide for war against fellow citizens. The theory of democratic peace does not claim the genuine "peaceful character" of democratic states. The theory points that democratic states are similarly inclined to violence towards non-democratic states (Levy 1988).

Secondly, it should be noted that the Muslim population in the Southern Philippines assert that they were forcefully incorporated in the Philippine state immediately after the independence of the country from the United States. For the Muslims, Mindanao is a separate nation. This event may represent a breach of Kant's second preliminary article in his work "Perpetual Peace" (1795) that says, "*No independent states, large or small, shall come under the dominion of another state by inheritance, exchange, purchase, or donation.*" It can be interpreted that Mindanao was inherited by the Philippine state from the American colonial administration, particularly in the context of the self-rule that was practiced during the colonial period. Therefore, it should be questioned whether the current democratic setting of the Philippines will lead to "perpetual peace", within the context of post-colonialism. Why is there a tendency for the constitutional republican setting of the Philippines to nurture violence?

This chapter argues that there is a need for a more analytical approach in answering whether democracy nurtures violence with regards to the Philippines. Democracy does not automatically exclude a violence-generating power preponderance that is extracted from established hierarchical relations. Particularly in the Philippines, nation-building was initiated by a specific national group that was successful in defining the constitutional and political setting of the state; thus, indirectly establishing hierarchical bureaucracies.

The hegemonic national group assumes the self-evidence and implicitness of the realized normative order, particularly in the context of a lack of opposing challengers. With this assumption, it is not democracy that nurtures violence but the hierarchical relations between identity groups. Democracy can however intensify violence through the 1) legitimization awarded to the "majority" group which 2) abuses of the "constitutional process" created by the refusal to accommodate the claims of minorities.

In the Philippines, democratic settings and existing hierarchical bureaucracies are not mutually exclusive, to the contrary, they are mutually complementary. The democratic setting of the state did not prevent the Philippine Congress from declaring in 1955 that Muslims were not capable of participating in social life because of the backwardness of their culture. This assumption justified structural imbalances through the legitimacy that was provided by the assumed inferiority of the Muslim culture.

The political system in the Philippines, although considered democratic, is unitary and centralistic. The dominant nation group (with their political allies) as (qualitative) majority can use democratic principles to justify direct, structural and symbolic violence. It can also instrumentalizes democratic principles to refuse claims for recognition. Claims for recognition are subjugated to the constitutional process. For example, the 2008 breakdown of peace negotiations between the government and the Moro Islamic Liberation Front (MILF) was associated with the Memorandum of Agreement on Ancestral Domain (MOA-AD) declared unconstitutional by the Philippine Supreme Court. Several hundred thousand people were internally displaced following the armed confrontation between the military and rebel groups, as well as elements of the rebel groups attacking Christian villages, prompting the military to attack Muslim areas. Eventually, a year later, both parties agreed to cease armed confrontation. The action of the Philippine Supreme Court shows how democratic processes can actually instigate violence. The constitutional process is never a guarantee of the cessation of violence.

5.6 The Need for a Paradigm Shift – The Concept of a "Non-Competitive Nation-Building"

The Southern Philippines provides an interesting example of how violence contributes to the development and maintenance of identity in a self-sustaining conflict cycle. Violence is assumed to be a necessary instrument for nation-building. Such an assumption is however an example of existing paradigms that should be re-visited. Any reconciliatory peace processes such as the one desired in the Philippines requires a critical evaluation of self-evident and self-enforcing institutions, state policies, and societal mechanisms. This section of the project aims to summarize these paradigms that refer to features of nation-building that initiates and maintains violence. The concept of "non-competitive" nation-building is introduced to reify several paradigm shifts. This is a theoretical concept that emerges from experience.

The point of departure for this concept is the notion that nation-building is a multidimensional non-linear process. It is comprised of both deliberately planned decisions and accidental events that led to the actual reification of what is called nation-building. As a process, nation-building can also develop otherwise. Nationhood need not be a result of a violent process. The four different streams of the study of the nation (see chapter 3) refer to the different means of how legitimacy and political loyalty can be demanded by the nation-state. The plurality in the study of nationhood implies the same plurality in an understanding of what a nation is; therefore enabling a concept of nation-hood that is most appropriate in former colonies such as the Philippines. The context of nation-building in former colonies can be summarized as follows:

- The dominant role of a specific national group is acquired through the 'divide-and-rule' strategy during the colonial period and during wars for independence.
- The dominant role of a specific national group is maintained and consolidated by the successful bureaucratization of the group's normative order and a lack of potential challengers.
- One of the remnants of colonialism is the rather artificial state boundaries that were determined by the geo-strategical calculations of the colonial powers rather than by socio-identity conditions.
- The forceful incorporation of other national groups within the state territory leads to contesting narratives that determine social interactions between groups.
- Social cohesion is believed to be guaranteed only through homogenization, for instance through the national educational system.

With the above mentioned elements comprising nation-building in former colonies like the Philippines, paradigms are formulated from context. Acknowledging the claim of Thomas Kuhn (1996) in his work "*The Structure of Scientific Revolution*" that the concept of the 'paradigm' is not applicable in social science, the concept of the "social paradigm" of Handa (1986) confirms the necessity of looking at social phenomenon such as nation-building through a multidimensional process outlook. Handa (1986) focuses on social circumstances that precipitate a shift of paradigm, and effects on the shift on social institutions.

A shift of paradigm involves a change in the perception of the reality of individuals and groups. Assuming that a social paradigm is an outcome of cognitive processes implies an understanding of the paradigm in the sense of *Weltanschauung* (worldview). A shift of paradigm therefore involves a change in the worldview or at least in how a specific worldview is to be framed. It involves changes in the interpretation of a set of experiences, as well as the change in the evaluation and expression of the beliefs and values that maintain social institutions and frame social interactions.

5.7 Nationalistic Paradigms (P) – Discovering Patterns of Misrecognition

Identity conflicts involve paradigms that are responsible for the maintenance of distorted social relations. These paradigms reflect the system-structural and hegemonial conditions that frame conflicting relations between groups. Paradigms are therefore system related. Their identification requires a systems analytical approach. The following patterns of misrecognition are system-related conditions that require critical evaluation.

The understanding of the ruling national group that it represents society at large refers to the equation of society with nation-states (Smith 1979) *(P1)*. This paradigm confirms two other paradigms according to which equilibrium or cohesion in the society is needed to ensure stability *(P2),* and that the national group that understands itself as the society and is therefore accountable for ensuring cohesion in the societal system *(P3)* that is understood as a whole with interrelated parts (Giddens 1984; Durkheim 1996). Being accountable for social cohesion, the national group sees the necessity to establish political and constitutional order that expresses the group's normative worldview *(P4)*. The national group will tend to be unwilling to tolerate and to maintain (e.g. finance) a bureaucratic system that does not represent its worldview. What follows is the evaluation of the other system as inferior and ineffective *(P5)* through narratives. The securitization of the normative order follows the perception of threat. Securitization eventually leads to the legitimization of the use of direct violence *(P6)*. Furthermore, having in mind that the mere existence of democratic institutions is enough to accommodate minorities *(P7),* the nation-state fails to see existing hierarchical relationships, leading to asymmetries in symbolic and cultural capital that cause structural and symbolic violence.

The above mentioned nationalistic paradigms are the underlying causes of conflict in former colonies such as the Philippines. It is not the intention of this chapter to call for the elimination of the concept of nationality, nationalism, nation, nation-hood or nation-building, but rather to find a concept that removes the underlying causes of conflict, or at least a concept of nation-building that allows plurality and discharges violence. The next step is to derive a concept of nation-building that promulgates the shift of these paradigms to enable societal transformation leading to sustainable conflict management.

5.8 A Concept of "Non-Competitive" Nation-building

Nation-building is a reality in former colonies. While European nation-states had hundreds of years to pursue nation-building, newly independent states with inherited boundaries and security vacuums to fill are expected to express nationhood in a very short time period. Former colonies are addressed as nation-states in the international system, although several of these states are still in the process of consolidating governance mechanisms. Kreisky (2008, p.152) recognizes that the system of the nation-state was able to assert itself subsequently during the decolonization process. Nevertheless, the performance of governance structures tends to be evaluated using European standards. While the actual boundaries of European nation-states were the outcome of hundreds of years of contestation (that lasted until the end of the Second World War), former colonies are stuck in predetermined boundaries through existing international laws that divide communities and families (McEwen 1971).

Although the international system tries to recognize the difficulties of the lines "on the ground," the boundaries are defended "with the principles of finality, stability and effectiveness, which, according to international tribunals, have in the past been declared to govern territorial disputes" (Brownley & Burns 1979, p.18). The imminent implication of rather static boundaries is the legitimization of violence, which is aggravated by the lack of judicial channels at an international level. Assuming that paradigms are capable of changing, nation-building does not need to be backward-looking and manipulative.

5.8.1 The Nation-State and Institutional Pluralism

Equating the nation with the society (P1) maintains hierarchies in that society. This equation consolidates the advantageous position of the center against the disadvantaged position of the periphery. The understanding of the equation of the nation-state with society leads to what Karl Renner (1952, p.320) refers to as the idea of the economic state coalescing with the idea of the nation-state. Renner (1952, p.321) further suggests that the idea of the "exclusive right" of the nation to the national economic space is expressed in the structuring of the economy. A non-competitive concept of nation-building requires the separation of politics from economics, welfare and other spheres of public life. Economic competition should not find itself in the political arena. Economic contestation should not reflect the political contestation of national groups, but should rather reflect contestation of economic stakeholders such as business companies, corporations, and labor unions. A formula has to be found to separate political and economic institutions to ensure institutional pluralism.

This suggestion does not call for the total separation of the economy from the influence of politics, at least not if politics remain biased, nor is it suggesting the state be dismantled through the deregulation of institutions (Altvater & Mahnkopf 2002, p.26). In a context of a state that is perceived as the property of the hegemon, economic processes should not be determined in the political realm to devitalize structural and symbolic violence. Existing disparities between nation groups should be compensated by "mediating institutions" (which will be discussed below), to counter preexisting structural and symbolical deficiencies.

In the Philippines, the mind-set that there is a single Filipino society leads to a failure to evaluate economic practices that discriminate against minority groups. Membership to a specific ethno-linguistic group is then reflected in class membership. Perceiving the nation-state as the modern Filipino society legitimizes structural and symbolic violence. A single Filipino society implies blindness towards evaluating economic disparities from the perspective of the ethnic minority. A shift in this understanding to one which says there is one family of several societies will lessen the incentive for "society-grabbing" by the dominant national group.

5.8.2 Stability vs. Resilience

Understanding the necessity of maintaining equilibrium or social cohesion (P2) in ensuring stability leads to nation-building becoming a euphemism for homogenization. Under the popular word 'integration', the diversity of identities is seen as the cause of antagonism instead of the "violence of homogenization and discrimination brought about by narrow nationalism" (Dionisio 2004, p.14). The word 'equilibrium' is one of these terms that seem to be so clear that no one asks what is actually meant by this term.

In game theory, John Nash (1950) introduced in his dissertation *Non-cooperative Games* the concept of equilibrium according to which equilibrium is achieved when no single actor has anything to gain by changing their own strategy unilaterally. If each actor has chosen a strategy and no actor can benefit from changing its strategy while the other actors keep theirs unchanged, then the current set of strategy choices and the corresponding payoffs constitute the '*Nash-equilibrium'*. The concept of 'Nash of equilibrium' focuses on the perspective of actors when making decisions. However, it remains unclear how equilibrium is to be conceptualized in a context of nation-building in former colonies such as the Philippines.

In hegemonic nation-building, equilibrium seems to be impossible, because the conditions are biased against all actors except the hegemon. The hegemon will tend to understand equilibrium as 'stability', that is when events are predictable and reliable. Stability connotes a quality or a state where there is resistance to any change and that constancy in the behavior of actors is desirable. Stability is the condition in which the status quo is not challenged.

The concept of non-competitive nation-building calls for a shift of paradigm. The desire for stability legitimizes the use of violence through the hegemon, which sees itself as the defender of stability in the system (P4). Non-competitive nation-building involves a dominant national group not seeking hegemonic stability but 'resilience'. Borrowing the concept of resilience from psychology, it refers to the ability to recover from trauma or crisis (Bonnano 2004). In the context of state-building, resilience refers to the ability of the system to resist breakdown brought by crises such as the isolated outbursts of violent confrontation. Resilience is different to stability, because it connotes adaptability to challenges brought on by changes in the system. Adaptability, in turn, is guaranteed by building capacities to anticipate and identify sources of vulnerabilities.

Nationhood, as Dionisio (2004, p.15) argues, requires "the constant reinvention of ... institutions. New ways of thinking should be matched with new ways of doing things." The capacity of institutions to evolve independently from the hegemon alleviates biased political and constitutional orders. In contrast to stability, resilience acknowledges the inevitability of constant change and the uncertainties brought by a specific change. Stability implies maintaining the status quo, whereas resilience alters the status quo to adapt to changes.

A dominant national group that understands itself as accountable to the cohesion of the societal system emerges as the hegemon, because in ensuring cohesion, there is a need to predetermine the "glue" in the form of a normative order that would bind all groups. The hegemon establishes political and constitutional mechanisms that they perceive will reify the normative order. As mentioned above, cohesion is assumed by the dominant group as necessary for the stability of the system. Stability, however, maintains the status quo, and those groups that stopped recognizing this "glue" will be perceived as threats to stability. This is where securitization is used to legitimize the use of violence (P6).

5.8.3 Resilience and Leadership

The concept of a non-competitive nation-building implies that although there is a need for an actor to act as guarantor, it is not for the sake of cohesion and stability, but for the sake of resilience. While stability requires a hegemon, resilience needs a leader. A leader, unlike a hegemon, delegates responsibility to the so-called "mediating institutions" (Berger 1998). Such institutions are mechanisms that regulate the co-existence of different normative orders. They allow society to negotiate a settlement. A hegemon is not capable of establishing such an institution, because it will be inevitable assessed as biased. Asserting that the national group is responsible for ensuring stability is necessary to eliminate patterns of misrecognition. The delegation of role of ensuring the resilience of the system to mediating institutions reduces hegemony and eventually enables hegemonic groups to assume leadership.

Mediating institutions may be central to civil society (Then 1998, p.xviii). These groupings play an important role in integrating different segments of society which find themselves constantly in bargaininging. Mediating institutions may also be based on traditional customs and norms in managing conflict (Then 1998: xviii). Each society has invented modes of dealing with conflict. Although such modes can both mitigate and aggravate conflict based on who established such modes, these can be reviewed and modified (see Penetrante 2010). Such modes are already deeply instilled in society, and with slight modifications, can be more easily accepted than modes exported from the outside.

5.8.4 The Nation and the Identity of Solidarity

Mediating institutions requires the establishment of the "public sphere" (Habermas 1962), particularly in Mindanao, where more than 75 percent of Christian Filipinos have no personal relationship with Muslim members of society. The segregation between groups impedes the establishment of a much needed public sphere where Filipinos of all religions and ethno-linguistic groupings can meet to discuss issues of mutual interest. The public sphere mediates between the "private sphere" and the "sphere of public authority" (Habermas 1989). The state with all its structures (such as the police and military) maintains discursive relations with the private sphere which is represented by the civil society in this public space.

The current political landscape in the Philippines hinders the consolidation of a public sphere, particularly because the state classifies all kinds of opposition as "communist" insurgency. The failure of achieving a single Filipino identity is commonly attributed to the perception that it "does not pay to be a Filipino". Another possible reason is the failure to find an overarching mode of social communication among individuals across all tribal and non-tribal ethno-linguistic groups in the Philippines. This confirms the near absence of the Habermasian public sphere in the country. Existing communicative practices of the hegemonic national group lead to the exclusion of perceived non-members. Furthermore, some practices include imposing communication barriers on other groups, which increases the resources needed to participate as equal social peers in the public sphere.

Interestingly, the assumption that the public sphere is unproblematic in democratic states such as the Philippines is rather misleading as the case of the Philippines illustrates (P7). The democratic setting of the states is not a guarantee for the consolidation of the public sphere, particularly if democracy fails to eliminate hierarchical relationships between national groups.

Non-competitive nation-building intends to move from a primordialist understanding of the nation as an identity to an understanding of the nation as "*an identity of solidarity*." The task of nationhood should include a preparedness to reinvent institutions and to meet the demands of the current generation to ensure the continued existence of the nation. The understanding of what a nation means is constantly evolving, and this evolution should be reified in the state institutions. For example, in the Philippines, the question citizens should formulate is not "what is a Filipino?", but rather "why be Filipino?". Solidarity based on a single overarching Filipino identity remains weak in the Philippines. One possible reason for this is the state's failure to provide its citizens with an acceptable reason to remain Filipino (Dionisio 2004, p.6). Dionisio mentions a study conducted by Ma. Luisa Doronila in 1992 that suggests that given a chance, Filipino schoolchildren would rather be reborn as Japanese or Americans. There is no reason for Cebuanos, Muslims and other groups to embrace the Filipino identity when it brings them no positives effects. As Dionisio (2004, p.14) argues, "nationhood should therefore be antithetical to ubiquitous destitution."

5.8.5 Nation-building and History – Reframing Narratives

A non-competitive nation-building furthermore involves rethinking history. The hegemon's interpretation of history reflects how the nation-state interprets narratives (P5). Narratives function as a driving force in the identity-building process of groups. History is seen only "from the clear vantage point of someone who has figured out the road to the future" (David 2001). Nationhood is not the search for a destiny, but rather an attempt to create one's own destiny (Dionisio 2004, p.7). The existence of several identity-groups within the state territory implies diverging narratives. In a competitive setting, the hegemon tends to sell its own "dogmatic" narratives as the absolute truth, negating other narratives.

Formal education is equally efficient in undermining the acceptance of other existing cultures. For instance, in Philippine schools, younger generations are told stories and inculcated with values that ignore and denigrate the cultural traditions of their ancestors (Dionisio 2004, p.5). The use of Tagalog in all schools enhances this perception of inferiority, particularly when their native language is prohibited. The configuration of the national curriculum is determined solely on the capital, and there are no mechanisms for accommodating local narratives such as stories of Cebuano heroes. For instance, the stories of Igorot men and women who fought with the Katipunan during the 1898 revolution remain unheard in Philippine schools (Cabreza 2007). Another example is how Mindanao is narrated in the Philippines. Filipino leaders see Mindanao merely as "an unfinished task in the agenda of national integration" (Dionisio 2004, p.7).

Using Nietzsche's (2005) [1873] notion of "critical history" and Renato Constantino's (1975) pragmatic concept of a "usable past," Dionisio (2004, p.5) argues that history should not be considered an instrument of uncovering the truth of the past. History is a tool through which the memory of a people who are constantly reflecting on ways to achieve nationhood is written and rewritten. She continues that Nietzsche's critical review of history challenges individuals and groups to be brave enough to remember all those painful and shameful episodes in history, with the intention of gaining an understanding as individuals and of achieving goals as a nation. A nation needs to continuously evaluate its historical narratives as a guide for the present and the future.

Dealing with contesting narratives is essential if citizens want to be sure of who they want to become. Although some individual narratives are arguably incompatible with others, they do not necessarily need to be offensive to each other. Mediating institutions can reconfigure offending narratives through reframing them positively. Furthermore, a culture complocit in the latent demonization of minorities should be neutralized. The media should be self-critical when reproducing narratives. For instance, in a news story about a series of earthquakes in the Philippines in July 2010, the reporter Alcuin Papa (2010) wrote about personal stories of local residents. Latently, he reproduced a narrative of Christian Filipinos towards Muslims in including the statement of a local resident saying "some of our Muslim neighbors fired their weapons to drive away bad spirits." This statement is unnecessary in objective news coverage. This statement connotes the narrative attribution of the gun culture to the Muslim population without taking into account an objective analysis of how many Muslims actually have guns compared to Christians. This statement confirms the tendency of the media to attribute individual actions to the whole group, leading to latent biased perceptions. Although the media is an important fundament of democracy, when democratic fundaments lead to structural and symbolic violence, how 'democratic' elements are actually contributing to the protraction of a conflict should be evaluated. Media personnel should be sensitized to the existence of the symbolic violence they are intentionally or unintentionally reproducing. Mass communication serves as "the purveyor of images" (Dionisio 2004, p.7) that are ultimately expressed as narratives.

5.9 Interim Conclusion – Legitimizing Violence through Nation-Building

In the context of the Philippines and of several Third World countries, the use of violence in the initiation of nationhood is not always necessary. The absence of violence is imaginable when pursuing nation-building. In this chapter, it is argued that violence does not arise through the idea of nation-building, but rather through the hierarchical relationships resulting from nation-building. Nation-building does not always need to build hierarchical relationships which necessarily elaborate the hegemonial position of a specific national group.

The theoretical foundation of violence implies the need to understand why violence is chosen as the instrument to reach a goal. The production process of violence is explicable in the context of means and ends (Arendt 2009b, p.8). Nevertheless, the role of violence in politics is assumed to be so self-evident that violence as means is spared from critical analysis. Although, as Thomas Hobbes (1966) wrote, covenants without the sword are but words, violence is never in a position to sustainably persuade actors to reach a consensus – swords cannot reach covenants, and they eliminate words.

References:

Alston, P., 2007. Promotion and Protection of All Human Rights, Civil, Political, Economic, Social and Cultural Rights, Including the Right to Development, Available at: http://www.inquirer.net/verbatim/A-HRC8-Philippines_Advance.pdf [Accessed September 20, 2013].

Altvater, E. & Mahnkopf, B., 2002. Globalisierung der Unsicherheit, Münster: Westfälisches Dampfboot.

Arendt, H., 2009a. Elemente und Ursprünge totaler Herrschaft. Antisemitismus, Imperialismus, totale Herrschaft 13. Auflage., München & Zürich: Piper Taschenbuch.

Arendt, H., 2009b. Macht und Gewalt, München & Zürich: Piper Taschenbuch.

Berger, P. ed., 1998. The Limits of Social Cohesion, Colorado and Oxford: Westview Press.

Bonnano, G., 2004. Loss, Trauma, and Human Resilience: Have we underestimated the human capacity to thrive after extremely adverse events? American Psychologist, 59, pp.20–28.

Bourdieu, P., 1991. Language & Symbolic Power, Cambridge, MA: Harvard University Press.

Brownley, I. & Burns, I., 1979. African Boundaries, London: Royal Institute of International Affairs & Billing and Sons Limited.

Buckel, S. & Fisher-Lescano, A. eds., 2007. Hegemonie gepanzert mit Zwang. Zivilgesellschaft und Politik im Staatsverständnis Antonio Gramscis, baden-Baden: Nomos Verlagsgesellschaft.

Cabreza, V., 2007. CPLA Head's Arrest Leads to Restudy of ´87 Pact. Philippine Daily Inquirer.

Constantino, R., 1975. The Philippines: A Past Revisited and the Continuing Past, Quezon City, Philippines: Tala Publishing.

Czempiel, E.O., 1996. Kants Theorem und die zeitgenössische Theorie der internationalen Beziehungen. In M. Lutz-Bachmann & J. Bohman, eds. Frieden durch Recht: Kants Friedensidee und das Problem einer neuen Weltordnung. Frankfurt am Main: Fischer Taschenbuch Verlag, pp. 300–323.

Damazo, J., 2003. Breaking Free. Philippine Daily Inquirer. Available at: http://archives.newsbreak-knowledge.ph/2003/03/30/breaking-free/ [Accessed September 20, 2013].

David, R., 2001. Five Questions on People Power 2. Philippine Daily Inquirer.

David, R., 2004. Nation, Self and Citizenship: An Invitation to Philippine Sociology, Pasig City: Anvil Publishing Inc.

Dionisio, J., 2004. Introduction: the Project of Nationhood. In R. David, ed. Nation, Self and Citizenship: An Invitation to Philippine Sociology. Pasig City: Anvil Publishing Inc., pp. 3–22.

Durkheim, E., 1996. Über soziale Arbeitsteilung 2. Auflage., Frankfurt am Main: Suhrkamp.

Elwert, G., 1997. Gewaltmärkte: Beobachtungen zur Zweckrationalität der Gewalt. In T. von Trotha, ed. Soziologie der Gewalt. Sonderheft Nr. 37 der Kölner Zeitschrift für Soziologie und Sozialpsychologie. Opladen: Westdeutscher Verlag, pp. 86–101.

Galtung, J., 1990. Cultural Violence. Journal of Peace Research, 27(3), pp.291–305.

Giddens, A., 1984. The Constitution of Society, Berkeley, CA: University of California Press.

Goar, C. & Sell, J., 2005. The Tipping Point: How Little Things Can Make a Big Difference. Sociological Quarterly, 46(3), pp.525–543.

Goodwin, J., 2001. No other Way Out, Cambridge: Cambridge Univeristy Press.
Habermas, J., 1962. Strukturwandel der Öffentlichkeit. Untersuchungen zu einer Kategorie der bürgerlichen Gesellschaft, Frankfurt am Main: Suhrkamp.
Habermas, J., 1989. The Structural Transformation of the Public Sphere: An Inquiry into a Category of Bourgeois Society, Cambridge: Polity Press.
Handa, M., 1986. Peace Paradigm: Transcending Liberal and Marxian Paradigms. In International Symposium on Science, Technology and Development. New Delhi: OISE University of Toronto, Canada.
Hobbes, T., 1966. Leviathan oder Stoff, Form und Gewalt eines bürgerlichen und kirchlichen Staates, Frankfurt am Main: Suhrkamp.
Jean, F. & Rufin, C. eds., 1999. Ökonomie der Bürgerkriege, Hamburg: Hamburger Edition.
Kaldor, M., 2000. Alte und neue Kriege. Organisierte Gewalt im Zeitalter der Globalisierung, Frankfurt am Main: Suhrkamp.
Kant, I., 1983. Perpetual Peace, and Other Essays on Politics, History, and Morals, Indianapolis & Cambridge: Hackett Publishing.
Kreisky, E., 2008. Geschwächte Staaten, schwächelnde Männlichkeit und neue Kriege. In W. Sützl & D. Wallnöfer, eds. Gewalt und Präzision. Krieg und Sicherheit in Zeiten des War on Terror. Vienna: Verlag Turia & Kant, pp. 137–163.
Kreuzer, P. & Weiberg, M., 2005. Framing Violence: Nation- and State-building. An Asian Perspective., Frankfurt: Peace Research Institute Frankfurt.
Kuhn, T., 1996. The Structure of Scientific Revolutions 3rd Edition., Chicago, IL: University of Chicago Press.
Levy, J., 1988. Domestic Policies and War. Journal of Interdisciplinary History, 18(4), pp.563–573.
Magee, J. & Galinsky, A., 2008. Social Hierarchy: The Self-enforcing Nature of Power and Status. The Academy of Management Annals, 2(1), pp.351–398.
Mair, S., 2003. The New World of Privatized Violence, Friedrich Ebert Stiftung. Available at: http://www.fes.de/ipg/ONLINE2_2003/ARTMAIR.PDF [Accessed September 21, 2013].
McEwen, A., 1971. International Boundaries of East Africa, Oxford: Clarendon Press.
Nash, J., 1950. Equilibrium Points in n-person Games. Proceedings of the National Academy of Sciences, 36(1), pp.48–49.
Nietzsche, F., 2005. The Use and Abuse of History, New York: Cosimo Inc.
Papa, A., 2010. Quakes Shake Southern Philippines. Philippine Daily Inquirer. Available at: http://www.asianewsnet.net/home/news.php?id=13283 [Accessed September 21, 2013].

Penetrante, A.M., 2010. Court-Annexed Mediation in the Philippines – Community Involvement in the Judicial System – Recommendations for Bridging the Gaps I. W. Zartman, ed. PINPoints, The Impacto f History, Memory, and Culture in Negotiation(34), pp.13–15.

Percy, K., 2007. Correspondents Report – Philippine Gun Culture Examined. Australian Broadcasting Corporation. Available at: http://www.abc.net.au/correspondents/content/2007/s1921262.htm [Accessed September 21, 2013].

Renner, K., 1952. Mensch und Gesellschaft. Grundriß einer Soziologie, Wien: Verlag der Wiener Volksbuchhandlung Ignaz Brand.

Ridgeway, C. & Berger, J., 1986. Expectations, Legitimation, and Dominance Behavior in Task Groups. American Sociological Review, 51(5), pp.603–617.

Smith, A., 1979. Nationalism in the Twentieth Centry, Oxford: Martin Robertson.

Then, V., 1998. Introduction. In P. Berger, ed. The Limits of Social Cohesion. Boulder, CO: Westview Press, pp. xv–xix.

Tiedens, L. & Fragale, A., 2003. Power Moves: Complementarity in Dominant and Submissive Nonverbal Behavior. Journal of Personality and Social Psychology, 84, pp.558–568.

Tilly, C., 1985. War Making and State Making as Organized Crime. In P. B. Evans, D. Rueschemeyer, & T. Skocpol, eds. Bridging the State Back In. Cambridge: Cambridge University Press, pp. 169–191.

Weber, M., 1968. Economy and Society: An Outline of Interpretive Sociology, New York: Bedminster Verlag.

Zelditch, M., 2001. Processes of Legitimation: Recent Developments and New Directions. Social Psychology Quarterly, 64(1), pp.4–17.

6 Mediation as Intervention of Choice – A Critical Analysis of Mediation in Identity Conflicts

Mediation as the intervention of choice to resolve identity conflicts assumes that human societies have found their own ways and means to avert and/or to resolve conflicts. The existing body of literature claims that the cause of conflicts and the mechanisms for resolution are deeply rooted in the culture and history of every society. Conflict management is not a phenomenon exclusive to the West. The *Panchayat* in India (see Baxi & Galanter 1979; Hayden 1984; Moore 1985), the mediation committees in China (Clark 1989; see Li 1978), the *Jirga* in Afghanistan (see Carter & Connor 1989; Elphinstone 1992) and the *Katarungang Pambarangay* community mediation in the Philippines (see Pe & Tadiar 1988; Penetrante 2010) are traditional forms of conflict resolution that are embedded in modern institutions.

Conflicts and their resolution are culturally and politically specific (Harris 1968; Spiro 1986). Since conflicts are forms of social relationships, they are bound to reflect changes in societal structures, as traditional modes of conflict resolution are themselves evolving over time. Ultimately, these modes may also reflect new dynamics of violence and power hierarchies. For instance, community-level mediation through the "Katarungang (Justice) Barangay System" in the Philippines is slowly transforming itself into an instrument of the local political warlords, bent on consolidating power in the area (Penetrante 2010). Furthermore, local communities are becoming increasingly militarized through the establishment of community armies called "*Barangay Defense Mechanism*", and this limits the effectiveness of community mediation as a means of enhancing societal communication.

6.1 Studying Mediation

The literature on mediation suggests a diversity of approaches and perspectives (Kolb & Rubin 1991). The approaches include purely scholarly studies, policy implications and the reflections of mediators themselves (Bercovitch 2009). Furthermore, the body of literature creates the impression of newly discovered "non-Western" perspectives on conflict management.

The purpose of this chapter is to find a comprehensive and yet focused concept of mediation that can be used to analyze the intervention measures employed in protracted and intractable identity conflicts such as that of the Southern Philippines. This chapter recognizes the difficulties in finding a suitable common definition that encompasses all the different forms or types of mediation that have been conducted so far in the Southern Philippines. For example, the mediations conducted in Malaysia and Libya are not comparable to those conducted by local NGOs and private individuals. The mediation strategies of NGOs are heterogenous in their own right. The rationales and motivations of all these different actors are so diverse that a common understanding among intervening actors is hard to find. This diversity is perceived to limit the scope of the scientific study of mediation due to its perceived "conceptual imprecision" and "lack of transparency" (Bercovitch 2009: 341).

Furthermore, there is still considerable disagreement among scholars, and a state of disorientation and confusion among practitioners, as to what constitutes effective mediation and how to evaluate it (Bercovitch 1992). The lack of consensus on the concept of mediation follows the discussion of whether a consensual definition of mediation is actually needed to determine standards and to enable quality assessment. To find criteria for evaluation and to determine standards, a definition or a concept of what mediation constitutes is necessary.

The profile of the mediator is diverse on its own right. Aside from personalities such as Marthi Athisaari and Jimmy Carter (see Antrim & Sebenius 1992; Bercovitch 1992) who are not primarily professional mediators but are rather to be considered as "mediators through the context," professional mediators can be lawyers, psychologists, sociologists, clerics, economists and academics. Mediation can be practiced through different professional modes, further contributing to the diversity of mediation as a field of study. This professional diversity in conducting mediation confirms its position at the intersection of various disciplines such as political science, sociology, psychology, law and economics. In addition, the field of mediation application reflects such professional modes. Family mediators are likely to have a different educational and training background compared to business mediators. The diverging practices of professional mediators impede the institutionalization of standards, quality management and control comparable between professional groups and between countries.

Aside from the above mentioned impression that mediation originates exclusively from the United States, there is the notion that mediation is a newly invented mode of conflict management. There exist several forms and modes of mediation in Africa, Asia and in ancient Europe. Moore (1996, p.20) notes that mediation has a long and varied history in almost all cultures of the world. As Bercovitch (1992, p.1) enumerates, references to acts of mediation can be found in the Bible (ca. 2000 BC), for example in 1 Timothy 2:5-6 where Jesus Christ was mentioned a mediator between God and man: "For there is one God, and one mediator between God and man, the man Christ Jesus; who gave himself as ransom for all, to be testified in die time." Furthermore, mediation is found in Homer's Iliad (ca. 750 BC) and in Sopochles' Ajax (ca. 500 BC). In both works, mediation was mentioned as the ideal way of dealing with conflict (Dickson 1990). Mediation was furthermore the principal way of resolving personal disputes in ancient China.

The different practices of mediation are to be found deeply embedded in all societies. Some traditional practices of mediation were integrated in the legal system of the Philippines (see Penetrante 2010). Some practices are used to complement overwhelmed courts such as the *Gachacha* in Rwanda and the *Jirga* in Afghanistan. Indonesia, considered the largest Muslim country, blended traditional means of decision-making and dispute resolution with Islamic practices. The *musyawarah* process, a consensually based conflict management procedure (Moore & Santosa 1995), is practiced throughout the country to make decisions and resolve disputes on both local and national issues (von Benda-Beckmann 1984; Slatts & Porter 1992).

Mediation has become an increasingly common form of dispute resolution particularly in the United States and several European countries. Countries such as Germany, Poland and Austria have introduced court-annexed mediation through which cases can be forwarded by the judge to mediation for an out-of-court settlement. The advantages of mediation include increased privacy and confidentiality, greater flexibility when formulating outcomes, less costs for disputing parties, less work load for the courts, and increased sustainability of achieved agreements. Nevertheless, the social-embeddedness of mediation practices is also considered to be a hindrance in conducting comparative studies of mediation practices, because too narrow a definition could reduce some tradition forms of mediation to mere deviations from the "standard." Furthermore, a too broad definition of mediation limits its comparability and applicability.

Mediation in the international system pertains to other contexts of mediation. However, although issues differ between national and international mediation, similar processes of reconciling interests between conflicting parties can be observed at both levels. The United Nations prefer the use of mediation to settle disputes between countries. Mediation has been conducted by states, individuals, regional organizations and non-government organizations to resolve international conflicts or internal conflicts that are feared to spread to neighbouring countries, thus, threatening international stability. Internal conflicts, including identity conflicts, are often feared to destabilize regions as countries confronted by internal conflicts are for example often used by terrorists as safe havens.

The intention of this chapter is to critically assess mediation as an instrument of choice in settling identity conflicts. It should be analyzed whether mediation in identity conflicts is really as advantageous as it is characterized to be. The reduced costs and decreased formality through mediation are believed to be factors that are likely to encourage minority groups to bring their grievances to the courts. As Seth (2000) notes, it is hoped that mediation will become a means through which to rectify some of the injustices that minority groups experience in the judicial system.

6.2 Conceptualizing Mediation

The following table summarizes the definitions of leading authors on mediation. An 'actor' here refers to the agents that conduct mediation. 'Structural context/issue' refers to the framework that makes an intervention such as mediation necessary. 'Procedure' points to the form of action that the mediator applies to induce the flow of the process. 'Process' is the way that is chosen to reach an outcome.

Table 6.2: Definition and Conceptualization of Mediation

Author	Actor	Structural Context/ Issue	Procedure	Process	Outcome
Young (1967)	Not a direct party actor	Crisis	Facilitation	Reduction of Removal of Problems of the Bargaining Relationship	Termination of crisis
Mitchell (1981)	Third party	Disruptive conflict behavior	Intermediary activity		Compromise; settlement
Blake & Mouton (1985)	Third party	Problem	Investigation, Definition and Recommendation	Intervention	Mutually acceptable solution
Douglas (1957)	Outsider	Dispute	Assistance	Intervention	Agreement
Moore (1986)	Acceptable, impartial and neutral third party	Contention ("contending")	Assistance (no authority)	Intervention	Voluntarily, mutually acceptable settlement

Singer (1990)	Third party / Outsider (who lacks power to make decisions)	Dispute	Assistance	Involvement	Decisions
Spencer & Yang (1993)	Third Party	Dispute	Assistance	"Go-between" (Relationship broker)	
Bingham (1985)	Neutral Third Party	Negotiation	Assistance		
Folberg & Taylor (1984)	Neutral person	Dispute	Assistance	Development of Options and Alternatives	Consensual Settlement
Schelling (1960)	Third Party	Communication Gap	Communication Arrangement		Pay-off
Bercovitch (1992)	Individual, Group, State or Organization	Dispute	Change, Affect or Influence Perceptions and Behaviour	Conflict Management	Conflict Management

Mediation according to Oran Young (1967, p.34) is "any action taken by an actor that is not a direct party to the crisis, and that is designed to reduce or remove one or more of the problems of the bargaining relationship and therefore to facilitate the termination of the crisis itself." Young's definition implies the necessity of neutrality that can be ensured by finding a mediator who is not a direct party to the crisis. Furthermore, Young's definition implies an active intervention to alter the "problematic" status quo. In this regard, the definition of Bingham (1985, p.5) involves a very concise understanding of mediation as the "assistance of a `neutral´ third party to a negotiation."

Ann Douglas (1957, p.10) preconditions a situation lacking peace when conducting mediation. She defines mediation as "a form of peace-making in which an outsider to a dispute intervenes on his (or her) own or accepts the invitation of disputing parties to assist them in reaching agreement." Like Young, she argues that to guarantee the desired outcome, neutrality must be ensured. She suggests the intervention of an outsider who does not belong to a specific normative order. An 'outsider' means someone who is not likely share norms or practices with the group. Unlike Young's actor, who is not a direct party to the crisis but can share the same outlook and worldview, for Douglas it is someone who has a different perspective.

Linda Singer (1990, p.20) goes further and attempts to concretize the meaning of neutrality and impartiality by defining mediation as a "form of third-party assistance [that] involves an outsider to the dispute who lacks the power to make decisions for the parties" (emphasis added). For her, mediation seeks a situation where the conflicting parties autonomously reach decisions in the form of an agreement. Spencer and Yang (1993, p.195) point out the the role of the mediator in the process by defining mediation as "the assistance of a third party not involved in the dispute, who may be of unique status that gives him or her certain authority with the disputants; or perhaps an outsider who may be regarded by them as a suitably neutral go-between." Connecting this definition to that of Singer (1990), it is an interesting question whether the given "authority" to the mediator (as understood by Singer) is compatible with the notion of Spencer and Yang on the lack of power to make decisions.

Charles W. Moore (Moore 1996, p.6) moves the focus to the process and attributes of mediation by defining it as "the intervention of an acceptable impartial and neutral third party who has no authoritative decision-making power to assist contending parties in voluntarily reaching their own mutually acceptable settlement." His definition implies the significance of finding the appropriate process to ensure the acceptability of the outcome. With the "right" process, the "right" outcome inevitably follows.

Blake and Mouton (1985, p.15) share Moore's perspective by defining mediation "as a process involving the intervention of a third party who first investigates and defines the problem and then usually approaches each group separately with recommendations designed to provide a mutually acceptable solution." They have a concrete understanding of the different stages of the process. The mediator is expected to guide the conflicting parties through these stages and he or she being a third party to the conflict ensures the acceptability of the intended outcome.

Folberg and Taylor (1984: 7) define mediation "as the process by which the participants, together with the assistance of a neutral person or persons, systematically isolate disputed issues in order to develop options, consider alternatives, and reach a consensual settlement that will accommodate their needs." In this definition, they see mediation as the process that eventually leads to a consensual settlement. Consensuality requires neutrality and the active participation of the mediator in developing options for the conflicting parties. For them, neutrality is not undermined by active participation in developing options.

Following an outcome orientation, Christopher Mitchell (1981, p.287) defines mediation as any "intermediate activity [...] undertaken by a third party with the primary intention of achieving some compromise settlement of the issues at stake between the parties, or at least ending disruptive conflict behaviour." What is new in Mitchell's definition is the identification of the minimal goal of mediation – to end a disruptive conflict behavior. At the other end of the pole, the goal of mediation is to reach a compromise settlement.

Coming from a game theoretical perspective, Tom Schelling (1960, p.22) claims that mediation "is probably best viewed as an element in the communication arrangements, or as a third party with a pay-off structure of his own." This definition implies that mediation may be conducted not merely by an actor, but also by structural arrangements that foster communication between conflict parties. He admits that neutrality is less likely because a mediator envisages benefits through its role as mediator.

The definition of Jacob Bercovitch involves a very comprehensive understanding of what mediation is. He defines mediation as a "process of conflict management, related to but distinct from the parties' own efforts, where the disputing parties or their representatives seek the assistance, or accept an offer of help, from an individual, group, state or organization to change, affect or influence their perceptions or behavior, without resorting to physical force or invoking the authority of law" (1992, p.7). Interestingly, his definition implies the equation of the process with the outcome. Unlike other authors, he did not mention any concrete outcome such as an agreement or a settlement. The process of changing or influencing the perceptions or behavior that led to the conflict is the desired outcome itself. Furthermore, his definition did not mention neutrality nor impartiality. This is a major deviation from all other definitions of mediation.

This project uses the following definition of mediation:

> *Mediation is a process of conflict management that involves strategic facilitation of contestation through acceptable actors or structures transforming contestation to a legitimate phenomenon.*

Following the common denominator of all the definitions in mediation is best understood as a process through which a specific outcome can be achieved. Strategic facilitation implies an active maneuvering of activities in which an acceptable mediator aims to reframe the understanding of contestation as a threat to it being a legitimate part of social interactions in the context of diversity.

It is not neutrality and impartiality that counts but rather whether the mediator is credible enough to deliver the expected performance. A biased mediator is not necessarily counterproductive to mediation. Mediation may become a source of impasses in managing identity conflicts. Therefore, a more systemic, comprehensive and critical analysis of mediation has become a precondition in the resolution of identity conflicts.

6.3 How Mediation Works

The scientific study of mediation as an intervention between conflicting parties is regarded as limited in its scope due to its perceived "conceptual imprecision" and "lack of transparency" (Bercovitch 2009, p.341). This diversity in terms of approaches and perspectives (Kolb & Rubin 1991) leads to confusion as to how mediation should be defined. In conflicts at an international level, the use of mediation is codified through Article 33(1) of the United Nations Charter. This article exhorts all member-states to settle their disputes through mediation. Empirical data indicates that states are more than willing to apply mediation (Bercovitch 1986) in resolving conflicts. It may be applicable to inter-state conflicts involving boundaries etc., however, when it comes to intra-state conflicts involving separatism, affected states seem to be reluctant to pursue mediation at the beginning of the conflict, fearing bestowing the status of belligerency to rebel groups. States facing insurgencies tend to opt first for violence to protect the "integrity" of the state. When these states realize that it cannot (yet) be won through military means, it negotiates. Furthermore, the international system tends to maintain the status quo (including boundaries) and the balance of power that is perceived to maintain the international order. The international system intends to maintain the "territorial integrity" of states, as separatism is usually assessed as a threat to international peace and stability.

New states that unilaterally declared independence usually find it difficult to achieve recognition from other states. Unilateral declaration of independence is seen as a major breach to international norms, particularly because many states are confronted by separatist movements within their own territory. For example, in the case of Kosovo, the Argentine Foreign Minister Jorge Taiana said in February 2008 that "if we were to recognize Kosovo, which has declared its independence unilaterally, without an agreement with Serbia, we would set a dangerous precedent that would seriously threaten our chances of a political settlement in the case of the Falkland Islands" (B92 Net 2009).

India is confronted by separatist sentiments in Tamil Nadu, stated on 31 July 2008 through its Ambassador Swarup that "India abides by the principles of international law and does not recognize Kosovo's secession" (B92 Net 2008). Interestingly, the recognition of the unilateral declaration of independence by Kosovo is seen to undermine peace talks in several countries such as in Spain and in the Philippines. On 19 February 2008, Alberto Romulo, the Secretary of Foreign Affairs stated that the recognition of Kosovo could complicate peace talks with Muslim separatists in Mindanao. He continued that "while the Philippines does not oppose the idea of independence for Kosovo, it would prefer a settlement...taking into account the internationally accepted principles of sovereignty and territorial integrity" (Reuters 2008).

Mediation of identity conflicts must accommodate several aspects of the broader political context. Furthermore, mediation must be studied as an aspect of a broader structure of negotiation and the parties' own efforts to manage their conflict (Bercovitch 1992, p.3). The Kosovo case reiterates the legitimacy of mediation and negotiation as the sole method to solve such conflicts. International courts such as the International Court of Justice accept cases involving conflicts between states, and not between states and sub-state actors. This leads to the pressure for sub-state actors to resort to other means of managing conflicts, which also includes unilaterally declaring independence.

6.3.1 The Different Stages of Mediation – Bringing Structure to the Process

To address conflicts appropriately, the intervening actors need a conceptual road map or "conflict map" (Wehr 1979) that: (1) identifies the multiple underlying causes of the conflict (Moore 1996, p.58); (2) suggests the relevant stakeholders to the conflict; (3) enumerates the issues and interests involved, which point to the barriers to settlement; and (4) indicates the possible procedures that can be used to resolve the conflict. The systems analytical evaluation of identity conflicts confirms the necessity of a mixture of interventions.

Referring to Moore's (Moore 1996, pp.60–61) summary of the causes and the appropriate modes of intervention, it should be noted that causes of conflict usually come as part of a package, which confirms that conflicts are rather multidimensional. It is the convention that a specific conflict encompasses contestation related to relationships, data, interests, structures and values. In this sense, there is a necessity to find a "healthy" combination of available interventions.

The following table introduces the causes of conflict that Moore (1996, p.60) suggests. Relationship conflicts are caused by strong emotions; misperceptions or stereotypes; poor communication or miscommunication and repetitive negative behavior. Relationship conflicts are reflected in a social context whereas social interactions are distorted. Data conflicts are caused by lack of information; misinformation, different views on what is relevant; different interpretations of data; and different assessment procedures. The other causes of conflict – value, structure, interest - elevate contestation.

Moreover, the table enumerates the types of interventions corresponding to the causes of conflict. The common denominator among these interventions is the need to establish a mechanism of cooperation to enable communicative interaction between conflicting parties. For example, legitimizing the emotional aspect of conflict resolution and providing a process for the expression of emotions are conditions that are necessary to a cooperative dialogue. Agreement on developing common criteria to assess data requires a minimum level of cooperation. Developing trade-offs to satisfy interests of different strengths require cooperative interactions between conflict parties. Establishing a fair and mutually acceptable decision-making process requires a cooperative spirit and the assumption that all parties will adhere to the agreed process.

Table 6.3: Causes of Conflict and Interventions (modified from Moore 1996)

	Causes	Intervention
Value conflicts	different criteria for evaluating ideas or behavior; exclusive intrinsically valuable goals; different ways of life, ideology, or religion	Avoid defining problem in terms of value; Allow parties to agree and to disagree; Create spheres of influence in which one set of values dominates; Search for superordinate goal that all parties share
Relationship conflicts	strong emotions; misperceptions or stereotypes; poor communication or miscommunication; repetitive negative behavior	Control expression of emotions through procedure, ground rules, caucuses, and so forth; Promote expression of emotions by legitimizing feelings and providing a process
Data conflicts	lack of information; misinformation; different views on what is relevant; different interpretations of data; different assessment procedures	Reach agreement on what data are important; Agree on process to collect data; Develop common criteria to assess data; Use third-party experts to gain outside opinion or break deadlocks
Interest conflicts	perceived or actual competition over substantive (content) interests; procedural interests; psychological interests	Focus on interests, not positions; look for objective criteria; Develop integrative solutions that address needs of all parties; Search for ways to expand options or resources; Develop trade-offs to satisfy interests of different strengths
Structural conflicts	destructive patterns of behavior or interaction; unequal control, ownership, or distribution of resources; unequal power and authority; geographical, physical or environmental factors that hinder cooperation; time constraints	Clearly define and change roles; Replace destructive behavior patterns; Reallocate ownership or control of resources; Establish a fair and mutually acceptable decision-making process; Change negotiation process from positional to interest-based bargaining; Modify means of influence used by parties (less coercion, more persuasion); Change physical and environmental relationship of parties (closeness and distance); Modify external pressures on parties; Change time constraints (more or less time)

An analysis of the stages of mediation enables a more focused intervention. A modified version of Moore's (1996, pp.66–67) figure on the twelve stages of mediation (Figure 6.1) illustrates the link between the causes of conflict and the stages of mediation, proving the nature of mediative intervention as a process. Although the above mentioned causes of conflict usually come as package, they can be distributed in the different stages. For example, stage 1, 6, 7 and 10 will tend to be characterized by relationship conflicts. In establishing relationship with the disputing parties, the mediator may be increasingly confronted by misperceptions or stereotypes. At the beginning of actual mediation, poor communication or miscommunication between the parties are common. When it comes to the identification of issues and the setting of agendas for upcoming talks, strong emotions are connected with a desire to be heard. Emotionality should be taken as relevant to the negotiation process, as it suggests that the issues are of immense significance.

Figure 6.1: Stages of Mediation (modified by the author from Moore 1996, pp. 66-67)

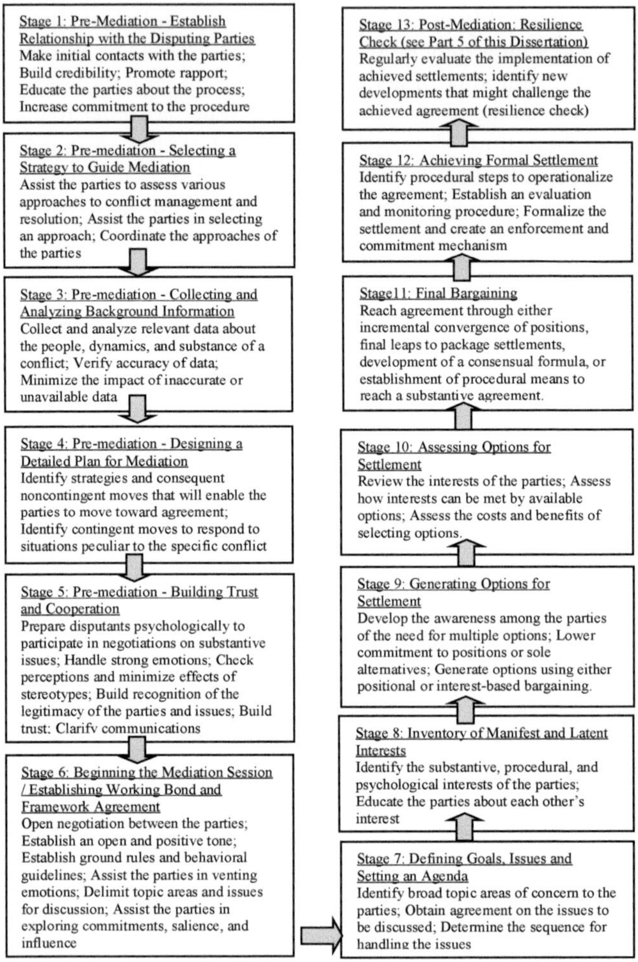

Interest conflicts may tend to dominate the mediation process in stages 8 and 10. During the identification of manifest and latent interests, conflicting parties may feel intense competition between interests when parties are not yet convinced of the legitimacy of the interests of the others. Conflicting parties may focus on the procedure, and contest whether mediation is the appropriate method to fulfill their interests and to achieve their goals. In addition, in the stage where suggested options for settlement are to be evaluated, conflicting parties may find themselves asking how such a settlement will fulfill their interests.

6.3.2 Conditions for the Use of Mediation in Identity Conflicts

The use of mediation in identity conflicts requires the existence of several conditions:

a) There is a conflict manifested through the use of violence.

The decision to use mediation requires the existence of a reason for using it. Mediation needs a conflict, which involves struggles between two or more people over values, or competition for status, power, or scarce resources (Coser 1967). Moore (1996, pp.16–17) suggests that mediators intervene in conflicts that have reached various levels of development and intensity – latent, emerging, and manifested.

Latent Conflicts

Latent conflicts are those with underlying tensions that have not fully developed and have not escalated into a highly polarized conflict (Curle 1971). However, mediators are not likely to be invited by conflicting parties to intervene if the conflict has not violently escalated. In particular, a government established by the hegemonic national group in identity conflicts will tend to ignore latent conflicts. While the decision to engage in mediation involves the perception that the potential new situation will be better than the status quo, in latent conflicts, the status quo may be considered better than any new situation, delaying the use of mediation. Furthermore, any claim for recognition by a minority group is considered illegitimate by the dominant group under the banner of universality and state coherence. Therefore, it can be argued that mediation is less likely to occur at this level of conflict.

Emerging Conflicts

Emerging conflicts are disputes that involve the identification of conflicting parties and conflict issues, and the acknowledgement that there is a dispute. However, cooperation is not always evident in emerging conflicts. In addition, no problem-solving mechanism is available at this point in time, as such a mechanism requires a learning process based on cooperation, which may be still in its infancy. Escalation is most likely to occur in emerging conflicts if a resolution on procedures is yet to be found. Emerging conflicts involving identity contestation are yet not likely to lead to mediation. If the hegemonic group realizes that there is a conflict that it cannot further ignore (as it is having a negative effect on the hegemony), the group will attempt to eradicate the conflict through the claim of universality which is likely to lead to the use of force.

Recognizing a minority group as belligerent is considered to bestow political legitimacy on armed sub-state actors. This recognition is inevitably interpreted as undermining the territorial integrity of the state, because subgroups are elevated to the status of states. Therefore, it is less likely that mediators will be invited by the government, because this inevitable gives political legitimacy to rebel groups.

Manifest Conflicts

Manifest conflicts are those in which parties are actually engaged in an active and ongoing dispute. Conflicting parties are well-identified, may have started to negotiate, and may have reached an impasse. A mediator is invited to change the negotiation procedure or guide the conflicting parties to break a specific deadlock. However, defining manifest conflicts through the involvement of mediators is misleading. Conflict should be categorized independently from the desired instrument to resolve it. Manifest conflicts should be defined as those where violence in all its forms (direct, structural and symbolic) has been used. Mediation is likely to be used when the efforts of the conflicting parties to unilaterally (e.g. military offensives or legislative reforms to accommodate claims of minorities) or bilaterally (e.g. direct negotiations) end the conflict have failed.

b) Dispute is long, drawn out and complex, with disputing parties convinced that a mediated outcome is much better than the status quo.

Identity conflicts do not occur overnight. It is an accumulation of experiences of the social interactions of groups. It is when sentiments are labeled and consolidated, and peaceful claims for recognition remain ignored or refused, that the use of violence to put forward claims is legitimized. What follows is sporadic violence and low-intensity warfare. Furthermore, complexity arises when there is no clear line between the victims and the perpetuators, with both groups responsible for violence. It is when the manifest conflict escalates and when it becomes too complex for the conflicting parties to handle that they welcome mediation.

c) The parties' own conflict management efforts have reached an impasse.

Mediation is likely to be used only after the parties' own conflict management efforts have reached an impasse or have proven to be ineffective in meeting acceptable outcomes for all parties. Existing traditional mechanisms of conflict management prove to be insufficient to accommodate grievances because of the complexity of the issues. Traditional mechanisms and legal settings may have been politicized, undermining its legitimacy.

d) Neither party is prepared to countenance further costs or loss of life.

Mediation will be likely sought when the continuation of the status quo means further costs or loss of life. The concept of 'ripeness' is necessary (although not sufficient) to initiate mediation and negotiation. The conflict is 'ripe' for mediation when its continuation inflicts further unwanted costs in the forms of death casualties, decreasing popular support, increasing international sanctions, and decreasing vitality of the economy. It is when the status quo is suffering that alternative solutions become attractive. As Zartman (2000) explains, parties resolve their conflict only when they are ready to do so – when alternative means of achieving the desirable outcome are blocked, and the parties find themselves in a costly predicament (Zartman 2001, p.8). The concept of a Mutually Hurting Stalemate (MHS) is based on the notion that when the parties find themselves locked in a conflict from which they cannot extract victory and this deadlock is painful for both, they seek an alternative policy or *way out* (see Touval & Zartman 1985; Zartman 1989; Zartman 2000; Zartman 2001).

e) Both parties in mediation can obtain a better outcome than would otherwise be the case (Bercovitch 1992, p.8).

Aside from the concept of a mutually hurting stalemate, the conflict is ripe for mediation (and negotiation) when the conflicting parties see Mutually Enticing Opportunities (Ohlson 1998; Zartman 2000) in the potential outcome of mediation. For Touval & Zartman (1985) and Saunders (1991), the enticement comes in the form of a new ingredient provided by a persistent mediator, and that new ingredient is the chance for improved relations with the mediating third party itself.

While the ripeness theory refers to the decision to negotiate, it does not guarantee results. The perception of the ripeness for negotiation does not ensure the commitments of the parties to actually reach a settlement through the process. Parties may still opt to drop out of mediation. Therefore, the opportunity through the settlement must be more attractive than opting out of the process.

f) The mediator will be able to alter the power and social dynamics of the conflict relationship by influencing the beliefs or behavior of conflict parties, by providing knowledge or information, or by offering a more effective negotiation process in settling contested issues.

For mediation to be useful to the resolution of identity conflicts, the mediator needs to be capable of altering the power and social dynamics of the conflict relationship. This is for instance not possible when the mediation itself is a strategy of a one conflicting party to achieve something other than the settlement of the conflict. If mediation is used only to gain more time, a better military position or to produce weapons to ensure military victory, then mediation will inevitably fail. The intention to pursue military offenses by any means undermines any outcome of mediation. The intention to negotiate for "side-effects" (Walliham 1998) eliminates the ability of the mediator to alter power and social dynamics. Some parties, as Walliham (1998, p.257) suggests, may engage in negotiations even though they are determined to avoid any agreement, or at least consider any agreement as incidental to their reason for negotiation. Mediation requires the condition that conflicting parties have genuine intentions to achieve a settlement.

6.4 Rationale and Motives of Mediation in Identity Conflicts – Altruism or Pure Politics?

To see mediators as altruistic actors who do not have vested interests is misleading. Why should a mediator wish to intervene in the disputes of others? Humanitarian values may genuinely be the case in a few instances of mediation, but normally even this interest intertwines with other less altruistic interests. However, that mediators pursue their own interests is not necessarily a negative phenomenon. For instance, Norway may be seen as altruistic in its mediation in the Philippines. However it considers the flow of "economic refugees" from the Philippines as a threat to its own economic stability. Therefore, it perceives its intervention in the Philippines legitimate, because it may lead to the decrease of migration.

Depending on who is the mediator, there exists different sets of motives. Identity conflicts involve different types of mediators: states, international governmental organizations, NGOs, and individuals. One commonality is that all these actors involve human beings. As Bercovitch (1992, pp.7–14) summarizes, individuals representing states or international organizations may wish to initiate mediation because

a) They have a clear mandate to intervene in disputes such as the constitution of the Arab league or of the Organization of African Unity which contain an explicit clause mandating its members to mediate in regional disputes (Kaufmann & Duncan 1989). The intervention of the Organisation of The Islamic Conference (OIC) in Southern Philippines is mandated through Article 1-16 of its charter which intends to assist Muslim minorities and communities outside the Member States of the OIC "to preserve their dignity, cultural and religious identity" (OIC 2010).
b) They may want to do something about a dispute whose continuance could adversely affect their own political interests. For instance, the intervention of Norway in Sri Lanka in 2001 is connected with Norway's interest in halting migration from Sri Lanka to Norway. Furthermore, Malaysian officials are worried about the flow of refugees from Southern Philippines to Sabah, as well as the increased proliferation of small arms and lights weapons in the Southeast Asian region (see Greene & Penetrante 2011).
c) They may be approached directly by one or both parties and asked to mediate. In late 1999, Husaini Hassan of the Free Aceh Movement Council (MP-GAM) contacted the Finnish government then under the presidency of Martti Ahtisaari about whether Finland could offer its services in negotiations between GAM and the Indonesian Government. In 2004, after Ahtisaari's term as president of Finland, Farid Husain and Juha Christiansen contacted the former president, and this contact led to the President actually mediating between GAM and the Indonesian government.
d) They may see the importance of preserving intact a structure of which they are a part. The frequent mediation attempts by the United States in disputes between Greece and Turkey which are both members of NATO are intended to maintain unity in the alliance. The mediation efforts of Malaysia may be intended to secure stability in the ASEAN region.
e) They may see mediation as a way of expanding, maintaining, and enhancing their influence, or by gaining the gratitude and political allegiance of one or both protagonists. For instance, the frequent efforts by the United States to mediate in the Arab-Israeli conflict are perceived to be in connection with the interest of the United States in maintaining its influence in the Middle East.

Mediators, like other political actors, engage in mediation and spend resources because they expect to gain something from it (Bercovitch 1992, p.9). Therefore, any third party intervention should always be critically assessed, whether its intervention actually serves to resolve the conflict or whether it contributes to the intractability of the conflict. Mediators should be able to transparently explain their own interests. The conflicting parties should then assess for themselves whether the mediator is actually pursuing its own interests based on motives that are counterproductive to the whole process. It should be noted that such an evaluation should be done regularly because interests change over time.

A more significant analysis refers to the motives of the conflicting parties themselves in engaging in mediated negotiations. Why would they seek or accept mediation? As Bercovitch (1992, p.9) argues, disputing parties may have reasons for assuming that a mediator's presence will be helpful. The parties may want to pursue mediation for the following reasons:

a) Mediation is considered a low-risk and flexible form of conflict management that will actually help conflicting actors to understand their conflict. A third party perspective may bring new (objective) insights to the conflict.
b) One or both parties expect the mediator to influence the other to give in.
c) One or both parties may consider mediation as a public expression of their commitment to genuine conflict management.
d) Their participation during mediation may be considered a source of legitimacy, particularly by those separatist groups desiring international recognition of their sentiments.
e) The conflicting parties may want an outsider to take some of the blame for failure of mediation.
f) The conflicting parties may opt for mediation because a mediator can be used to monitor, verify and guarantee any eventual agreement (Touval & Zartman 1985; Stulberg 1987).
g) One or both parties may consider mediation as a strategy to buy more time to regain military strength.
h) One or both of the conflicting parties may see that the engagement of a specific state as mediator will limit the influence of this mediating actor in the area. Accepting the role as mediator for instance may halt the military assistance of the mediating state to a specific party.

After assessing the motives of both the mediators and the conflicting parties, it can be argued that by virtue of mediating, a mediator becomes another actor in the peace process. A mediator can either accelerate the process or delay it. It can contribute resources that either prevent the outburst of violence or actually prolong the conflict. A mediator may find the reached settlement insufficient, and may actually manipulate the decision-making process to achieve what it perceives to be appropriate.

6.5 Dilemmas of Mediation Standards - Quality Assessment as Guarantee for Success?

Coming back to the several definitions that were summarized in chapter 8, mediation is predicated on the following attributes – *neutrality and impartiality of mediators, autonomy of the conflicting parties, confidentiality of the process, voluntariness, and a power balance between conflicting parties.* Such attributes are referred to as the foundations of mediation, and as the precision of professional ethics (Taylor 1997; Stimec 1999). Mediation is regarded as being "perfect" when it encompasses the above-mentioned attributes. A critical assessment of such attributes is necessary to identify existing dilemmas that are responsible for mediation, and may be contributing to the intractability of the identity conflict.

6.5.1 Neutrality and Impartiality of Mediators

The neutrality and impartiality of mediators are attributes that ensure the acceptability of intervention in any conflict. Only neutral and impartial mediators are perceived to be successful in guiding the decision-making process. However, as Johan Galtung (1998) argues, the only possible way for an individual to become neutral is through death. The mediator is bestowed with a sense of justice or a 'feeling for justice' (Stimec 1999), and a value system through which absolute neutrality is impossible to achieve (Grillo 1991). The mediator in the case of perceived unfairness and injustice will inevitably consciously or unconsciously express his or her opinion, which will accordingly influence the process (Stimec 1999).

According to the "model standards" introduced by Milne (1985), the mediator can elude predetermined bias by making this bias transparent. Furthermore, differentiation should be made between bias on the substance and bias on the process. As long as bias on the process (mediation as procedure) is avoided, a minimum level of neutrality is guaranteed. Particularly in international mediation involving identity conflicts, neutrality is a non-negotiable attribute. However, as the Philippine cases show, this is not the case. States are not altruistic in their interventions. Malaysia is not a neutral party in this conflict, as it has financially and militarily supported the MNLF in the past. Malaysia is also considered a patronage state of the Muslim community in the Philippines (Evangelista 2008). Nevertheless, the Philippine government considers Malaysia as "sufficiently neutral," because Malaysia has shifted its focus onto procedure.

Related to neutrality is impartiality. The literature in mediation suggests that the absence of impartiality is detrimental to mediation. 'Impartiality' is defined as the non-preference of mediators towards an outcome and party (Taylor 1997). The mediator must avoid any form of influence, lest he or she becomes a conflicting party. States that act as mediators in other countries are expected to achieve desirable outcomes in the form of an agreement, in order to legitimize the resources they are spending.

The expectation of achieving an outcome reduces the impartiality of state mediators. However, as Bercovitch, Kremenyuk and Zartman (2009) explain, the reasons for the failure of mediation in Cyprus and Camp David are the absence of endurance and perseverance, the absence of any substantial expectations, and the unwillingness of mediators to use sanctions and incentives. The conflicting parties were not prepared to contemplate fresh approaches, and the dilemma therefore lies between impartiality and efficiency.

6.5.2 Autonomy of Conflicting Parties

A mediator generally has limited or no authoritative decision-making power. The mediator cannot unilaterally mandate or force parties to resolve their differences or enforce decisions (Moore 1996, p.17). Decisions are to be made solely by the conflict parties. This characteristic distinguishes the mediator from the judge or arbitrator, who is generally empowered to make a decision for the parties on the basis of a prior agreement or on societal norms, rules, regulations, laws or contracts. The lack of decision-making authority on the part of mediators makes mediation attractive to many parties in disputes, because they can retain ultimate decision-making power (Moore 1996, p.18).

Mediation lacking the opportunity to influence the decision-making process is expected to fail. Not only are States accountable to their constituents and must legitimize the resources provided for the mediation, but the efficiency of mediation suffers when the mediator is reduced to the role of mere listener. However, the autonomy or the lack of autonomy of the mediator does not need to be an impediment to the autonomy of the conflict parties. The differentiation between substance and procedure should again be highlighted. Mediation involves the manipulation of the process through which the structure is continuously modified to accommodate the specificities of context. The modification of the process however may undermine neutrality and impartiality because such a modification involves influencing the social interactions and dynamics of the process. Nevertheless, a "minimum level of neutrality" is achieved when influence is limited to the procedure and does not encompass the substance.

6.5.3 Confidentiality of the Process

Confidentiality is a major attribute of mediation. The mediator is expected to treat information expressed in the mediation process as confidential. He or she may not forward any information to outsiders. The consultation with experts outside of the mediation process is therefore problematic. In an international context involving identity conflicts, transparency is necessary to ensure the sustainability of the outcome, but also to prevent the emergence of actors who feel they were not properly incorporated in the decision-making process.

Furthermore, negotiators at the table usually represent a larger group. The government negotiating panel represents the government and the larger population, while the negotiating panel of the rebel group represents the minority group. However, the confidentiality of negotiation is necessary to ensure the safety of the negotiators, and to avoid external assessment of premature decisions. The latest collapse in peace talks in the Philippines was brought about by the confidentiality of the peace negotiations. The Malaysian mediation pushed for the "Memorandum of Agreement on Ancestral Domain" (MOA-AD), through which important concessions were made by the Philippine government negotiating panel through the intended establishment of the "Bangsamoro Juridical Entity" (BJE). The agreement was declared unconstitutional by the Philippine Supreme Court on the grounds of the lack of consultation with stakeholders (Torres 2008).

The dilemma lies between the necessity to ensure confidentiality and the necessity to promote transparency. 'Transparency' means that procedures and their implications, the role of the mediators, the risks and expected advantages and disadvantages, as well as the alternatives to mediation are addressed. Transparency allows conflicting parties to trust the mediation process. Transparency becomes problematic, however, when it leads to inefficiency. Transparency may for example give certain actors more resources to delay and sabotage the process.

6.5.4 Voluntariness

Mediation requires voluntary participation and agreements made out of free will. Parties are not forced to negotiate, mediate, or settle by any internal or external party to the dispute. Voluntariness offers the conflicting parties an "exit strategy" in case they perceive the mediation process as not effective in achieving their interests. As Stulberg (1981, pp.88–89) notes, "there is no legal liability to any party refusing to participate in a mediation process since a mediator has no authority to unilaterally impose a decision on the parties, and he cannot threaten the recalcitrant party with a judgment." However, in several cases, conflicting parties are forced to negotiate by the international community. The concept of a 'mutually hurting stalemate' that is assumed to be a condition for conflicting parties to negotiate and undergo mediation has a coercive element in it. Nevertheless, as long as parties are not coerced into signing an agreement they are reluctant to sign, then a "minimum" level of voluntariness is guaranteed.

6.5.5 The Power Balance between Conflicting Parties

In order to derive sustainable decisions from mediations, all parties must have some means of influence, either positive or negative, on the disputants at the table. This is a prerequisite for a settlement that recognizes mutual needs (Lovell 1952). Moore (1996, p.68) continues that unless a weaker party has some power or influence, recognition of its needs and interests will occur only if the stronger party is altruistically oriented. The mediation literature proposes the balancing of the asymmetric power relations between conflicting parties through mediation (Duss-von Werdt 2000).

Power is based on the perception whether individuals can pursue their interests. Balancing power requires however the measurability of power. Measurability requires access to all relevant information, which is not always possible to achieve. Furthermore, power has different sources and applications. Power can be measured by the number of weapons and the amount of money an actor has. Power can be derived through norms and principles, from legitimacy and legality, and from bureaucracy. Power can be derived from deficits and a lack of resources, through which the lack of resources is effectively used as a reason for not participating in or for delaying the process (negative power). Hence, the meaning of power is explicable only through its context. For instance, the military resources of the United States would not play a significant role in negotiations on climate change. This confirms the argument of Stimec (1999), that the existence of power sources does not automatically imply the actual existence of power.

In identity conflicts, the stronger party is usually the government of the state that controls the state military. Nevertheless, the weaker party which is in this case the rebel group must already have some effective power sources, because if it did not, the government would not consider negotiating. A negotiating government realizes that it cannot win the conflict through military means, or without inflicting politically unacceptable costs. Therefore, the weaker party has something that convinced the government to start negotiating. Furthermore, as Faure and Klaousen (2002) argue, weaker parties may achieve more than stronger parties. Being weaker doesn't necessarily mean the party is in a disadvantageous position. The weaker party may use context to demand more concessions from the stronger party.

In examining the methods a mediator can use to balance power between disputants, it is important to distinguish between the situations where a mediator assists in recognizing, organizing, and marshaling the existing power of a disputant and where a mediator becomes an advocate and assists in generating new power and influence. The latter strategy inevitably removes the impartiality of the mediator, whereas the former keeps the mediator within the power boundaries established by the parties (Moore 1996, p.69). Finding the appropriate position between the two poles is an important endeavor for the mediator. Mediation can only work when interdependency between conflicting parties has been established, paving way for cooperation.

6.6 Critical Views on Mediating Identity Conflicts – Gaps through the Bridge

Mediation involves gaps that arise as the negotiation process unfolds. Mediation of identity conflicts is for example confronted by limitations when it attempts to find a new social contract that aims to remove the hegemonic structures that have caused the conflict in the first place.

6.6.1 Mediation and (In)justice

Richard Delgado (1985; 1988) criticizes mediation from the psychological perspective. Primarily focusing on the origins of prejudice, he claims that in the long run, mediation is not capable of correcting the deep-rooted prejudices that stem from historical developments. Latent and manifest bias towards minorities has been consolidated by societal norms. A society with consolidated bias towards minorities is more likely to promote expressions of bias, for example through social engineering or violence. A society that tolerates bias will eventually tolerate violence. This society will be more likely to lack social modes and formal rules to prevent violence.

Mediation as an alternative mode of dispute resolution, as argued by Delgado, will not necessarily lead to the establishment of social norms that prevent future violence towards minorities. Mediation inevitably diverts the attention away from the judicial system as the "higher public conscience", designed to restrain any form of prejudice and violence. Furthermore, Delgado suggests that there is a societal norm of 'fairness' that is incorporated into courtroom symbols and procedures - such as the flag, the black robe and the room setting - that disappears in mediation (1985). In addition, the justice system contains both external and internal constraints designed to prevent judges to exhibiting either prejudice or bias (Seth 2000). In the moments of intimacy and informality that occur during mediation, the positive influence of symbols and procedures disappear. Delgado (1988) recommends that it is better for members of minority groups to seek recourse through the judicial system.

Owen Fiss (1984) does not believe that mediation and other forms of alternative dispute resolution (ADR) are preferable to a court ruling. Mediation should not be institutionalized on a wholesale and indiscriminate basis, because it cannot guarantee that the settlement is not coerced. The idea that a potential settlement could be struck by someone without authority and accountability also problematises mediation. Mediation cannot guarantee that justice is rendered, particularly when the bargaining conditions in mediation reflects the conditions of broader society (Fiss 1984, p.19).

In identity conflicts such as in the Philippines, it is not clear how Malaysian mediation will be able to address the deep-rooted bias in society at large towards Muslim groups and other minorities. to the contrary, frustration about the slugishness and inefficiency of first track mediation led in some cases to the outburst of violence. The agreement on ancestral domains (MOA-AD) also aggravated distrust in society at large. The idea that Christians will be minoritized by the new juridical body further led to the deepening of bias.

6.6.2 Mediation and the Pro-Rights Approach

The proponents of the "pro-rights" approach claim that for those conflicts involving members of a disadvantaged group, formality, symbols and the procedures of courtroom litigation create a forum that is preferable to that of mediation. Several authors argue that mediation became popular with government and court authorities particularly in the United States at the point when minorities and other disadvantaged groups began using the court system more extensively to pursue their claims. For instance, feminist scholars such as Catherine MacKinnon (1989) and Anne Bottomley (1989) suggest that the increasing use of mediation in the context of family law reduces issues of women's rights from public to private matters. Therefore, mediation is paradoxically undermining the rights it seeks to protect.

Furthermore, it is argued that as disadvantaged groups lose power within the process of informal adjudication, they also lose power and control in society at large (Abel 1982). Mediation can extend the direct influence of the state into broader society. All institutionalized mechanisms, whether formal (e.g. courts) or informal (e.g. mediation), involve state regulation. Mediators in several countries are obligated to meet standards determined by the state. In some cases, like in the Philippines, mediation that is formalized through its integration in the legal system is paradoxically leading to its instrumentalization by the hegemonic group (see Penetrante 2010).

Owen Fiss (1984) reminds us that settlements reached by negotiating parties through mediation may in some cases not reflect the interests of the groups being represented. Minority groups are ensnared in "contractual relationships" (Fiss 1984, p.21) that impair their autonomy: Rebel groups representing marginalized minority groups during mediation tend to follow vested interests that are in some cases counterproductive to the peace process. Fiss continues that the fact that the conflicting parties are groups creates problems settlements may be challenged by factions within the group.

Identity conflicts involve groups that have less access to power in society at large. Such minority groups are exposed to different forms of violence and social engineering. The aspect of mediation that emphasizes informality (Abel 1982) and compromise mistakenly encourages parties to conceive of the setting of social and political values as the tasks of the majority (Sparer 1984). Minorities are then asked to negotiate for a compromise in a case by case basis. Mediation effectively avoids public discourse on the principles, values and power imbalances that inherently define the conflict. Hence, social change may be significantly impeded through the lack of social struggle. The formalization of any social struggle that is obstructed by mediation is necessary to bringing social change. To conclude, it is only through the adversarial process that minorities and other historically disadvantaged groups are able to achieve social change.

6.6.3 Mediation, Power Imbalances and Sustainability

The judgment of the court is not the end of the court's involvement. The involvement of the court may continue indefinitely, which is not problematic within an institutionalized legal system. Mediation and ADR cannot provide the same basis for the continuing involvement. The responsibility of the mediator often ends with the achievement of the settlement. The passing of legal judgment does not end the struggle, but rather changes its terms and the balance of power (Fiss 1984, p.21). The same conflicting parties may decide to come back to the court and demand fulfillment, for example, compensation. The court as an institution must continue to supervise the parties after judgment. As a formal matter, power is used to punish violations of the court's judgment. Mediation cannot provide any resources to ensure the implementation of any settlement. Furthermore, Fiss (1984, p.22) argues that mediation impedes vigorous law enforcement. When mediated settlements collapse, courts are hesitant to force parties to abide to the settlement. As Fiss continues, courts do not see a mediation-based bargain between parties as sufficient foundation for the exercise of their institutional coercive powers.

Another criticism leveled against mediation is summarized in the so-called "oppression story", which claims that mediation cannot lead to "fair" outcomes when there are considerable power imbalances between the parties (Bush & Folger 1994, pp.22–24). The mediation process will preserve the existing "relative balance of power between the parties" (Levine 1984, p.146) that reflects the social context during the bargaining process. Mediation cannot and should not change existing power relations.

In identity conflicts, mediation between a minority group and a powerful government shows a vastly powerful asymmetry that cannot be balanced through mediation. The relaxation of formal and procedural safeguards in mediation may lead to the mediation process benefiting stronger parties, who take advantage of their position in order to coerce weaker parties (Augusti-Panareda 2004). It is argued that mediation works best when equals are bargaining with one another (Mather 1984). However in identity conflicts, the usual case involves power asymmetry. The informality and consensuality of the mediation process accentuate existing power imbalances between the parties (Pinzon 1996). As Levine (1984, p.151) argues, mediation is therefore not only ill-adapted for handling power imbalances, it also seems to foster and preserve them.

6.6.4 Mediation and Accountability

Courts use public resources, and employ only public officials chosen through a rigid qualification and selection process, and who are accountable to the general public. There are mechanisms of public control to ensure the neutrality and impartiality of decision-makers. Judges undergo years if not decades of training and regular examinations to ensure their qualifications. Judges possess a power that has been defined and conferred upon them by public law, not by a private agreement (Fiss 1984, p.22). Mediation, as Fiss continues, may be successful in resolving private conflicts. However, when violation of human rights and when structural discriminatory practices are involved, mediation cannot provide an adequate platform for conflict resolution. The courts interpret and embody authoritative texts in the constitution, as codified by the law-making bodies. A settlement will deprive a court of the ability to interpret and embody these texts, and to ensure that justice is done. A settlement does not always encompass justice. Mediators lack accountability: in several countries like the United States, mediators were successful in avoiding state regulations on standards and accountability.

In identity conflicts, when mediators are proven to have contributed to the protraction of the conflict, there are no means by which to hold them accountable. Because mediators in identity conflicts are more likely to conduct mediation free of charge, the conflicting parties' only leverage to hold the mediators accountable is in seeking other mediators. Furthermore, assuming of the role of mediator seems to have developed into a "cleansing" of the past actions of that mediator. For example, Malaysia and Libya supplied Muslim rebels with arms and weapons. Considering the thousands of people who died through these arms and weapons, these countries should be held accountable. However, because of their involvement as mediators, past activities are glossed over.

6.7 Interim Conclusion – Mediation as Intervention of Choice in Identity Conflicts

Alternatives to mediation (negotiation) to resolve identity conflicts are seen as ineffective. A rebel group is not likely to submit itself to the legal institutions of a state that it perceives to be biased and partial. The international system is paradoxically biased against sub-state groups through the principles of national sovereignty and territorial integrity. Elevating the causes of insurgent groups to the international level usually requires their claim for independence to be excised from the agenda.

Direct negotiations are inhibited by claims of recognition in the context of asymmetrical power conditions. Direct negotiations are ineffective in situations where parties consider the other party as the problem. Weaker parties are all too easily branded as out-laws, criminals and terrorists, and their causes labelled as illegitimate, leaving these individuals vulnerable to arrest and punishment.

Parties need assistance in structuring talks so that they can concentrate on substantial issues. Mediation, in all its forms, promises to provide additional resources to the conflicting parties. It allows the establishment of communication channels between conflicting parties, particularly when communicating with the enemy is considered to be politically undesirable. Mediation opens new channels for rebel groups and governments to become sensitized to the needs and interests of the other without sharing geographical proximity.

Mediation may prolong conflict, particularly when underlying dilemmas that exacerbate the complexity of identity conflicts are not adequately addressed. Because mediation is connoted positively, these dilemmas are often ignored. When mediators are countries, they are entrapped in the sovereignty principles of the international system that paradoxically lead to bias against sub-state actors whose demands of independence are connoted as threats to stability and international order. States do not mediate without vested interests. In this regard, there is a need to evaluate these interests and determine whether they are compatible with the interests of the conflicting parties. When states intervene, they inevitably become parties to the conflict.

In addition, the use of mediation usually implies that the conflict has already escalated and manifested itself. In such cases, grudges and frustrations are already deeply embedded in the mind-sets of the parties. A third party is more likely to be invited to mediate when other alternatives have already failed. Mediation is usually employed when it is almost too late to resolve the conflict through talks, increasing the challenge for mediators. Hence, identity conflicts may be biased against mediation. Moreover, the criteria of standards lauded by mediation literature – neutrality, impartiality, confidentiality and so on - may actually prolong the conflict. In this sense, adherence to these criteria requires a regular critical assessment of the dynamics involved. Mediation must address context.

References:

Abel, R., 1982. The Contradiction of Informal Justice. In *The Politics of Informal Justice*. New York: NYU University Press, pp. 267–295.

Antrim, L. & Sebenius, J., 1992. Formal Individual Mediation and the Negotiator's Dilemma: Tommy Koh at the law of the Sea Conference. In J. Bercovitch & J. Rubin, eds. *Mediation in International Relations: Multiple Approaches to Conflict Management*. London: Macmillan, pp. 97–130.

Augusti-Panareda, J., 2004. Power Imbalances in Mediation: Questioning Some Common Assumptions. *Dispute Resolution Journal*, 59(2), pp.24–31.

B92 Net, 2009. Argentina Rules out Recognition. *B92 Bet*. Available at: http://www.b92.net/eng/news/politics-article.php?yyyy=2008&mm=02&dd=29&nav_id=48079 [Accessed September 20, 2013].

B92 Net, 2008. India to back Serbian UN GA bid. *B92 Bet*. Available at: http://www.b92.net/eng/news/politics-article.php?yyyy=2008&mm=07&dd=31&nav_id=52346 [Accessed September 20, 2013].
Baxi, U. & Galanter, M., 1979. Panchayat Justice: An Indian Experiment in Legal Access. In M. Cappelletti & B. Garth, eds. *Access to Justice: Emerging Issues and Perspectives*. The Florence Access to Justice Project. Alphen aan den Rijn: Sijthoff & Noordhoff, pp. 314–386.
Von Benda-Beckmann, K., 1984. *The Broken Stairways to Consensus: Village Justice and State Courts in Mjnangkabau*, Cinnaminson, N.J.: Foris Publications.
Bercovitch, J., 1986. International Mediation: A Study of the Incidence, Strategies and Conditions of Successful Outcomes. *Cooperation and Conflict*, 21, pp.155–168.
Bercovitch, J., 2009. Mediation and Conflict Resolution. In J. Bercovitch, V. Kremenyuk, & I. W. Zartman, eds. *The SAGE Handbook of Conflict Resolution*. London: SAGE Publications, pp. 340–357.
Bercovitch, J., 1992. Mediators and Mediation Strategies in International Negotiations. *Negotiation Journal*, 8, pp.99–112.
Bingham, G., 1985. *Resolving Environmental Disputes*, Washington D.C.: Conservation Foundation.
Blake, R. & Mouton, J., 1985. *Solving Costly Organizational Conflicts: Achieving Intergroup Trust, Cooperation, and Teamwork*, San Francisco: Jossey-Bass Publishers.
Bottomley, A., 1989. What is Happening to Family Law? *Canadian Journal of Family Law*, 61(8), pp.1–52.
Bush, R.A.B. & Folger, J., 1994. *The Promise of Mediation: Responding to Conflict through Empowerment and Recognition*, San Francisco, CA: Jossey-Bass Publishers.
Carter, L. & Connor, K., 1989. *A Preliminary Investigation of Contemporary Afghan Councils*, Peshawar: ACBAR.
Clark, J., 1989. Conflict Management Outside the Courtroom in China. In *Social Control in the People's Republic of China*. London: Prager Press, pp. 57–69.
Coser, L., 1967. *Continuities in the Study of Social Conflict*, New York: The Free Press.
Curle, A., 1971. *Making Peace*, London: Tavistock Publications.
Delgado, R., 1988. ADR and the Dispossessed: Recent Books about the Deformalization Movement. *Law and Social Inquiry*, 13(1), pp.145–154.

Delgado, R., 1985. Fairness and Formality: Minimizing the Risk of Prejudice in Alternative Dispute Resolution. *Wisconsin Law Review*, pp.1359–1404.
Dickson, K., 1990. A Typology of Mediation in Homer. *Oral Tradition*, 5(1), pp.37–71.
Douglas, A., 1957. The Peaceful Settlement of Industrial and Intergroup Disputes. *Journal of Conflict Resolution*, 1(March), pp.69–81.
Duss-von Werdt, J., 2000. Mediation und Macht. *Zeitschrift für Konfliktmanagement (ZKM)*, 1, pp.4–7.
Elphinstone, M., 1992. *An Account of the Kingdom of Caubul*, Karachi: Oxford University Press.
Evangelista, K., 2008. Indonesia pushed to mediate MILF talks. *Philippine Daily Inquirer*.
Faure, G.O. & Klaousen, P., 2002. The Andorra-European Community Trade Agreement. In I. W. William & J. Rubin, eds. *Power and Negotiations*. Ann Arbor: University of Michigan Press, pp. 107–128.
Fiss, O., 1984. Against Settlement. *Yale Law Journal*, 93, pp.1073–1090.
Galtung, J., 1998. *Frieden mit friedlichen Mitteln. Frieden und Konflikt, Entwicklung und Kultur*, Opladen: Leske und Budrich.
Greene, O. & Penetrante, A.M., 2011. Arms, Private Militias and Fragile State Dynamics. In O. Greene & N. Marsh, eds. *Small Arms, Crime and Conflict. Global Governance and the Threat of Armed Violence*. Berlin, Heidelberg & New York: Routledge.
Grillo, T., 1991. The Mediation Alternative - Process Dangers for Women. *Yale Law Journal*, 100, pp.1545–1610.
Harris, M., 1968. *The Rise of Anthropological Theory*, New York: Thomas Crowell Company.
Hayden, R., 1984. A Note on Caste Panchayats and Government Courts in India. *Journal of Legal Plurarlism*, 22, pp.43–51.
Kaufmann, S. & Duncan, G., 1989. Third Party Intervention: A Theoretical Framework. In A. Rahim, ed. *Managing Conflict*. New York: Praeger, pp. 273–290.
Kolb, D. & Rubin, J., 1991. Mediation through a Disciplinary Prism. *Research on Negotiation in Organization*, 3, pp.231–257.
Levine, M., 1984. Power Imbalances in Dispute Resolution. In *A Study of Barriers to the Use of Alternative Methods of Dispute Resolution*. South Royalton, VT: Vermont Law School, pp. 137–158.
Li, V., 1978. *Law without Lawyers*, Boulder, CO: Westview Press.
Lovell, H., 1952. The Pressure Lever in Mediation. *Industrial & Labor Relations Review*, 6(1), pp.20–29.

MacKinnon, C., 1989. *Towards a Feminist Theory of the State*, Cambridge: Cambridge University Press.
Mather, L., 1984. The Importance and Political Implications of Dispute Definitions. In *A Study of Barriers to the Use of Alternative Methods of Dispute Resolution*. Royalton, VT: Vermont Law School Dispute Resolution Project.
Milne, A., 1985. Model Standards of Practice for Family and Divorce Mediation. *Conflict Resolution Quarterly*, 8, pp.73–81.
Mitchell, C., 1981. *The Structure of International Conflict*, London: Macmillan.
Moore, C., 1996. *The Mediation Process. Practical Strategies for Resolving Conflict* Second Edition., San Francisco: Jossey-Bass Publishers.
Moore, C. & Santosa, M.A., 1995. Developing Appropriate Environmental Conflict Management Procedures in Indonesia. *Cultural Survival*, 19(3), pp.23–29.
Moore, E., 1985. *Conflict and Compromise: Justice in an Indian Village*, New York: New York University Press.
Ohlson, T., 1998. *Power Politics and Peace Politics*, Uppsala: University of Uppsala.
OIC, 2010. *OIC in Brief*, Organisation of Islamic Conference. Available at: http://web.archive.org/web/20071021030710/http://www.oic-oci.org/english/main/oic_in_brief.htm [Accessed September 21, 2013].
Pe, C. & Tadiar, A., 1988. *Katarungang Pambarangay: Dynamics of Compulsory Conciliation*, Quezon City: Publishers' Printing Press.
Penetrante, A.M., 2010. Court-Annexed Mediation in the Philippines – Community Involvement in the Judicial System – Recommendations for Bridging the Gaps I. W. Zartman, ed. *PINPoints*, The Impacto f History, Memory, and Culture in Negotiation(34), pp.13–15.
Pinzon, L.A., 1996. The Production of Power and Knowledge in Mediation. *Conflict Resolution Quarterly*, 14, pp.3–20.
Reuters, 2008. Philippines tiptoes around Kosovo Recognition. *Reuters*. Available at: http://www.reuters.com/article/2008/02/19/us-kosovo-serbia-philippines-idUSMAN6439620080219 [Accessed September 23, 2013].
Saunders, H., 1991. *Guidelines B*, Washington D.C.: Kettering Foundation.
Schelling, T., 1960. *The Strategy of Conflict*, Cambridge, MA: Harvard University Press.
Seth, R., 2000. *Mediation: The Great Equalizer? A Critical Theory Analysis*, Canadian Forum on Civil Justice. Available at: http://cfcj-fcjc.org/clearinghouse/drpapers/critical.htm [Accessed September 21, 2013].
Singer, L., 1990. *Settling Disputes: Conflict Resolution in Business, Families, and the Legal System*, Boulder, CO: Westview.

Slatts, H. & Porter, K., 1992. *Traditional Decision Making and Law*, Jakarta: Gadja Mada University Press.

Sparer, E., 1984. Fundamental Human Rights, Legal Entitlements and the Social Struggle: A Friendly Critique of the Critical Legal Studies Movement. *Stanford Law Review*, 36(1/2), pp.509–574.

Spencer, D. & Yang, H., 1993. Lessons from the Field of Intra-National Conflict Resolution. *Notre Dame Law Review*, 67, pp.1495–1512.

Spiro, M., 1986. Cultural Relativism and the Future of Anthropology. *Cultural Anthropology*, 1, pp.259–286.

Stimec, A., 1999. Grenzen der Mediation. *Zeitschrift für Mediation*, 4, pp.212–218.

Stulberg, J., 1987. *Taking Charge! Managing Conflict*, Lexington, MA: D.C. Health.

Stulberg, J., 1981. The Theory and Practice of Mediation: A Reply to Professor Susskind. *Vermont Law Review*, 6, pp.85–117.

Taylor, A., 1997. Concepts of Neutrality in Family Mediation: Contexts, Ethics, Influence, and Transformative Process. *Mediation Quarterly*, 14(3), pp.215–236.

Torres, T., 2008. SC Final Ruling. *Philippine Daily Inquirer*.

Touval, S. & Zartman, I.W., 1985. *International Mediation in Theory and Practice*, Boulder, CO: Westview Press/Foreign Policy Institute, School of Advanced International Studies, Johns Hopkins University.

Walliham, J., 1998. Negotiating to Avoid Agreement. *Negotiation Journal*, 14(3), pp.257–267.

Wehr, P., 1979. *Conflict Regulation*, Boulder, CO: Westview.

Young, O., 1967. *The Intermediaries: Third Parties in International Crisis*, Princeton, NJ: Princeton University Press.

Zartman, I.W., 1989. *Ripe for Resolution* 2nd ed., Oxford: Oxford University Press.

Zartman, I.W., 2000. Ripeness: The Hurting Stalemate and Beyond. In P. Stern & D. Druckman, eds. *International Conflict Resolution after the Cold War*. Washington D.C.: National Academy Press, pp. 225–250.

Zartman, I.W., 2001. The Timing of Peace Initiatives: Hurting Stalemate and Ripe Moments. *Th Global Review of Ethnopolitics*, 1(1), pp.8–18.

7 Managing Intractable Identity Conflicts – A Concert of Measures in the Southern Philippines

The conflict between the Muslim separatist groups and the Philippine government has proven to be resistant to any kind of sustainable settlement or resolution. Several peace negotiations, which in the last four decades have led to specific agreements, all collapsed within a specific time frame. The regular outbreak of violence has hardened public opinion on both sides. The anti-Muslim sentiments are very deeply embedded in the society at large. The notion that the Philippine state is an occupying entity, which limits Muslims in their way of life, still persists in the mind of the Bangsamoro.

Identity conflicts such as that in the Philippines don't need to be intractable. The concept of intractability conflicts is well discussed in the conflict literature (see Azar, 1986; Burton, 1987; Pruitt and Olczak, 1995; Pruitt and Kim, 2004; Crocker et al., 2009). Intractability refers to the renewed outbreak of violence after rounds of negotiations, which led to concrete agreements. As Crocker, Hampson & Aall (2009, p. 493) suggest, "intractable conflicts are conflicts that have persisted over time and refused to yield to efforts – either by the direct parties, or, more often, third-party assistance – to arrive at a political settlement." This chapter intends to analyze why intervention efforts such as mediation are failing to resolve the conflict. In some cases, intervention efforts are actually prolonging the conflict.

7.1 Causes of Intractability – Mapping out the Bangsamoro Conflict

Identity conflicts can become intractable, when at least one of the following conditions applies (Crocker et al., 2009, pp. 494–496):

1) Geography and Geopolitics
The escalation of violence in the Philippines in the late 60s was triggered by the *Jabidah* massacre. This event is related to the border dispute between the Philippines and Malaysia. Geographical and geopolitical causes of intractability are neighboring wars, ethnic diaspora and ideological alignments. Wars lead not only to refugees entering neighboring

counties' territory, but they may also lead to agents of violence seeking refuge abroad, which could spark diplomatic tensions in the region. Furthermore, if the state is considered a "patronage state", nationalist political groups in the patronage state may demand intervention to show solidarity to their peers in the other country.

2) Deep-seated Identity and Grievance
Identity conflicts may be manipulated by political entrepreneurs in order to gain popular support. Michael Brown (1996, p. 575) blames "bad leaders", who inflame latent or overt differences in order to build their own powerbase for intractability of conflicts. While "bad leaders", who instrumentalize ethnic differences are not really rampant, "good leaders", who actively pursue reconciliation such as Desmond Tutu and Nelson Mandela in South Africa, are not really present in the Philippines. The lack of renowned personalities in the Philippines, who could confront deep-seated grievances, may be blamed as well for the intractability of the conflict. The existence of bad leaders causing intractability can be equated with the lack of good leaders.

3) Poverty and Denial of Basic Human Needs
Furthermore intractability of conflicts can be traced from the systematic denial of basic needs as well as the discrimination against certain groups in society. In addition, the lack of a legitimate channel to address grievances through the political process (Stewart and Brown, 2007) is a conventional cause of intractability. Violence as an instrument to address grievance becomes a viable option. The establishment of biased state structures, such as the legal and constitutional system, may label such grievances as illegitimate under the banner of universalistic nationalism. Identity conflicts such as that in the Philippines tend to witness blaming the minority groups for their own poverty. In the Philippines, minority groups such as the *Aetas*, the Muslim ethno-linguistic groups, and other indigenous groups find existing mechanisms of addressing grievances insufficient to bring about changes to their situation. While minority groups recognize the internationalization of their demands can both simultaneously encourage internal mobilization and weaken the salience of the state by creating international forums for sub-state grievances (Smith, 1986), the accommodation of grievances require structural reforms in the society. The inflexibility of the Philippine constitution to allow structural reforms to enable the political process to address the grievances of mi-

norities contributes to the intractability of the conflict. Although the legitimization process is supported by the existence of supranational organizations and international norms, which provide a forum and focal point for sub-national claims, such forums and focal points are still framed within the principle of national sovereignty and territorial integrity.

4) Avarice of Predatory Warlords
The franchising of violence to local political warlords through the Philippine state prolongs the conflict. It changes the dynamics and complicates any resolution effort to resolve and manage the conflict cleavages between groups in the south of the country. The so-called predatory warlords, who profit from the political economy of violence through arms sales, smuggling, and other illicit commercial practices and transactions, resist intervention efforts they think will lead to a disadvantageous outcome. They become conflict parties, when they manage to fill the security vacuum established through the absence of the Philippine state, which is preoccupied with the armed struggle of MNLF and MILF. Predatory warlords in the country maintain their own private armies, which can create competition with rival warlords and may easily lead to "clan wars" (rido) (see Torres, 2007). While localized feudalistic structures are established, NGOs and journalists, who criticize these structures become targets of extrajudicial killings. Political warlords in the Philippines, who profit from the culture of impunity, prolong the conflicts by providing more venues to apply violence.

5) Polarized Zero-Sum Notions of Identity
Intractable conflicts imply mutually exclusive (zero-sum) expression of identities. Unquestioned assumptions regarding key cultural and religious symbols, which perpetuate both the sense of resentment and demonization of the others, contribute to the polarization of identities. For instance, the staging of the "*Moro-Moro*", which refers to a type of folk drama performed in villages throughout the Philippines, reifies the constant competition between Christians and Muslims in the country. The play, initially written by Spanish friars in the 17th century, is highlighted by a battle between Muslims and Christians, which dramatizes the capture of an Islamic stronghold by a Christian army (Encyclopedia Britannica, 2010), depicts the victory of good against evil (Baet, 2010). Such framing of group relations to good and evil consolidates polarization. The play ends with the victory of the Christians against the "evil" Muslims. The

lack of critical assessment for such traditional practices and symbols nurtures polarization promoting intractability.

6) Failures in Earlier Peace-making Efforts
The failure of earlier interventions increases frustration on all sides. It increases the caveats to start negotiation anew because negotiation requires a minimum level of trust. However, failed interventions reduce the degree of trust that has previously existed. With a past failed negotiation still dominating the discourse, the conflicting parties refer to this failed negotiation in formulating new demands. The negotiation process is then delayed by the inappropriate focus on the procedure of negotiation rather than on the substance of the conflict. Basic requirements and preconditions for negotiations are re-negotiated, which consumes both time and energy on the part of the new intervening actors and conflicting parties. Instead of bargaining on the content and substance of the conflict, the negotiation becomes dominated by "cleaning up" the remnants of the previous failed effort. Moreover, failed efforts may lead to the lowering of expectations in the subsequent talks, where strategies are adapted to achieve the desired outcome. In this case, when an outcome has been reached, the conflicting parties realize that the outcome is not sustainable because of it being insufficient to address the underlying problems. Expectations, which are too low, on the agreement lead to a self-fulfilling prophecy. Lowered expectations due to the failures of earlier efforts may lead to further failures.

7) Local Decision-maker's Zero-Sum Mind-set
Intractable conflicts involve a zero-sum mind-set of local decision-makers, which is, what their opponents gain, they lose. Local decision-makers defy settlements because they believe their objectives are fundamentally irreconcilable with some provisions of the settlement. This is one of the causes for the intractability of the conflict in the Philippines. Particularly Christian local leaders in Mindanao fear that concessions made to the Muslim minorities would eventually mean the decrease of their power. Furthermore, local Muslim political leaders, who are not affiliated to the MNLF and MILF, fear a loss of power. The fear that any political office on the juridical body negotiated by the MILF would be exclusive for MILF members and dominates the motivation of local decision-makers to resist any settlement. They become spoilers because they seek to prevent any uncertain future situation. Intractability therefore involves a specific settlement, which is perceived to decrease the power and influence

of local decision-makers, implying a lack of more alternative perspectives for specific stakeholders. Nevertheless, shifting zero-sum to positive sum perspectives involve the reframing of mind-sets. This can be achieved by involving local decision-makers in the negotiation process as early as possible.

8) Deficits in Governance Mechanisms
The political system of the Philippines involves personified "clan" politics involving family dynasties assuming political offices. There is de facto no functioning political party system in the country. The implication of this institutional deficit is the increased significance of political warlords, who fill up the political space that political parties should be taking. This institutional deficit fosters the resources of hardliners from all sides. Moderate Muslim elite members are prevented from extending their influence because of limited recruitment opportunities for political offices. Instead local political warlords and armed MNLF/MILF members have dominated the political scene in the South. The centralistic design of the political system in the Philippines reflects the nationalistic terms of reference for state-hood in the country. Aggravated by the rather static conditioning of the constitution brought about by "angst" (fear) of any reform, governance mechanisms are unable to adapt to the constantly evolving conditions in the country. However, any constitutional reforms should be assessed very carefully. For example, the proposed introduction of federalism in the country may be a viable option, however, only under certain conditions. Federalism may eventually lead to the arsenal upgrade of local political warlords, who will have more resources and (bureaucratic) legitimacy to use in order to maintain power and deter rivals. Although federalism may address representation deficiencies, it may expand security deficits not only in Mindanao but in other provinces of the country. Hence, as long as the needed "non-violent" alternatives to the current dominating agents of violence are missing, the conflict will most likely continue.

In sum, as Crocker et al. (2009, p. 496) argue, the causes of intractability may totally differ to the original cause of the conflict. The sources of intractability prolong the conflict by adding more complexity, which remains unaddressed in current intervention efforts. Therefore, intractability requires a different set of efforts, which must complement the mediation and negotiation process.

7.2 Mediation and other Intervention Efforts in the Philippines

The case of Southern Philippines shows a variety of non-coercive means of intervention are needed to manage identity conflicts. The available methods of peaceful settlement for identity conflicts are numerous and varied. The UN charter recommends the following three methods for peaceful management of international conflicts[5]: (a) direct negotiation among the conflicting parties; (b) various forms of mediation, good offices, and conciliation; and (c) binding methods of third-party intervention such as arbitration and adjudication (Bercovitch, 2009, p. 340). Other forms of peaceful interventions are various tracks of diplomacy, back-channeling, expert advice, consultation, and activities of NGOs, which would facilitate negotiation such as monitoring, development projects and grass-root mediation. These methods are practiced by numerous and diverse actors such as individuals, civil society through local and international non-governmental organizations, international organizations as well as states (Dixon, 1996). These methods may promote diplomacy and may be instrumental in achieving a cessation of hostilities, a peace agreement, or a full settlement of a conflict. Such methods are furthermore instrumental in creating conditions that favor reconciliation in the long term through the building of "capacities for peace" or as Crocker et al. (2009, p. 497) suggest "a supportive political climate and constituency for peace-making." A systemic illustration of the different methods of peaceful intervention can be found through the following matrix (Table 7.1):

[5] For the purpose of this book project, international conflicts involve not only inter-state conflicts, but also intra-state conflicts which are likely to endanger the maintenance of international peace and security. The conflict in Southern Philippines has effects on other South-east Asian countries in form of the inflow of refugees and proliferation of small arms and light weapons in the region.

Table 7.4: Mapping Out Non-violent and Non-coercive Conflict Management in Southern Philippines

	Security	Political / Governance	Socio-economic	Socio-cultural
International	**Mediation** through the OIC (Malaysia, Indonesia, Libya), **Peace monitoring** through Australia; **Good Offices** through Norway **Positive Inducement** through the United States, Malaysia, OIC	**Mediation** through the OIC (Malaysia, Libya) **Vocalization** through INGOs **Positive Inducement** through the United States, Malaysia, OIC, Australia, Spain, EU	**Positive Inducement in form of Foreign Direct Investments** through the United States, China, Spain, Australia and Canada, as well as Mirant; **Partnerships** between International NGOs such as Synergos and local NGOs and local leaders (e.g. leadership training at the AIM-Mirant Center for Bridging Societal Divides) **Vocalization** through INGOs	**Cultural and Religious programs and projects** through international organizations and foundations such as the *Gaddafi International Foundation for Charitable Associations* and *Arab Foundations Forum* (AFF) **Vocalization** through INGOs
Regional	**Mediation** through Malaysia; **Peace Monitoring** through Malaysia, Indonesia, Brunei, and Japan	**Mediation** through Malaysia; **Monitoring and Public Consultation** of regional agencies of ASEAN in Mindanao such as the ASEAN Human Rights Mechanism (PWG)		
National	**Direct negotiations** between the GRP and MNLF, MILF **Abjudication** and **Arbitration** through Philippine courts	**Direct negotiations** between the GRP and MNLF, MILF influencing legislation **Abjudication** and **Arbitration** through Philippine courts **Legislation**	**Partnership** between the Mindanao Economic Development Council and the GRP	**Enhancing of Socio–Cultural Research and Development Activities** in Mindanao through the GRP

		Referral to the Judicial System		
Local	**Peace-monitoring** (e.g. ceasefire watch) through local NGOs; **Vocalization** through NGOs **Mediation** between communities through local NGOs; **Mediation and Arbitration** between individuals through the traditional Datu-system (similar to Barangay Community Mediation	**Public Consultation and Partnership** between GRP, local government units and NGOs **Vocalization** through NGOs	**Local Investments** through local investors **Community Development Projects** through local NGOs **Vocalization** through NGOs	**Education projects** through local NGOs; **Establishment of Research Institutes for Mindanao Culture** at local university; **Cultural programs** of local NGOs such as cultural festivals; **Dialogue Projects** through local churches (both Christian and Muslim) **Mediation and Arbitration** between individuals through the traditional Datu-system to enhance grass-root reconciliation; **Mediation** between communities through local NGOs to enhance reconciliation **Vocalization** through NGOs

The table is an attempt to map out the on-going responses undertaken by a wide range of actors in Southern Philippines. It should be noted that the responses of the international and regional third-parties such as Malaysia, Libya and the OIC, although significant in their own rights, are not able to cover all aspects of the conflict. For example, while Malaysia is concentrating on the security and governance aspects of the conflict, this country as a mediator does not address grass-root reconciliation in Mindanao.

Other third-party states such as the United States, Japan, Australia, the European Union and Norway provide "positive inducements" in form of economic and military aid (e.g. the "*Balikatan,*" an annual military exercises between the United States and the Philippines), diplomatic support or diplomatic pressure in the international system (e.g. OIC granting the MNLF an observer status in its organization leading to its recognition, or the policy of Libya and Malaysia for supporting only claims on autonomy and not independence), and assistance in civil administration (e.g. the EU's support of governance projects in Mindanao). Another example is the fruit nursery, which was opened in 1998, was facilitated and funded by the United States Agency for International Development (Vitug and Gloria, 2000, p. 108).

Civil society has emerged as capable of covering all aspects of the conflict, from security to cultural, as table (8) illustrates. NGOs are involved in public consultation with the government and representatives of armed groups. Philippine NGOs are in a very unique position as they can influence the legislative process through the possibility of holding seats in the Philippine congress through the "party-list system" in the country, which aims to increase legislative representation of marginalized sectors. NGOs and INGOs conduct "*vocalization*", which involves public third-party appeals or demands for the disputants to negotiate or to implement agreements (Gartner and Melin, 2009, p. 568) while regularly naming and blaming both the government and the armed groups, when concessions are not reached.

Furthermore, NGOs monitor existing agreements and publish violations committed by both sides. NGOs have made an agreement with both sides not to conduct armed confrontations in the so-called "*peace zones*" to decrease human casualties in the conflict (Santos, 2005). On the socio-economic side, NGOs have conducted development and livelihood projects particularly in impoverished isolated communities. NGOs, particularly local churches (both Christian and Muslim), have maintained partnerships between communities and dialogue projects to enhance communication between groups.

Another intervention is adjudication and arbitration, which involves the use of the international or national legal system to manage the conflict by generating binding decisions to which the disputants must adhere (Cede, 2009, 2012). Aside from adjudication and arbitration, the referral to the judicial system is a very important instrument in persecuting criminal offenses. A current incident, which affirms the importance of this method, is the massacre of 57 men and women by more than 100 armed militia of a warlord allied to Philippine President Gloria Macapagal-Arroyo on 23 November 2009 (International Crisis Group, 2009). The victims were the families and friends of the rival candidate Esmail "*Toto*" Mangudadatu, who decided to run for governor of *Maguindanao* province, for the 2010 May elections. The province, which is part of the ARMM, has been in the control of the Ampatuan family for decades. The clan is considered to be a very powerful local political dynasty, which was an important ally of the Philippine government under President Arroyo. The 36 municipalities of the province and the ARMM itself are led by extended clan members. The immediate response of the Philippine government was the declaration of a state of emergency in *Maguinda-*

nao and in the neighboring province *Sultan Kudarat*, giving the Philippines military the mandate to restore and maintain order, especially the local police, who were compromised through the involvement of some policemen in the massacre. After some weeks, martial law was lifted and the case was brought to the courts.

7.2.1 First-Track Mediation in the Philippines – Dealing with "Biased" Mediation

The international system is a system of states. Particularly, when internal conflicts such as civil wars are perceived to threaten stability and international order, states intervene. Because mediation is perceived as the intervention of choice in internal conflicts, several states such as Norway and Sweden are increasingly engaging in mediation. Several regional powers such as India (in Sri Lanka), Malaysia (in the Philippines) and South Africa (in Zimbabwe) recognize the necessity to intervene in order to guarantee the stability and order in the region. Some states are mediating because of political interests or of cultural bonds either to the state or to the minority group.

Critical to any successful intervention is the perception by the conflicting parties that the intervening state has no direct interests at stake. However, it does not suggest that the intervening state is completely indifferent to the outcome (Slim, 1992, pp. 225–226). This is particularly not problematic to small states such as Norway and Sweden compared to the superpowers. The mediation efforts of the United States and the former Soviet Union attracted special attention because of their status as "superpowers" (Touval, 1992, p. 232). Any mediation effort and/or any other coercive actions by the United States are easily seen as instruments to extend its influence. This can be called as the "superpower syndrome."

The continuity of mediation efforts can be jeopardized not only by the prevalent public opinion but also by a sudden change of administration, whereas the new administration's policy in other domains is hostile or counterproductive to the mediation efforts. For instance, while Malaysia was continuing its mediation efforts in the Philippines, the government strengthened its immigration rules prompting the mass deportation of one million "illegal immigrants" (Amnesty International, 2004), where hundreds of thousands of Filipino refugees were forced to return to Mindanao. Malaysia's mediation efforts in the Philippines require the adaptation of Malaysia's policies to its activities as mediator, if it wants its efforts not be undermined.

States engage in mediation as a pursuit of national or foreign policy interests. In some cases, an emerging settlement may be against the state's policy; therefore, the mediating state may block that specific settlement. Furthermore, the prospective state mediator may be too closely aligned to one party or too directly involved in the conflict to be capable of meeting the minimum conditions of a balanced agreement (Crocker et al., 2009, p. 498).

Small states such as Libya and Malaysia are perceived as preferable mediators compared to major states. Slim (1992, p. 207) argues that small states as mediators resort to persuasion instead of power and coercion. He continues that unlike superpowers, small states can offer conflicting parties more prospect of success because of the strategic weakness of small states. The Philippine case shows that small states derive their mandate from the international context of conflict. Libya, Malaysia and Indonesia derive their mandate to intervene through the principle of *Ummah* (the community of Islamic faithful, the sense of a "people" or "nation") as codified in the charter of the Organization of the Islamic Conference (OIC). These small state mediators are to a significant extent biased towards a specific conflict party – Libya and Malaysia for the benefit of the Muslim rebel groups and Indonesia for the benefit of the Philippine government. These states have to a significant extent become a party to the conflict. Nevertheless, the Philippine government realized that the best way to integrate "patronage" states that are serving as diplomatic, financial and moral supporters of the Muslim rebel groups is to involve them as mediators. The Philippine government was successful in limiting the influence of these patronage states by allowing them to assume the role of mediators.

While Libya and Malaysia actually mediated on separate occasions, Indonesia served primarily as a balancing factor to deter bias in favor of rebel groups. Indonesia, as a traditional ally of the Philippine government expressed its interest in preserving the sovereignty and territorial integrity of the Philippines in the series of meetings of the OIC. Like the Philippines, Indonesia is confronted by similar problems such as the conflict in Aceh. Without the interference of Indonesia in the OIC meetings, the mediation would have been a failure.

The intervention efforts of Libya, Malaysia and Indonesia are framed within the structure of the OIC. This organization is biased towards the Muslim population, particularly when the MNLF, which was granted the observer status (similar to the Palestine Liberation Organization), not only granting the rebel group diplomatic recognition on the international level, but as well direct access to OIC members. Nevertheless, the involvement of the OIC as mediators in the Philippines, as well as the efforts of Indonesia and other ASEAN members of the OIC to preserve the national sovereignty and territorial integrity of the Philippines led to the limitation for the support of the OIC to the Muslim rebel groups. Furthermore, the events in September 11, 2001 led to political constraints particularly in financing rebel groups such as the MNLF and MILF.

7.2.1.1 Libya's Mediation of the GRP – MNLF Conflict

The involvement of Libya started in 1971, when Colonel Muammar Qaddafi heard on BBC Radio that 70 Filipino Muslims had been killed by Christian vigilantes inside a mosque in the town of Manili, Cotobato (Vitug and Gloria, 2000, p. 60). Qaddafi as leader of the revolution in Libya took the mission to empower Muslim communities in many parts of the world against oppression. Furthermore, the founder of the MNLF Nur Misuari was a known communist during his days as professor at the University of the Philippines. The involvement of Libya in the Philippines is therefore to be classified as cultural and ideological in nature.

Immediately, Libya spent millions of to arm the MNLF and provided a safe haven and training for Muslim rebels in Tripoli. Supported by Malaysia, which was still angry with Manila for plotting to destabilize Sabah (Vitug and Gloria, 2000, p. 61), Libya initiated at many OIC meetings the inclusion of the situation of Muslims in the Philippines as an agenda. In the spirit of *ummah*, Muslims overseas were called to support their beleaguered brothers in the Philippines (Vitug and Gloria, 2000, p. 60). In 1973, at the Fourth Islamic Conference in Benghazi, Libya pushed for the adoption of an OIC resolution expressing "deep concern over the reported repression and mass extermination of Muslims in Southern Philippines and [urging] the Philippine government to halt these operations immediately" (OIC, 1974).

The Marcos government could not afford to ignore the concerns of Muslim countries particularly because of the dependence of the country on oil imports from the Middle East. The OIC Resolution No. 474 created a funding mechanisms for the Muslim community in the Southern Philippines. It imposed a mandate on OIC states to pressure the Philippine government. After trips of government officials to the Middle East from January 14 to 20, 1975, Marcos realized in context of the oil crisis that any attempt to improve the Philippine's diplomatic ties with the Middle East countries depends on a settlement with the MNLF and that the MNLF was receiving financial and material support from its major supporters in the OIC (Vitug and Gloria, 2000, p. 62). The Philippines experienced series of oil embargos until the 80s. While launching a series of military offensives against the MNLF, the Marcos government decided to hold talks with the MNLF within the guidelines of the OIC led by Libya.

According to Melchor (Vitug and Gloria, 2000, p. 33), who was a member of the Philippine negotiating panel in Libya, Libya's game plan was simple. Libya wanted to make Nur Misuari another Arafat. Ali Abdussalam Treki, Libya's foreign minister, who had succeeded at that time in getting Arafat to speak to the UN General Assembly in Geneva in 1974, wanted to repeat this success with Misuari.

In the next few years, talks between the Philippine government and the MNLF were held. In November 1976, President Marcos dispatched his wife, First Lady Imelda Marcos as a diplomatic bridge in the Middle East, where a meeting between her and Qaddafi was organized in order to ask Qaddafi to convince the MNLF to agree to sign a peace agreement with the government. This meeting led to the final stage of the negotiations, which culminated in December 1976.

In the final stage of the negotiations between 15 and 23 December 1976, Ermita, a political aid for the head of the government panel Defence Undersecretary Barbero, noted that the government panel vigorously objected to provision 15, which called for the establishment of a "provisional government" in the areas covered by the autonomy pact. The government panel's request for a recess due to Christmas was refused by Libya. Barbero plotted a sea "escape" from Tripoli to Malta to board a plane to Manila. But Libya was able to tap the rooms of panel members and learned of the escape plan. Libya called Marcos in Manila to convince Barbero to sign the agreement. Marcos instructed Barbero to go ahead and sign the agreement on one condition that an additional provision be added in the final draft (Vitug and Gloria, 2000, p. 34). Referred to as Paragraph 16 of the Tripoli Agreement, it says that "the Philippine government shall undertake all the necessary constitutional process to implement the entire agreement" (Conciliation Resources, 2010). Nevertheless, this paragraph can be considered as a big hole in the agreement, because it gave the Philippine government resources to delay the implementation. The 1976 Tripoli Agreement was eventually signed in presence of the Secretary-General and the members of the Quadripartite Ministerial Commission of the OIC.

The popular revolt against Marcos in 1986 led to the reinstallation of a democratic regime in the Philippines. Nevertheless, the negotiations for the Final Peace Agreement were difficult and slow. A stalemate lasted for the next 16 years. The peace process gained a new momentum, when presidential candidate Fidel Ramos met with Qaddafi in Tripoli in 1992. Ramos revealed in his 1996 book "*Break not the Peace*" that "I was to divulge the details and purpose of my trip to the public only, when the peace agreement was fairly sure of success four-and-a-half years later." For Ramos, the confidentiality of the meeting was necessary to avoid any pressure form the parties, as well as to allow flexibility during negotiations (see Ramos, 1996).

In October 1992, Ramos dispatched to Tripoli a three-person team to follow-up the earlier meeting with Qaddafi. Libya, however, was confronted by Nur Misuari's refusal to be in the same room with one of the three members of the government panel, Representative Eduardo Ermita of Batangas. Misuari referred to Ermita as "the enemy of the Bangsamoro people." A senior MNLF leader says that there was an order from Qaddafi that the MNLF sit down with Ermita (Vitug and

Gloria, 2000, p. 29). The meeting was concluded with an agreement to hold the second round of exploratory talks.

Libya clearly changed its position and strategies after years of isolation from the West. The United States broke off relations with Libya in 1986 and imposed economic sanctions in response to a series of terrorist incidents. Furthermore, the United Nations Security Council imposed sanctions to Libya in 1992 following the bombings of a Pan Am flight over Lockerbie, Scotland. The UN sanction included a flight ban to Libya further aggravating its isolation from the international community. With this background, Libya changed its course and opted for the role of a peace-broker in 1992 under the term of President Ramos. In 1994, several agreements and the interim ceasefire agreement were reached through formal talks.

The Final Agreement on the Implementation of the 1976 Tripoli Agreement between the Government of the Philippines and the MNLF was finally reached in Manila on September 2, 1996, twenty years after the signing of the Tripoli agreement. Finally, Libya witnessed the formal end of its intervention in the Philippines. Nevertheless, Libya maintains its interest in the development of the Southern Philippines by sending in peacekeepers to Mindanao in order to monitor the 2003 ceasefire agreement between the Philippine government and the MILF following the withdrawal of Malaysian monitors (ABSCBN News, 2008). Several foundations from Libya, such as the Qaddafi Foundation, maintain investment projects in Mindanao. Libya mediated the end of the Sipadan hostage crisis in 2000, where the Abu Sayaff, a break-away faction of the MILF, took 21 hostages from Sipadan, Malaysia and brought the hostages to an Abu Sayaff base in Jolo, Sulu. Libya ended the crisis by offering 25 million US as “development aid” (BBC, 2000).

Without the formal involvement of Libya, the peace process in Mindanao would have been a failure. Although Libya is biased for the benefit of the Muslim rebel groups, its involvement as mediator 1) coerced the Philippine government to recognize the sentiments of the Muslim population, 2) coerced the MNLF to drop off its demand for independence paving way for negotiations, 3) limited its own financial and military support to the MNLF, and 4) led to the 1976 and 1996 Peace Agreements.

7.2.1.2 Malaysia’s Mediation of the GRP – MILF Conflict

Malaysia assumed the role of the mediator upon request of the MILF and the Philippine government. As a patronage state, Malaysia is to be classified as a biased mediator. It was in Sabah, Malaysia, where Muslim rebels sought refuge (Vitug and Gloria, 2000, p. 173). At the height of the Mindanao war in the 1970s, about

200,000 Muslim refugees flocked to Sabah. The Philippine government received information from captured combatants that MNLF fighters received from Malaysian sources at least 200,000 rounds of ammunition and more than 5,000 weapons ranging from hand grenades to machine guns (Vitug and Gloria, 2000, p. 173). In camps in Sabah, MNLF combatants underwent training from British-trained Malaysian officers. The village of Jiamperas became an enclave for the MNLF. A total of 477 rebels comprising the three batches of MNLF combatants were sent to Sabah from 1969 to 1974 (Vitug and Gloria, 2000, p. 175).

Malaysia was initially supportive of the initiatives made by Libya in OIC meetings. However, Malaysia's position changed over the course of time. As Vitug & Gloria (2000, p. 176) note, it wasn't Islam that moved the Malaysian leaders in encouraging Misuari to opt for a peace settlement. According to them it was realpolitik. Malaysian Prime Minister Dr. Mahathir Mohammad and Philippine President Fidel Ramos became good friends. Their meetings within the framework of the ASEAN promoted good relations between the two leaders. The good personal chemistry between the two leaders proved to have been significant in the crucial periods of the peace negotiation.

Furthermore, the change of policy of Malaysia is fostered by the domestic policies in the country. The threat posed by Islamic extremism and the economic dominance of the Christian Chinese population in Malaysia paved the way for pragmatic institutional arrangements in the country. Malaysia's policy towards the MNLF reflects the secular institutional setting that Malaysia has chosen to address the multi-ethnic and multi-religious composition of the country. The same formula is sought by Malaysia in the Philippines to address the problem of Filipino Muslims.

In 2001, President Gloria Macapagal-Arroyo requested Malaysian Prime Minister Mahathir Mohammad to intervene in the Mindanao peace process. Mohammad eventually agreed and sent peacekeeping missions to the Southern Philippines. Since then he hosted several rounds of peace talks in Kuala Lumpur. When a ceasefire agreement was reached in 2003, Malaysia sent police and military personnel to lead the 80-man and woman strong International Monitoring Team, which helped monitor the proper and effective implementation of the agreement on the cessation of hostilities in Mindanao (Fernandez, 2009). Both the Philippine military and the MILF credited Malaysia's and IMT's presence for the dramatic reduction of armed confrontations in the region until the July 2008 attacks by MILF renegades on civilian communities in North Cotobato and Lanao Del Norte prompting the end of the ceasefire.

The peace negotiations between the Philippine government and the MILF have been in a stalemate since 2008 after the Malaysia brokered MOA-AD was declared unconstitutional by the Philippine Supreme Court. The Philippine negotiating panel, nevertheless agreed with the MILF's earlier pronouncements that Malaysia should remain as the principal mediator. The MILF chief of civil-military affairs Eid Kabalu credited Malaysia with performing well as mediator in the peace talks and therefore, the MILF prefers Malaysia assuming the mediatory role. However, the newly installed Philippine President Benigno Aquino III left the option open that Malaysia will be replaced (The New Straits Times, 2010) as mediator and identifying Indonesia as a possible replacement following sentiments from various nationalist sectors on the issue of Sabah. Malaysia is often cited by Philippine officials as a mediator with vested interests because of the unresolved claims over Sabah, which somewhat compromises Malaysia's neutrality. Eventually, Malaysia retained its mediator role with Datu Tengku acting as facilitator.

Malaysia's bias position being the patronage state of the Muslims in the Philippines has been circumvented by its own domestic policies. Malaysia cannot politically afford any further military support for the Muslim rebel groups. Nevertheless, it cannot completely avoid any involvement in the Philippines because of its historical ties to the conflict. Mediation as a legitimately seen intervention effort in conflicts has provided Malaysia with the channel to maintain involvement without jeopardizing domestic policies.

The difference, which can be observed between the Malaysian mediation and the Libyan mediation, is that Malaysia seems to have lost political leverage to press and influence both sides to move toward a settlement. Compared to Libya, which several times succeeded in persuading conflicting parties to move forward through the use of political resources defined by the dependence of both parties to Libya, Malaysia lacks effective political sources to influence the parties to reach an agreement.

In the case of the Malaysian mediation, the MILF seems to have learned from the experiences of the MNLF and has adapted to the constraints of state sponsorship. The main financial sources of the MILF are not state sponsors, like in the case of the MNLF, but rather foundations and international Muslim NGOs. These NGOs are based in OIC member states and are more difficult, if not impossible to regulate. Furthermore, the MILF collects contributions from local Muslim entrepreneurs and multinational corporations investing in their controlled areas. As Vitug & Gloria (Vitug and Gloria, 2000, p. 119) observe, "the war itself brings economic opportunities to the MILF." For instance, when a Korean construction company started work in 1993 on a 1.7 billion Pesos (30 million US Dollar) government irrigation project in Malitubog-Maridagao in Carmen, Cotobato, an area under MILF influence, the MILF provided security for the company and was paid for it.

In addition, Malaysia seems to have lost influence with the Philippine government. Although Malaysia could forward the issue to the OIC member states, which could lead to oil embargos, the Philippine government seems to have found an assurance that this will not happen. The rivalry between the MNLF and MILF was solved at the OIC by declaring the MNLF the "sole representative of the Bangsamoro" (Business World, 2000). Malaysia's Foreign Minister Datuk Seri Syed Jamid Albar said the OIC will reject MILF's bid for OIC observer status. Therefore, any impasse with a rebel group not formally recognized by the OIC remains unproblematic in these terms. The political and diplomatic isolation of the MILF in the Muslim world is an advantage for the Philippine government because it sees no danger of oil embargos similar to the 70s.

Malaysia's mediation is currently evolving from a biased mediator to an impartial mediator. However, it can also be argued this evolution is caused by the gradual loss of political leverage of Malaysia towards the conflicting parties. The last perceived political leverage through the presence of Malaysian members in the International Monitoring Team (IMT) has proven to be inefficient, because of the willingness of several countries such as Norway, Japan and Australia to take over. It would be interesting to know, what other political leverages are available for Malaysia in order to get out of the stalemate and push forward the negotiation process.

To conclude, bias mediators such as Malaysia can still manifest impartiality, when they have stakes in being impartial. Furthermore, the historical and cultural bias of Malaysia for the benefit of the Muslim population is balanced by Malaysia's political bias for the benefit of the Philippine government linked with its interest to adhere to international norms on national sovereignty and territorial integrity. It confirms international mediation efforts by states still following the *Westphalian* notion of sovereignty. Moreover, both the Philippines and Malaysia are founding members of the ASEAN. Malaysia starts to internalize the main normative foundation of the ASEAN – non-interference in domestic issues. Malaysia recognizes the Moro insurgency as an internal issue. In the end, although Malaysia has a long record of military and diplomatic assistance to the MNLF and the MILF, Malaysia is still a state. It prefers to resolve the Philippine conflict without hurting itself.

7.2.2 Mediation by Regional Organizations – The Organization of Islamic Conference (OIC) in the Philippines

With states facing constraints in mediating intractable identity conflicts, international and regional governmental organizations such as the United Nations, the

African Union or the Organisation of Islamic Conference (OIC) are increasingly consolidating their efforts to mediate the conflicts. Not only are international and regional organizations enjoying clear legitimacy, they are seen as to be capable of providing the necessary resources for a successful mediation. Nevertheless, although international and regional organizations can invoke their intervention from charters and resolutions, these bodies are still consisted of states. Therefore, the principles of national sovereignty and territorial integrity will remain relevant as these bodies cannot independently provide resources, because they depend on the "goodwill" of their member states.

As showed in the UN's efforts in East Timor, the United Nations and other international and regional organizations are not immune to politicization. The United Nations failed to prevent the Rwandan genocide and continues to fail to prevent potential mass killings in Sudan, because of delaying tactics by some states. Indonesia was not willing to engage in any talks involving the United Nations after the independence of the Timor-Leste (Aspinall and Crouch, 2003). The United Nations is furthermore seen as incapable of providing a non-biased intervention in identity conflicts because the United Nations is after all a system of states. Hence, sub-state groups seeking independence see the United Nations as naturally biased against them.

Several regional organizations, such as the African Union and the Organisation of Islamic Conference (OIC), have a clear mandate to intervene in disputes. Other regional organizations such as the ASEAN have a more limited mandate. For instance, ASEAN's main principle involves the non-interference in internal issues of the member states. In this relation, the OIC feels it has a mandate to intervene in the Philippines, whereas the ASEAN sees the conflict in the Southern Philippines as an internal problem. Interestingly, this principle is regularly reflected in the positions made by OIC members, who are at the same time member of the ASEAN, such as Indonesia, Malaysia, Thailand (observer) and Brunei.

As Amoo and Zartman (1996, p. 131) note, regional organizations are in a difficult position to mediate disputes among their members. In many cases, the disputing states do not see the regional organization as a mediating instance but rather as an instrument, which must be won. Since such organizations are forums for sovereign states and much less corporate entities in their own right, these organizations are under pressure from their own members to endorse rather than to mediate. Moreover, as the OIC intervention in the Philippines shows, regional organizations entrust mediation to a committee also composed of sovereign states. Therefore, it can be argued that regional organizations are a locus and a flag, not a corporate actor (Amoo and Zartman, 1996, p. 131).

7.2.2.1 The Organization of Islamic Conference (OIC)

Primarily motivated by the struggle of the people of Palestine, the OIC was founded on 25 September 1969 in Rabat, Morocco. It intends to foster solidarity among Muslims all over the world. One of the major reasons for founding the OIC was to settle conflicts mainly through mediation, negotiation and arbitration. In the 1960s, Saudi Arabia called for an "Islamic Summit" to coordinate the efforts of Islamic countries to convince Israeli forces to withdraw from Arab territories, to recognize the Palestinian people's right to return to their homeland, and the restoration of Jerusalem to Arab rule (OIC, 2010).

The burning of the Al Aqsa mosque in Jerusalem by Israeli radicals triggered the holding of the first summit in Rabat, Morocco in September 1969. Six months after the meeting, the First Islamic Conference of Ministers of Foreign Affairs was held in Jeddah to establish a permanent General Secretariat, to ensure a liaison among Member States and charged it to coordinate their action. The Conference appointed its Secretary General and chose Jeddah as the Headquarters of the Organization, pending the liberation of Jerusalem, which would be the permanent Headquarters. The OIC grew out of this international meeting of 24 heads of Islamic states. The organization with its 57 member states claim to represent the 1.3 billion Muslims in the world.

The key OIC members are Saudi Arabia, Kuwait, Iraq, Libya and Egypt. Saudi Arabia serves as the major financier and has assumed informal leadership of the Jeddah-based organization. With 57 member states, as well as 13 observer members, the OIC has the potential of being a formidable force in international politics. However, the Philippines appears to be the only success story of the OIC in its record of dispute settlement. As Vitug and Gloria (Vitug and Gloria, 2000, p. 71) note, the OIC's influence has substantially declined since the 1970s. The lack of coherence within the organization confirms regional organizations have difficulties in maintaining the self-preservation of the organization.

The legitimacy of the interventions of the OIC in conflicts is derived from its charter and resolutions. The OIC-charter of 1972 calls for the promotion of Islamic solidarity; and political, economic, social, cultural and scientific cooperation between member states. In 2008, OIC member states replaced its 1972 charter with the 2008 charter. The new charter refers for the first time to the protection of human rights. It calls for member states to guarantee and promote democracy, human rights, freedom, rule of law and good governance (Der Western, 2008). The new charter is seen as an indicator of the new profile the OIC is intending to pursue in the future.

7.2.2.2 The OIC and the Bangsamoro Problem

The OIC used different sets of strategies in order to resolve the conflict in the Southern Philippines. This includes good offices, mediation, inquiry, sanctions, positive inducements, consultation, monitoring and coordination of NGO activities. This combination of strategies is partly the result of different calculations on how the conflict can be resolved. The OIC's intervention is itself a non-linear process. Interventions are sometimes very intensive and manipulative. OIC member states imposed oil embargos on the Philippines to pressure the government into negotiation. It was the threat of a second OPEC embargo, which convinced President Marcos to negotiate with the MNLF and accept OIC mediation in 1975 (Santos, 1999). In some cases, the OIC was perceived to be distracted with other international issues and to be tired of its efforts, which gave the impression the OIC lowered its expectations in the negotiation process in the Philippines

The OIC's interest was drawn to Mindanao in 1972 following initiatives of Libya. In almost all of its annual conferences, a resolution expressing concern for the plight of the Filipino Muslims became part of its routine. These resolutions have legitimized financial and military aid to the MNLF, as well as embargos on the Philippines. Malaysia hosted the first batches of MNLF combatants. Saudi Arabia and Iran effectively boycotted the Philippines and halted oil exports to the Marcos administration. The Islamic Fund, established by the OIC, donated 1 Million US dollars in humanitarian aid to Muslim Mindanao. The OIC eventually granted the MNLF observer status in 1977, giving the rebels better access to the international Islamic community, led by wealthy oil-producing countries (Vitug and Gloria, 2000, p. 60). The OIC became a party to the conflict.

Libya opted to coordinate its intervention efforts with the efforts of the OIC, which intended to maximize its leverage, while gaining legitimacy. Libya perceived the OIC was the appropriate forum to forward the interests of the MNLF and the OIC has the appropriate resources to coerce the Philippine government. A historical analysis of the mediation efforts made by the OIC in the Philippines and how these efforts were determined by the interests of the member states shows international organizations are constantly influenced by changing conditions in the international system.

After the oil embargos, the Marcos government believed it had no choice but to negotiate and bring in the OIC to mediate. The OIC, a forum of sovereign states decided against supporting the MNLF's call for an independent Muslim state. Instead they offered to mediate the conflict (Tan, 1993). The MNLF was coerced to obey the decision of the OIC. As historian Samuel K. Tan (1993) acknowledges, the OIC is the formidable force behind the Moro struggle. The MNLF under Nur Misuari decided to give in. The MNLF leadership admitted in 1994 "the primary reason why we had to accept that resolution was because we were terrified at the prospect of being isolated from our brothers in the world" (Vitug and Gloria, 2000, p. 32).

The OIC created a committee of four states – Libya, Saudi Arabia, Senegal and Somalia to investigate the problem in the Southern Philippines. The OIC committee of four delegations visited Mindanao in 1973 and was treated like royalty. The tone of the succeeding OIC resolutions softened soon after. In the 1974 and 1975 meetings, the OIC expressed interest in a negotiated settlement without giving into the rebel's secessionist demands. In a 1974 conference in Kuala Lumpur, the OIC adopted Resolution 18, which called on the Philippines to meet with representatives of the MNLF in Jeddah, Saudi Arabia in order to arrive at a just solution to the Muslim problem "within the framework of national sovereignty and territorial integrity of the Philippines" (Vitug and Gloria, 2000, p. 32).

The resolution stressed the OIC's recognition, which was, the war in Mindanao was a problem internal to the Philippines. The OIC refused to support the MNLF demand for independence. Particularly Indonesia, itself a multi-ethnic state, argued the conflict between the Philippine government and the Muslims was an internal matter. Malaysia, now wooed back by the Philippines, proposed a draft resolution, which centered on the idea the problem was a Filipino one, not international, nor Islamic, and asked the OIC to encourage communication between the conflicting parties. James Piscatori (1986) observed "Malaysia and Indonesia have been instrumental in keeping the OIC from a complete break with the Philippine government." After the resolution, Malaysia blocked a major arms shipment which was on its way to Western Mindanao through Sabah (Vitug and Gloria, 2000, p. 32).

The reaching of the 1976 Tripoli Agreement further limited the bias of the OIC. Its participation was framed through this agreement. Prior the reaching of the 1996 Final Peace Agreement, the OIC was tired of supporting a protracted and floundering struggle. The OIC was pushing for a political settlement. On one occasion, the government panel was taken hostage by the OIC secretary-general Tohamy, who followed his own political agenda. As secretary general of the OIC, he wanted to have a success story under his leadership. He wanted to impose the Cyprus solution on the Philippines in order to solve the Muslim problem by dividing the Philippines (Vitug and Gloria, 2000, p. 33). Nevertheless, he was unsuccessful in pushing his agenda because the OIC has no corporate identity of its own. Its decisions similar to most international organizations are still determined by member states. The OIC did not want a solution, which would result in the dismembered of the Philippines since some of their members such as Turkey's (PKK) and Indonesia's (GAM) are confronted by similar problems.

In 1982, the OIC was confronted by a huge problem. The MNLF was no longer one solid organization. In a conference in Niamey, Niger, the OIC urged the MNLF to participate in talks with government as a "united front" (Vitug and Gloria, 2000, p. 64). Among others, the MILF fraction decided to break away from the MNLF because it was unsatisfied with the flow of the negotiations. For many hard-liners, negotiation is an act of surrender. The patriarchal leadership style of Nur Misuari, who was perceived to be listening more to the Libyans instead of high-ranking rebel officers promoted the break-away of hardliners from the MNLF. When it became clear that Nur Misuari had no absolute command of all the elements within the MNLF, the OIC declared the MNLF as the sole representative of the Bangsamoro. This declaration delegitimized the break-away factions.

The change of administration in the Philippines in 1986 brought hopes to the negotiations. The unilateral creation of the ARMM in 1989 showed the OIC the administration of the newly elected President Corazon Aquino was serious about honoring the 1976 Tripoli Agreement. The OIC in its meeting in Turkey in 1991 acknowledged the measures taken by the Philippines in resolving the Mindanao conflict. Faced with other problems such as those of Muslim communities in Kashmir, Afghanistan, Bosnia and Egypt and Israel, the OIC started to become more accommodating, even willing to diminish the importance of the Tripoli Agreement (Vitug and Gloria, 2000, p. 67).

In 1993, the OIC symbolically reduced the MNLF issue to a regional concern by designating Indonesia as chairman of the Committee of Six, in place of Libya. Indonesia and Bangladesh joined the committee of four. Muslim members of the ASEAN initiated this expansion of the committee arguing the four members were all outsiders to the region. Indonesian diplomacy is less Islamic than ASEAN. The parameter for Indonesia's intervention follows the ASEAN framework of non-interference in domestic affairs of its member states.

The chairmanship of Indonesia for the OIC Committee of Six placed the Philippine government in a more advantageous negotiating position as the OIC started to lose its muscle. The Indonesian chairman, Dr. Hassan Wirajuda noted the OIC requested the MNLF panel should understand the establishment of a provisional autonomous government would violate the constitution of the Philippines and therefore could not be accommodated by the GRP panel. As Santos (1999) notes, provisions invoked by the MNLF by claiming self-determination carries less weight than provisions invoked by the Philippine government by claiming non-interference in the domestic affairs of member states with respect for sovereignty and territorial integrity.

Nevertheless, the Final Peace Agreement of 1996 was reached. Immediately, the OIC, in its summit in Tehran, called on the Philippine government and the

MNLF to preserve the gains. The OIC declared its intention to maintain its observer status in the implementation of the agreement and urged member states and affiliated institutions to increase financial and technical assistance for the rehabilitation of the Southern Philippines (Vitug and Gloria, 2000, p. 69).

The OIC as an international organization became part of the conflict. In his account of the negotiations with the MNLF, President Ramos (1996) said "we had to give the OIC a direct stake in the outcome of the autonomy." President Marcos invited the OIC to mediate between the Philippine government and the MNLF. The following presidents of the country acknowledged the OIC must be part of the solution. After the 1976 Tripoli Agreement, the participation and political leverage of the OIC was significantly limited through the framework built by this agreement. Furthermore, the intervention of the "friends of the Philippines" such as Indonesia, Brunei and later on Malaysia, who had interests of maintaining stability and good relations in the ASEAN region led to further decrease of the political leverage of the OIC.

The OIC mediation in the Philippines is a biased intervention with elements of coercion in the form of embargos against the Philippine government and military support for the MNLF. Furthermore, the OIC anticipated the outcome of the peace negotiations and expressed its preference on how the outcome should look, a behavior that is often halfway between partisan and neutrality (Thompson and Zartman, 1975). With the OIC dictating the design of the settlement, it took sides, however, not to the conflict parties, but to its member states, which wish to adhere to the principle of national sovereignty and territorial integrity.

The OIC participation in the Southern Philippines provides experience to the organization in its goal to consolidate mediation as the appropriate instrument to resolve conflicts between member states. The OIC has expanded its support of various mediation efforts to other countries aside from the Philippines. For example, with the OIC's support, Qatar mediated between Djibouti and Eritrea to resolve their border dispute. The Qatari mediation led to the signing of an agreement between conflicting parties (Qatar News Agency, 2010). Furthermore, this chapter explores the idea of tapping the OIC to mediate between Israel and Palestine. Using the Philippines as an example, Israel may realize it cannot solve the conflict without the participation of Islamic states. Israel may realize by giving OIC member states stakes to be impartial, the political leverage of the OIC may be useful to resolve the conflict. Moreover, the OIC can be tapped to mediate between the conflicting parties in Afghanistan.

To answer the question posed at the beginning of this chapter, the political leverage of the OIC is to be seen in terms of the member states and not in terms of the organization. Libya's initiatives have brought the issue of the Muslims in the Philippines to the discussion table of the OIC. Libya led the Committee of Four, which monitored the peace process between the Philippine government and the MNLF. The involvement of the OIC led to the dropping of a substantial demand of the MNLF for independence. The OIC, although it took sides, had interest in preserving the national sovereignty and territorial integrity because it did not want to undermine the efforts of member countries such as Turkey and Indonesia, who have similar problems. Clearly, the OIC reflects a locus and the flags of the member states and not a corporate actor.

7.2.3 Non-Governmental Organizations as Mediators – The Imperative Partnership

NGOs represent individuals both within a country and across countries, who have similar feelings, cognitions, knowledge, skills or interests, and who meet together on a regular basis to promote the special interests of their members (Bartoli, 2009). NGOs are groups, which seek to influence the political process by providing expertise and resources to decision makers. These groups are seen as important elements of democratization because NGOs serve as a communication channel between the society and the state. This enables a distinct deliberation process, which legitimizes the political authority structures. However, the positive connotation on the works of NGOs is in some cases hiding the negative implications of some NGOs in the societal processes. For instance, while some provide assistance to the state, others are in opposition to the state. Furthermore, while some may effectively provide expertise, other NGOs may not really be qualified to provide specific services to the society. The level of access the NGOs have to distinct power sources is different among all NGOs (Aall, 1996). Furthermore, the mediation styles, which the NGOs are likely to follow, are contingent upon their cultural milieu (Avruch, 1998). In this regard, a critical analysis of the implications of the NGO activities is important.

The specific functions of NGOs in conflict resolution are often overlooked (Call, 2004). NGOs are seen as outside the negotiation process because they lack the capacity, legitimacy, and recognition to engage directly in the negotiation process. Twenty years ago, it was rare for a NGO to become involved in first-track mediation as they were seen as lacking the capacity to influence party behavior during the decision-making processes (Griffith, 2005). NGOs, unlike states and international organizations such as the UN or the OIC, are less capable of offering incentives or sanctions like aid, trade, threats of sanctions or military action to make the conflicting parties more amenable to negotiation and to an agreement (Crocker et al., 2009, p. 503).

Legitimacy deficits, which NGOs face, include problems brought about by unequal distribution of resources among the NGOs themselves. They are dependent on donors to maintain their existence. Because they need to compete for resources, they may be subject to pressures from donors, who are pursuing their own interests. Furthermore, some see an increased involvement of NGOs in decision-making processes as undermining democracy because they are not democratically elected actors. Finally, the accountability of NGOs remains a high issue. International NGOs move across borders and the lack of transparency in their structure confirms skeptical views. These deficits are summarized through the following questions: What are the political resources NGOs may provide? How can NGOs facilitate the negotiation process and the peace process as a whole? Is there a necessity to control and monitor NGOs?

7.2.3.1 NGOs as Mediators – The Advantages of the "Weak" Mediator

Despite resource related deficits, there are many examples of NGOs playing the principal roles in preparing or assisting talks such as the Carter Center in the 1999 agreement between Uganda and Sudan, the Community of Sant'Egidio in Mozambique, the Henri Dunant Center for Humanitarian Dialogue and Mahrti Ahtisaari's Conflict Management Initiative in Aceh. Various NGOs as Crocker et al. (2009, p. 502) argue may enjoy a comparative advantage. A "weak" mediation may be successful in genuinely engaging conflict parties in the process, thus paradoxically paving the way to a "stronger" process, which guarantees sustainability (Hume, 1994). NGOs are seen as operating independently from states, but can embody many of the elements, which are commonly associated with impartiality. The successful facilitation at the conclusion of the mediation process through the Community of Sant' Egidio in Mozambique led to the acknowledgement of the potential functions for NGOs in conflict resolution are often overlooked (Aall, 1996).

NGOs can assist in establishing informal channels of communication between parties without compromising the policies and interests of the parties. NGOs as mediators can profit from its independence from the state. NGOs can respond to the vacuum left by states unable or unwilling to provide the services necessary to engage all actors in a constructive peace process in a given conflict (Bartoli, 1999). Arguably, because they are not dependent on periodical democratic elections, they are free to act on principle rather than populism. NGOs may add legitimacy through inclusion of all actors in the political process, while not being bound by the constraints of the political system.

Governments recognize the involvement of NGOs provides the opportunity to explore options not always possible within formal political structures. Governments can make politically sensitive and unpopular measures through their support of specific NGOs, thus expanding the alternatives in the bargaining process. However, government support can increase the risk of bias accusations for the NGOs, which reduce its credibility across interest groups. Furthermore, NGOs may be free to follow longer-term strategies as opposed to short-term strategies of official actors, who have shorter operation timetables (Matthews, 2001). In addition, NGOs can generate a political process through the representation of people's interests, memories or needs, which are not properly represented in the official channels of negotiation. In this regard, a communication chain between actors, for instance in the situation of escalation, can be provided by NGOs. The lack of a coercive capacity is perceived by conflicting parties as positive, therefore paving the way to a "stronger" process of bargaining through the increased mobilization of political capital, which would not have been possible with the absence of NGOs (Hume, 1994; Bartoli, 2009). Surely the principle is a simple one: NGO's cannot act as political parties or pretend to represent groups in conflict, but they can do the work to enable effective engagement of conflicting parties in the negotiation process. The key is to have a clearly understood role.

Bartoli (2009, p. 407) notes that one of the greatest concerns in literature, which is dedicated to NGOs and their role in conflict resolution, is accountability. With some NGOs highly dependent on external funding, there can be no guarantee the NGOs will prioritize the interests of conflicting parties instead of securing funding significant for their existence. Furthermore, some governments attempt to "use" the NGO framework to hide their direct involvement. Particularly international NGOs with non-transparent funding sources may prolong the conflict, when they start pursuing vested interests. NGOs are highly dependent on external funding to continue their existence, thus leading to the danger of manipulating the process to achieve any outcome, which they can use to legitimize funding. Furthermore, the dependence on external funding may be detrimental to the continuity of the efforts, especially when the NGOs fail to find sources of funding.

For example, some NGOs represented in the Philippine Congress are linked to the former President Gloria Macapagal-Arroyo. Poll watchdog *Kontra Daya* (*Against Cheating*) released a party-list of organizations in 2010, which included NGOs representing marginalized society sectors in the Philippine Congress.. For instance, one of the winning NGOs, *Ang Galing Pinoy* is representated by a Pampanga congressman and a presidential son, Mikey Arroyo. As Bartoli (2009, p. 407) argues, the difference between genuinely independent and impartial NGOs and state-sponsored ones is not always clear.

More importantly, as Bartoli (1999) argues, the most constructive contribution of NGOs to conflict resolution is the concretization of the synergies, which emerge through all relevant actors in the environment. The main contribution of the NGOs is illustrated by the aggregation of its activities. The NGO process strategically facilitates the creation of a framework for continuity (Bartoli, 2009, p. 408) by bringing more actors to work on the different areas, which should be addressed in identity conflicts.

However, it should be critically analyzed, whether their mediatory role can be somewhat circumscribed by the lack of adequate resources, particularly when the NGOs mutated from merely organizing interactive problem-solving workshops (Kelman, 1992; Fisher, 1994) or facilitated dialogues (Roberts, 2002; Bohm, 2004) to Track 1 mediators. Bartoli (2009, p. 292) recognizes Track 1 mediation of NGOs as still relatively rare. There have not been many Track 1 mediation efforts of NGOs, which have actually led to a formal settlement.

7.2.3.2 NGOs in the Philippines: Dealing with Traditional Opposition to the State

The advocacy and work of NGOs in Mindanao have given impetus to peace talks, inter-religious dialogue, peace zones, ceasefire monitoring and empowerment of isolated communities in the conflict areas. Civil society groups pinpoint the negligence of micro-dynamics in the conflict for past interventions (Bück, 2007). Civil society groups in the Philippines have been successfully integrated in the Philippine political structure. According to Bück (2007), the Philippines is famous for its strong civil society.

However, the NGO framework may also be held responsible to the intractability of the conflict in the Philippines. For instance, unlike the MNLF, the MILF lacks state sponsorship. The MILF is dependent on the financial support from Muslim NGOs based in some OIC member states. Without accusing all Muslim NGOs of militarily supporting the MILF, their financial resources are almost impossible to regulate. As Ibrahim Karawan discusses (Vitug and Gloria, 2000, p. 118) because Arab countries are more concerned about state sponsorship of Islamist activities, the funding sources for militant Islamist groups have shifted to the private sector. With the increased importance of NGOs in funding the activities of the MILF, these NGOs have gained increased political leverage.

Unlike many other countries, NGOs in the Philippines are regarded as a form of opposition to the state in the political landscape due to their long history of resistance against the military regime of former President Ferdinand E. Marcos. The Securities and Exchange Commission (SEC) has a register of around 30,000 non-governmental organizations (NGOs) and 35,000 cooperatives for the Philippines. Werning and Reese (2006) furthermore explain this figure could even be as high as 249,000, if local groups and NGO-like organizations are considered (Werning and Reese, 2006, p. 237). The broadest regional NGO network in Mindanao, MinCODE, hosts 539 member organizations, such as cooperatives focusing on the improvement of the economic status of local residents and addressing the contemporary issue of economic grievances, which is indirectly contributing to conflict resolution in Mindanao. However, civic society groups can also represent armed groups or be affiliated with a political group. Such groups are regularly used by political actors to legitimize the outcomes of their actions, while pretending they have a mass support base (Cagoco-Guiam, 1999).

In recent events, the public outrage over the scope of the pork barrel scam confirms structural deficiencies in the political system with NGOs further gaining a negative reputation in the public. For more than 10 years, legislators and other public officials have regularly used bogus NGOs to divert their Priority Developlment Assistance Fund (PDAF), publicly called pork barrel, to their own pockets (see Doronila, 2013; Ubac, 2013; Carvajal, 2013). NGOs will need enormous efforts to regain credibility in the public sector.

The Philippine civil society has been particularly active in promoting peace talks. The Philippine government has responded to the civil society advocacy and lobbying on several occasions. Civil society groups such as the Gaston Z. Ortigas Peace Institute, sponsor a community of peace advocates – non-governmental and peoples' organizations, academic institutions and civil society networks – which contributes to institutionalizing peace work in the Philippines by asserting the role of the citizens in the peace process, engaging youth in several creative demonstrations for peace, and participating in joint-meetings with other NGOs. This includes policy-makers and representatives from the Muslim Moro community. Raising awareness in the public about the urgency of a ceasefire and continuation of the peace talks serves as a counter-strategy in the current resignation of the public opinion due to customization.

Civil society groups also call for representation as third-party negotiators during formal peace talks in order to ensure political solutions, which can be shared by all stakeholders in Mindanao rather than simply the MILF or the national government. The presence of NGOs in the legislative body of the Philippines gives NGOs more political leverage because there is a formally existing structural arena, where they can actually influence the process of policy-making. Interestingly, many of the negotiators and other decision-makers were members of the NGOs. In this sense, they are well acquainted with the works of the NGOs.

They also act as independent watchdogs, which monitor the implementation of agreements signed by the conflicting parties (Mindanao Times, 2005). In 2001 many civil society groups in Mindanao convened the *Bantay Ceasefire* (Ceasefire Watch), which serves as an independent monitoring agency. The agency is facilitated by the secretariat of the Mindanao Peoples' Caucus (MPC) and Initiatives for International Dialogue (IID). The ceasefire watchdog consists of a broad network of grassroots monitors, who join investigative missions in case of ceasefire violations. Bantay Ceasefire publishes its report and has successfully lobbied for the introduction of the international monitoring team led by Malaysia.

Some civil society groups such as the Immaculate Conception Parish (ICP) encourage inter-religious dialogue through group trauma therapy, common festivities and the experience of solidarity with grievances of members from the other groups (Bück, 2007, p. 124). In July 1996, the Catholic Bishops Conference of the Philippines and the Ulama League of the Philippines met at the Ateneo University in Quezon City. The meeting initiated the unprecedented partnership between these two religious organizations (Vitug and Gloria, 2000, pp. 151–153). In 1998, the forum opened their secretariat in Iligan. Protestant bishops eventually joined the forum in the following years. Since then, the forum offered to assist in peace talks between the Philippine government and the MILF by availing themselves as communication channels and resource persons.

Furthermore, civil society groups have successfully convinced conflicting parties not to engage in armed confrontation in several "peace zone areas", which serve as "buffer zones" between adversaries. Peace zones offer sanctuary for local residents regardless of religious or ethnic affiliations. Since the Final Peace Agreement of 1996 between the MNLF and the government, peace zones have become a prominent form of community-based peace building (Rood, 2004). NGOs may function as partners of international donors, who are reluctant of directly providing rebel commanders with money. Moreover, NGOs are tapped by MNLF commanders in identifying projects, which can be financed by international donors. For instance, the United Nations raised in 1998 and 1999 a total of 9.8 million US dollar for livelihood and employment generating programs for former MNLF combatants. Other donors such as the Islamic Development Bank (IDB) consulted with NGOs in their investment activities in the Southern Philippines. There is a consensus in Mindanao the peace process would have failed without donor support (Oquist, 2000). Nevertheless, international donors can be motivated to continue their efforts, if there are local partners, with which they could work with. Some international donors prefer to directly fund projects coordinated by local NGOs. Therefore, NGOs function as channels for funding projects.

7.2.3.3 NGOs and the Peace Process

The presence of NGOs in the Philippines increases political capital for the peace process. NGOs are regularly assisting conflicting parties, providing expertise and knowledge. While MNLF followed a conventional warfare blueprint and set up purely military camps, the MILF opted to enhance economic life for combatants. Vitug & Gloria (2000, p. 108) illustrate there is economic life in MILF camps. The MILF has built communities with religious, social, economic, and military structures, with schools, mosques and courts. The MILF however is dependent on the resources and expertise of NGOs. Several Arab NGOs and foundations from the Middle East are believed to provide financial resources to the MILF. Other Muslim NGOs such as the Youth Alliance for Peace in Mindanao are in constant communication with the MILF (Vitug and Gloria, 2000, p. 109). The involvement of NGOs in ensuring a multidimensional life for MILF combatants may enhance the MILF's ability to transform itself from an armed rebel group to a political party. NGOs may assist the MILF to learn how it is to "govern".

NGOs are able to function as informal channels, which are necessary in the negotiation process, particularly when official channels are "politically" obstructed. Therefore, it can be argued NGOs increase the political resources for the negotiating conflict parties. In turn, negotiation reduced hierarchies and asymmetries in relations between actors, increases their political capital in the form of trust and make the negotiation channel more attractive than coercive means. Furthermore, with support of the NGOs, multiparty and multilevel negotiations establish a more consolidated and acceptable political framework. For instance, NGOs are external parties to the first track negotiations and assume the roles of monitors for peace agreements complementing the international monitoring teams. NGOs have continuously increased the stakes of the government and the rebel groups to engage in negotiations particularly in situations of escalations. Most importantly, the NGOs are able to maximize the synergies of different groups through regular communication forums..

NGOs are indispensable actors to resolve any identity conflict. NGOs reflect the societal landscape in the country. They represent different interests, which require mechanisms of healthy interactions in order to allow societal cooperation and social trust. NGOs should not be perceived as threats by any government or any rebel group because they fulfill several functions, which governments and rebel groups cannot always fulfill. NGOs may complement and support the negotiation process between the government and rebel groups by providing monitoring, expertise and communication channels. More importantly, the NGOs give voice to the affected communities.

7.3 Interim Conclusion - Designing the Intervention Process

Peace (the elimination of violence) requires the introduction and maintenance of social and political systems, which are felt to be fair. How justice issues are handled in a political negotiation process affects the prospects of any subsequent consolidation of peace. However, not all justice issues can be addressed in a formal (track 1) negotiation. Returning to the scale of range table, each scale has its own justice issues. In scale 4, the primary justice issue is fair access to welfare and resources for individual citizens regardless of their group membership.

In scale 1, the primary justice issue is 'procedural justice', which the government and the rebel group need to find a fair process for enabling meaningful peace talks. This includes shouldering the expenses of trips and meetings, finding an appropriate place for the negotiation, securing the safety of the negotiators from both sides, and guaranteeing immunity of the negotiators from persecution. A significant discussion is, whether or not actors guilty of violent acts in the past should be given amnesty to promote peace negotiations. It is an important issue, however, it is seems logical these actors will not participate in negotiations without guarantee of immunity from persecution.

Furthermore, because the situation has created a "space of violence" (Gewalträume), it is questionable, whether violent acts occurring inside this space can be considered a "crime" because of the dissolution of any legal system in this particular area. Criminality requires a legal system, which determines, what is criminal. In addition, these actors will question the jurisdiction of the legal system of the "society at large", particularly when they were already able to reach a de facto state status.

In designing intervention, the distinction between "forward-looking" and "backward-looking" principles of justice should be made (Zartman and Kremenyuk, 2005). Forward-looking notions of justice, seek the establishment of new cooperative relations based on mutual interests between parties. It refers to "transitional justice", in which norms and instruments on the basis of which a society or new government, in transition from armed conflict and/or authoritarian rule are established. Such norms and instruments aim to prevent further atrocities, marginalization and secure justice in the future, for example, through a new justice system (Call, 2004). It aims for the creation of mechanisms, which would reconcile conflicting rationality. It includes the establishment of new power-sharing schemes based on the newly established reconciling mechanism of fairness and justice such as quota systems and formal reservation of government seats for minorities. Such power-sharing schemes should not be generally defined through separation of jurisdictions in the decision-making process. Power-sharing should mean no decision can be made without the approval of the other.

Addressing transitional justice in the negotiation process would not necessary be enough to bring consolidated peace. It requires "restorative justice", which implies backward-looking notions of justice. Backward-looking notions are usually framed as zero-sum because they seek justice retrospectively for past wrong-doings. For example, issues of accountability, compensation, reparation payments and legal punishment are some of the most contested issues at the negotiation table. Backward-looking involves measures for reconciliation between groups, communities, and individuals. It involves the re-introduction of trust and social capital between groups and individuals.

One challenge of restorative justice is the clear identification of the victim. In several cases of mass violence such as in the Philippines, there is no clear distinction between perpetrators and victims, particularly in situations of escalation. Furthermore, apologizing to a collectivity will not ensure the needs of individuals are confronted. Unofficial dialogues and problem-solving workshops with people outside government are discussed extensively in the literature as a necessary and effective means to address various deep-rooted needs (Albin, 2009, p. 583).

References:

Aall, P., 1996. Nongovernmental Organizations and Peacemaking. In C. Crocker, F. Hampson, & P. Aall, eds. *Managing Global Chaos: Sources of and Responses to International Conflict*. Washington D.C.: United States Institute for Peace, pp. 433–443.

ABSCBN News, 2008. Libya to Send More Peacekeepers to Mindanao. *ABSCBN News*. Available at: http://rp1.abs-cbnnews.com/nation/05/12/08/libya-send-more-peacekeepers-mindanao [Accessed September 20, 2013].

Albin, C., 2009. Peace vs. Justice - and Beyond. In J. Bercovitch, V. Kremenyuk, & I. W. Zartman, eds. *The SAGE Handbook of Conflict Resolution*. Los Angeles & London: SAGE Publications, pp. 580–594.

Amnesty International, 2004. *Malaysia. Human Rights at Risk in Mass Deportation of Undocumented Migrants*, Amnesty International. Available at: http://asiapacific.amnesty.org/library/Index/ENGASA280082004?open&of=ENG-2AS [Accessed September 20, 2013].

Amoo, S. & Zartman, I.W., 1996. Mediation by Regional Organizations: The Organization for African Unity (OAU) in Chad. In J. Bercovitch & J. Rubin, eds. *Mediation in International Relations: Multiple Approaches to Conflict Management*. New York: St. Martin's Press, pp. 131–148.

Aspinall, E. & Crouch, H., 2003. *The Aceh Peace Process: Why it Failed*, Washington D.C.: East-West Center. Available at: https://scholarspace.manoa.hawaii.edu/bitstream/10125/3503/1/PS001.pdf [Accessed September 20, 2013].

Avruch, K., 1998. *Culture and Conflict Resolution*, Washington D.C.: USIP Press.

Azar, E., 1986. The Lebanon Case. In E. Azar & J. Burton, eds. *International Conflict Resolution: Theory and Practice*. Brighton, Sussex: Wheatsheaf Books & Boulder, pp. 126–140.

Baet, A., 2010. *Larong Moro-Moro: The Shroud of Arnis de Mano*, Pembroke Pines, FL: Abundio Baet.

Bartoli, A., 1999. Mediating Peace in Mozambique: The Role of the Community in Sant'Egidio. In C. Crocker, F. Hampson, & P. Aall, eds. *Multiparty Mediation in a Complex World*. Washington D.C.: United States Institute for Peace, pp. 245–274.

Bartoli, A., 2009. NGOs and Conflict Resolution. In J. Bercovitch, V. Kremenyuk, & I. W. Zartman, eds. *The SAGE Handbook of Conflict Resolution*. Los Angeles & London: SAGE Publications, pp. 392–412.

BBC, 2000. Philippine Hostages Head for Libya. *British Broadcasting Corporation*. Available at: http://news.bbc.co.uk/2/hi/asia-pacific/898190.stm [Accessed September 20, 2013].

Bercovitch, J., 2009. Mediation and Conflict Resolution. In J. Bercovitch, V. Kremenyuk, & I. W. Zartman, eds. *The SAGE Handbook of Conflict Resolution*. London: SAGE Publications, pp. 340–357.

Bohm, D., 2004. *On Dialogue*, New York: Routledge.

Brown, M., 1996. *The International Dimensions of Internal Conflict*, Cambridge, MA: The MIT Press.

Bück, P., 2007. Civil Society and Conflict in Mindanao. In P. Kreuzer & R. Werning, eds. *Voices from Moro Land. Perspectives from Stakeholders and Observers on the Conflict in the Southern Philippines*. Petaling Jaya, Malaysia: Strategic Information and Research Development Center & Vinlin Press Sdn. Bhd, pp. 99–124.

Burton, J., 1987. *Resolving Deep-Rooted Conflict: A Handbook*, Lanham, MD: University Press of America.

Business World, 2000. Malaysian Envoy Junks MILF Bid for OIC Status. *Business World*. Available at: http://www.accessmylibrary.com/article-1G1-

62769578/malaysian-envoy-junks-milf.html [Accessed September 20, 2013].
Cagoco-Guiam, R., 1999. A Critical Partnership: Civil Society and the Peace Process. In Accord, ed. *An International Review of Peace Initiatives*. London: Conciliation Resources.
Call, C., 2004. Is transitional Justice Really Just? *Brown Journal of World Affairs*, 11(1), pp.101–113.
Carvajal, N., 2013. Napoles, 3 senators face day of reckoning. *Philippine Daily Inquirer*.
Cede, F., 2012. Evolving International Law of Intervention and Prevention. In M. Anstey & I. W. Zartman, eds. *To Block the Slippery Slope: Reducing Identity Conflicts and Preventing Genocide*. New York: Oxford University Press.
Cede, F., 2009. The Settlement of International Disputes by Legal Means - Arbitration and Judicial Settlement. In J. Bercovitch, V. Kremenyuk, & I. W. Zartman, eds. *The SAGE Handbook of Conflict Resolution*. London: SAGE Publications, pp. 358–375.
Conciliation Resources, 2010. Key Texts and Agreements. Available at: http://www.c-r.org/our-work/accord/philippines-mindanao/key-texts.php [Accessed September 20, 2013].
Crocker, C., Hampson, F. & Aall, P., 2009. Why Mediation Matters: Ending Intractable Conflicts. In J. Bercovitch, V. Kremenyuk, & I. W. Zartman, eds. *The SAGE Handbook of Conflict Resolution*. Los Angeles, London, New Delhi: SAGE Publications, pp. 492–505.
Der Western, 2008. Neue Islam-Charta: Erstmal Menschenrechte Aufgenommen. *Der Western*. Available at: http://www.derwestern.de/nachrichten/politik/Neue-Islam-Charta-erstmals-Menschenrechte-aufgenommen-id153 [Accessed September 20, 2013].
Dixon, W., 1996. Third-Party Techniques for Preventing Conflict Escalation and Promoting Peaceful Settlement. *International Organization*, 50(4), pp.653–681.
Doronila, A., 2013. Money Trail of Fugitive Napoles. *Philippine Daily Inquirer*. Available at: http://opinion.inquirer.net/59151/money-trail-of-fugitive-napoles [Accessed August 30, 2013].
Encyclopedia Britannica, 2010. *Moro-moro*, Available at: http://www.britannica.com/EBchecked/topic/392592/moro-moro [Accessed September 20, 2013].

Fernandez, E., 2009. RP, MILF keep Malaysia as Peace Mediator. *Inquirer Global Nation*. Available at: http://globalnation.inquirer.net/news/breakingnews/view/20090914-225174/RP-MILF-keep-Malaysia-as-peace-mediator [Accessed September 20, 2013].

Fisher, R., 1994. Generic Principles for Resolving Intergroup Conflict. *Journal of Social Issues*, 50(1), pp.47–66.

Gartner, S.S. & Melin, M., 2009. Assessing Outcomes: Conflict Management and the Durability of Peace. In J. Bercovitch, V. Kremenyuk, & I. W. Zartman, eds. *The SAGE Handbook of Conflict Resolution*. Los Angeles & London: SAGE Publications, pp. 564–579.

Griffith, M., 2005. *Talking of Peace in a Time of Terror: United Nations Mediation and Collective Security*, Geneva: Centre for Humanitarian Dialogue.

Hume, C., 1994. *Ending Mozambique's War: The Role of Mediation and Good Offices*, Washington, D.C.: USIP Press.

International Crisis Group, 2009. *The Philippines: After the Maguindanao Massacre, Update Briefing*, Available at: http://www.scribd.com/doc/24478372/The-Philippines-After-the-Maguindanao-Massacre-International-Crisis-Group [Accessed September 20, 2013].

Kelman, H., 1992. Informal Mediation by the Scholar/Practitioner. In J. Bercovitch & J. Rubin, eds. *Mediation in International Relations: Multiple Approaches to Conflict Management*. New York: St. Martin's Press.

Matthews, D., 2001. *War Prevention Works: 50 Stories of People Resolving Conflict*, Oxford: Oxford Research Group.

Mindanao Times, 2005. Groups Meet to Talk about MNLF lessons. *Mindanao Times*.

OIC, 2010. *OIC in Brief*, Organisation of Islamic Conference. Available at: http://web.archive.org/web/20071021030710/http://www.oic-oci.org/english/main/oic_in_brief.htm [Accessed September 21, 2013].

OIC, 1974. Resolution No. 474: The Problem of Muslims in the Philippines. Available at: http://www.oic-oci.org/english/conf/fm/All%20Download/Frm.04.htm#RESOLUTION%20No.%204/4 [Accessed September 23, 2013].

Oquist, P., 2000. *Options for a Win-Win Solution in Mindanao*, United Nations Development Program.

Piscatori, J., 1986. *International Relations of the Asian Muslim States*, Lanham, New York & Oxford: University Press of America.

Pruitt, D. & Kim, S.H., 2004. *Social Conflict: Escalation, Stalemate and Settlement*, Boston: McGraw Hill.

Pruitt, D. & Olczak, P., 1995. Beyond Hope: Approaches to Resolving Seemingly Intractable Conflict. In B. Bunker & J. Rubin, eds. *Conflict, Cooperation, and Justice*. Essays Inspired by the Work of Morton Deutsch. San Francisco: Jossey-Bass Publishers.

Qatar News Agency, 2010. OIC Chief Welcomes Qatari Mediation Between Djibouti and Eritrea. Available at: http://www.qnaol.net/QNAEn/Local_News/Politics1/Pages/OICChiefWelcomesQatariMediation0806290.aspx [Accessed September 21, 2013].

Ramos, F., 1996. *Break Not the Peace*, Quezon City: Friends of Steady Eddie.

Roberts, N., 2002. Keeping Public Officials Accountable through Dialogue: Resolving the Accountability Paradox. *Public Administration Review*, 62(6), pp.658–669.

Rood, S., 2004. Civil Society and Conflict Management. In *Third Study Group Meeting*. Washington D.C.

Santos, S., 1999. *Islamic Diplomacy: Consultations and Consensus*, London: Conciliation Resources. Available at: http://www.c-r.org/our-work/accord/philippines-mindanao/islamic-diplomacy.php [Accessed September 21, 2013].

Santos, S., 2005. *Peace Zones in the Philippines*, Quezon City, Philippines: Gaston Z. Ortigas Peace Institute & the Asia Foundation.

Slim, R., 1992. Small-State Mediation in International Relations: The Algerian Mediation of the Iranian Hostage Crisis. In J. Bercovitch & J. Rubin, eds. *Mediation in International Relations. Multiple Approaches to Conflict Management*. New York: St. Martin's Press, pp. 206–232.

Smith, A., 1986. *The Ethnic Origins of Nations*, Oxford: Basil Blackwell.

Stewart, F. & Brown, G., 2007. Motivations for Conflict: Groups and Individuals. In C. Crocker, F. Hampson, & P. Aall, eds. *Leashing the Dogs of War. Conflict Management in a Divided World*. Washington D.C.: USIP Press, pp. 219–241.

Tan, S., 1993. *The Internationalization of the Bangsa Moro Struggle*, Quezon City: University of the Philippines Press.

The New Straits Times, 2010. Aquino Showing a Lack of Soft Diplomacy Skills. *The New Straits Times*.

Thompson, W.S. & Zartman, I.W., 1975. The Development of Norms in the African System. In Y. El-Ayouty, ed. *The OAU after Ten Years*. New York: Praeger.

Torres, W.M. ed., 2007. *RIDO - Clan Feuding and Conflict Management in Mindanao*, Makati City, Philippines: The Asia Foundation.

Touval, S., 1992. The Superpowers as Mediators. In J. Bercovitch & J. Rubin, eds. *Mediation in International Relations. Multiple Approaches to Conflict Management*. New York: St. Martin's Press, pp. 232–248.
Ubac, M.L., 2013. Palace: "Three Furies" will prosecute people in non-Napoles NGO scandal. *Inquirer News*. Available at: http://newsinfo.inquirer.net/481885/palace-three-furies-will-prosecute-people-in-non-napoles-ngo-scandal [Accessed September 6, 2013].
Vitug, M. & Gloria, G., 2000. *Under the Crescent Moon : Rebellion in Mindanao*, Quezon City: Ateneo Center for Social Policy & Public Affairs : Institute for Popular Democracy.
Werning, R. & Reese, N. eds., 2006. *Handbuch Philippinen*, Bad Honnef: Horlemann Verlag.
Zartman, I.W. & Kremenyuk, V., 2005. *Peace vs. Justice: Negotiating Forward- and Backward-Looking Outcomes*, Lanham, MD: Rowman & Little Publishers.

8 Relating Agreements to the Peace Process – The Science and Art of Decision-Making

A more comprehensive, that is, an inclusive definition with a broad or wide mental grasp (Merriam-Webster 2013) in understanding non-violent and non-coercive interventions such as mediation requires a more systematic analysis of possible outcomes. As Mark Anstey (2006) claims, achieving a peace agreement is difficult, but it is no easier than implementing them. Adebajo (2006) suggests agreements should be detailed and inclusive. Agreements should address the root causes of conflicts, ensure parties are representative and are trustworthy. They should have a win-win element to optimize prospects of success. They should build on continuous dispute resolution systems to overcome problems of implementation, and be scheduled with deadlines and accountabilities for delivery.

This chapter suggests instead of starting with the question, what an agreement *should be* to serve its intended purpose, it should be first asked, what *it is*. Before creating "how-to-succeed" manuals, the operation of the mechanisms through which outcomes are produced should be documented (Underdahl 2002, p.110). Scholars tend to doubt the possibility of creating generalizations about conflict management and its outcomes (see Meyer 1960; Simkin 1971; Gartner & Melin 2009). Deriving generalizable knowledge from case studies is problematic because of pointing on the impediments of comparing reductionist contexts. However, comparing issues is different to comparing processes.

The Agreement as Negotiation Outcome

As Underdahl (2002, p.110) argues, the term outcome may itself be ambiguous. Because of this ambiguity, Easton (1965) and Sharkansky (1970) distinguished between the "output" of a decision-making process – that is the agreement negotiated – and the set of consequences for implementing this decision. This distinction answers, why actors have succeeded in concluding an agreement following several negotiation processes, when they still fail to implement the provisions of the agreement. The term agreement is used in two ways. He says it is frequently used to refer to an "exchange of conditional promises" (Iklé 1964, p.7), that is, a formal contract (treaty or convention) or at least a mutually recognized exchange of tacit commitments. Underdahl adds an agreement may also refer to the "meeting of minds" (Underdahl 2002, p.112), through which parties have reached a conclusion regarding a particular problem. The second understanding of agreement requires there is a problem, which should be dealt with.

The working definition of an agreement, which is assumed in this book project, is the following:

> *An agreement is a formal or informal statement (oral, written or even merely assumed) of an exchange of declared intentions, which directly or indirectly results from a process of a cooperative (and therefore interdependent) relationship-building to follow a specific course of conduct.*

The above formulated working definition of an agreement involves the output of a (collaborative) negotiation process, which opens a new stage towards reaching the desired status. An agreement can only be reached through cooperation between parties either with or without external assistance. Furthermore, even when no formal agreement has been reached at the end of a specific negotiation round, considerable progress may have been made on other issues, and important side effects, such as improving the general relationship between the parties or may have resulted in reaching a consensual knowledge. An agreement is to be seen as part of a bigger process.

8.1 Uncertainty and Negotiated Outcomes

The following quotation of the former US Defense Secretary Donald Rumsfeld (2002) serves best in explaining uncertainty:

> *"We know there are known knowns: there are things we know we know. We also know there are known unknowns: that is to say we know there are things we know we don't know. But there are also unknown unknowns — the ones we don't know we don't know."*

Uncertainty accompanies the negotiating parties in formulating decisions. Both consciously and unconsciously, policy-makers seek to address uncertainty, when calculating political decisions. Policy-makers attempt to "structure" uncertainties to the level, where decisions can be made. There are several sources of uncertainty in the negotiation process. For example, the lack of transparency of how outcomes are achieved hinders a more intensive scholarly study of conflict resolution because most actions and decisions are done behind doors (Young 1967). This results in a "mystique" and skepticism on the mediation, together with the lack of available data and low numbers of "successful" conflict management measures due to "statistical bias" on conflict management. Conflict management and the outcomes of these efforts have only recently become a focus of systematic scholarship (see Young 1967; Bercovitch 1997; Bercovitch & Gartner 2006).

Other sources of uncertainties are the actors themselves. In the course of time after the achievement of the negotiation, actors can adapt to new circumstances and such adaptation may significantly modify the impact of outcomes (Underdahl 2002, p.110). Because negotiated outcomes, particularly in identity conflicts, are usually legally non-binding, actors may find it more attractive not to adhere to the negotiated agreement. As no actor can predict the aggregate impact with great precision and confidence (Winham 1977), there can never be the assurance agreements will not collapse in the future. In addition, an argument reached may have "side-effects" detrimental to the whole peace process. Furthermore, even if the consequences may be more or less predicted, the evaluation criteria themselves may change over time (Iklé 1964).

Recognizing the existence of several kinds of uncertainties contribute to the intractability of identity conflicts, several strategies can be pursued to deal with uncertainty. Problems, which are known, may include concrete provisions to solve the identified problems. The known unknowns are the problems, which are perceived to exist. However, the degree, scope or the specific impact of the problematic issue remains unknown. For instance, the negotiating parties may anticipate future problems, which could arise. The agreement may then include contingency provisions such as social institutions or management systems, which would monitor and act on future problems to limit the damage the problem could inflict. It can be in the form of an insurance to cover the costs of an anticipated problem.

However, dealing with the unknown unknowns remains a challenge. These are problems, which cannot be anticipated, but could occur. If negotiations do not have any means to address these events, the agreements reached may eventually collapse. Agreements, which fail to address the unknown unknowns require a high degree of trust and consolidated modes of cooperation between negotiating parties, which is of course not yet the case for instance in the Philippines. For this dilemma, the mediator and the negotiating parties should complement the negotiation process with confidence-building measures as well as with a clear and efficient communication channels between negotiating parties. For example, the negotiating parties may choose to use back channels, which are particularly useful in periods of escalation and stalemate. Such back channels may be "common friends" of conflicting parties, which could meet informally to discuss reasons for the impasse and to find solutions to enable a "way out" (Zartman 2000) from the deadlock.

8.2 Reaching an Agreement – Options and Dilemmas

Conflict management, particularly mediation, typically results in one of two possible outcomes: *an agreement or status quo*. Gartner & Melin (2009, p.565) illustrate the outcome of conflict management measures as follows:

Figure 8.1: The Interaction of Third Party and Disputant Choices (Gartner & Melin 2009)

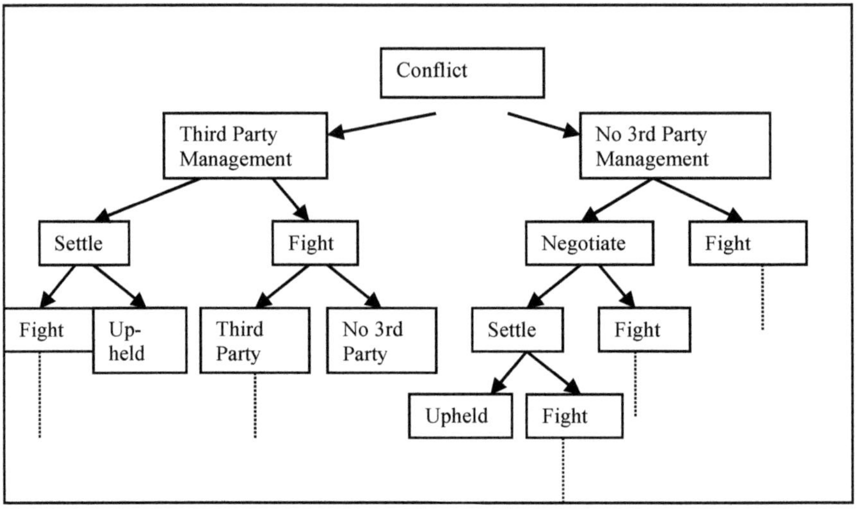

As this schematic model of the conflict management process illustrates, a third party can offer to help or be invited to manage the conflict at any point in a conflict. A situation of no agreement brings parties back to the status the achievement of a settlement, which is however not the end of the process. The settlement can either be upheld or collapse. In this case, the cycle starts from the beginning. A mediator may wish to re-start negotiation through informal or "exploratory" talks paving the way for formal negotiations. The conflicting parties may also seek other channels and approaches to resolve the conflict. For instance, the disputing parties might wish to seek other organizations or states to act as mediator.

The illustration of Gartner & Melin (2009) should be complemented by more possible scenarios. For example, when there is no intervention, one disputing party might decide to unilaterally confront the grievances of the minority group following intense pressure from the civic society. Legislative reforms may be initiated in order to enhance liberal institutions to address violence towards minorities. The regime may genuinely recognize the rights of minority groups. The restoration of democracy in the Philippines in 1986 induced an environment, which recognized minorities as equal social peers. President Corazon Aquino established the Autonomous Region of Muslim Mindanao as well as the Cordillera Autonomous Region (CAR) outside the negotiation table. Furthermore, the rebel group may accept such moves and unilaterally "give up" armed resistance. For example, the armed group in the CAR decided to accept the legislative reforms initiated by the (Cory) Aquino government. In this case, the conflict was resolved, even though there was no ceasefire or comprehensive peace agreement.

However, Figure 8.1 is limited in illustrating the alternatives to an agreement. The figure misleadingly imposes the only alternative to an agreement is the maintenance of the status quo. This remains problematic in the view of situations, where although no agreement was achieved, but norms were successfully established, which would be conducive to the whole peace process. Even though no agreement was reached, the disputing parties may then be capable of understanding the interests of the others, thus, facilitating future talks. It may be a case, in which correcting structural imbalances, benefit not only the rebelling minority group, but other sectors of the society as well. The introduction of anti-discriminatory laws and regulations in the Philippines may increase the economic competitiveness of other marginalized sectors.

Correcting historical structural imbalances, which have disadvantaged not only ethnic minority groups, but the working class and women may increase societal productivity. The horizontal linkages of issues in identity conflicts prove identity conflicts are never only about religion or ethnicity, but they also include socioeconomic dimensions. Therefore, the establishment of norms can be regarded as an alternative to an agreement. Particularly in some cases, where binding agreements are politically impossible to achieve, norm-setting "mutual understanding" may pose a more viable alternative to an agreement. Negotiation may produce an agreement, norms or the maintenance of the status quo. Without prejudging, which outcome is desirable, the complexity of the negotiation process shows an agreement is not always the most preferable outcome.

8.3 Negotiation Outcomes - Agreement, No Agreement and Collapsed Agreement

Negotiation rounds may lead to the following outcomes: *agreement, no agreement,* or *collapsed agreement*.

8.3.1 *Agreement*

Rounds, which led to an agreement, are usually celebrated as a success. However, an agreement may have both positive and negative externalities, both within the negotiation system as well as to other negotiation systems. Looking at this specific agreement through a process outlook approach, the agreement may:

1. Complement previous agreements (e.g. implementation plan)
2. Promote future agreements by transforming the situation into an enviroment, which is susceptible to negotiation (e.g. establishment of a framework or point of reference for future negotiations)
3. Establish precedents, which are productive for future negotiations within the negotiation system (e.g. an agreement that suddenly includes the necessity to undergo a "constitutional process")
4. Establish precedents, which are detrimental to other negotiation systems (negative externalities) (e.g. an agreement between the MILF may lead to massive protests from Christian settlers and indigenous groups in Mindanao, who are separately negotiating with the government).
5. Establish positive precedents in other negotiation systems (positive externalities) (e.g. an agreement between the government and the MILF, which for instance deal with agrarian reform, may induce an agreement between the government and the Communist Party of the Philippines (CCP) because the structural conditions now established are of interest for the CCP).
6. Empower hard-liners may eventually lead to the emergence of breakaway factions (e.g. the 1996 Final Peace Agreement formally led to the separation of the MILF and the MNLF).

8.3.2 *No Agreement*

Another possible outcome involves one or more negotiation rounds failing to produce an agreement. Following the same logic of argumentation, a situation of "no agreement" may include both positive and negative effects to the whole negotiation system. A situation of no agreement may:

1. Promote future agreements by pointing out the issues, which should be addressed and the "Mutually Enticing Opportunities[6]" (Zartman 2000) are not yet available (e.g. the negotiation round, which did not end with an agreement, may have identified needs, which should be addressed first, such as the recognition of the MILF as "equal negotiating partner").
2. Promote future agreements by elaborating or proving "failing" to reach an agreement is part of the process and therefore should not be taken as lack of intention to solve a problem (e.g. the failure to reach an agreement may not impede the negotiating parties from cooperating with each other. The possibility of cooperation in times of hardship may entice trust and confidence).
3. Establish norms and consensual knowledge, which are needed in the whole peace process (e.g. the conflicting parties realize the best way to pursue their interests is through negotiation).
4. Increase or consolidate distrust and may eventually increase the "hurdle for re-negotiation" (e.g. when the failure to reach an agreement is blamed on the other party and not the complexity of the problem).
5. Lead to the total breakdown of negotiation and meltdown of the peace process (e.g. when the failure to reach an agreement is interpreted as legitimacy to pursue military offensive measures)
6. Empower "weaker parties" at the negotiation table through the recognition of their "negative power", which is the power to delay the process, eventually leads to their recognition as "equal negotiating partner" (e.g. when the rebel group was not coerced to sign an agreement it perceives not serving its interest, this may lead to more confidence from the rebel group as well as the recognition the rebel group is as powerful as the government).

8.3.3 Collapsed Agreement

Finally, another scenario may be the situation, where negotiating parties were successful in reaching and signing an agreement. However, because of circumstances such as change of leadership, the agreement is then seen as detrimental to their

[6] Zartman (2000)(2000) argues negotiators must craft MEO to counter the concern they do not know ahead of time the outcome of a specific negotiation. MEO is important in the negotiation process as it could extend ripeness theory (Bercovitch 1997; Zartman 2001) into the agreement and post-agreement phases. MEO as a resolving formula is needed by the parties to see their needs are met by an agreement making the perceived outcome better than perceived the status quo.

interests. The agreement eventually collapses. This collapsed agreement may have both positive and negative impacts to the whole process. It may:

i) Point out the necessity to establish new institutions, new mechanisms, new mediators, or new representatives for both the government and the rebel group, as well as new negotiating settings (e.g. the collapse of the MOA-AD led to the dissolving of the negotiating panel of the Philippine government and the re-constitution of the International Monitoring Team as well as the establishment of the International Contact Group (ICG)).
j) Lead to an increase in distrust among parties more than in the situation of having no agreement (e.g. more doubts on the sincerity of the other party)
k) Increase uncertainties in future negotiations (e.g. who will be the members of the new negotiating panel, as well as concerns on the implementation of future agreements)
l) Lead to the expansion of contested issues, as well as providing more room for position-taking in negotiation rounds (e.g. the collapsed MOA-AD is still regarded by the MILF as valid. Furthermore, the Philippine government demands punishment of the MILF rouge elements, who attacked civilians in 2008).
m) Empower hard-liners and "rogue elements" among both parties (e.g. the collapsed MOA-AD gave "uncontrolled" MILF elements resources to attack towns).

8.4 Macro-Perspectives in a Long-Term Process – the Mindanao Case

The macro-perspective on the peace process calls for an assessment of the impacts from other agreements on the process as a coherent whole. It is not only for the understanding of the issues involved, but more importantly to anticipate potential problems through early-warning systems. Knowing regressions are normal features of the peace process, conflict parties may understand the occurrence of a specific goal cannot be completely determined by a single agreement. The failure to implement an agreement can be caused by some gaps in the content of the agreement, which should be addressed and accommodated to ensure sustainability.

The following table illustrates the agreements, which were reached within the peace process in Southern Philippines.

Table 8.5: Assessment of Agreements through the Long-Term Process Outlook: the Mindanao Case

Administration Period (President)	Name of Agreement	Intervention used	Parties	Content of Agreement	Purpose of Agreement	Spoilers / Spoiling Event leading to Set-backs	Immediate Events after the Agreement
1965-1986 (Ferdinand Emmanuel Edralin Marcos)	1976 Tripoli Agreement	Mediation/ Facilitation by OIC by invitation of MNLF	GRP and MNLF	Ceasefire, Call for Autonomy and Dropping of Claim for Independence	Initiation, Agenda-setting and Issue Clarification	Breakdown of ceasefire in 1877 amid Moro charges the GRPs autonomy plan allowed only token self-rule (escalation); splitting of the MILF from MNLF	Continuation of fighting in 1977; Establishment of the MILF faction in the Moro movement in 1977; Presidential Decree 1628 – declaring autonomy in some regions
1986-1992 (Corazon "Cory" Cojuanco Aquino)	1987 Jeddah Accord	Mediation/Facilitation by OIC	GRP and MNLF	Ceasefire, Discussion about "formula" of autonomy	Initiation, Formula-negotiation	Refusal of MILF to accept accord; Further division along tribal lines of the Moro movement (MNLF, MNLF-Reformist, MILF); 7 coup attempts by the military to re-establish a military regime in the country; Abu Sayaff 1991 bombing of M/V Doulous in Zamboanga City	Month-long offensive of MILF, which ended with another ceasefire; continuation of fighting in 1988; Organic Act for the Autonomous Region in Muslim Mindanao (ARMM) or Republic Act 6734 (GRP)
1992-1998 (Fidel	1992 and 1993 State-	Mediation/Fa	GRP and	1992 "exploratory talks";	Initiation, Agenda-		Memorandum Order No. 163,

Valdez Ramos)	ments of Understanding (Tripoli and Cipanas, Indonesia)	cilitation by OIC	MN LF	1993 interim ceasefire	setting and Issue clarification, Formula negotiation, Norm-setting		which defines the functions and responsibilities of the Presidential Adviser on the Peace Process (GRP); Executive Order 125, which defines the approach and administrative structure for the GRP's comprehensive peace efforts; the formulation of the "Sixth Paths to Peace" (GRP)
	Memorandum of Agreement of 1993 (Jakarta); 1993 Interim GRP-MNLF Ceasefire Agreement (Jakarta); 1994 Joint Guidelines and Ground Rules for the Implementation of the 1993 Interim Ceasefire Agreement; 1994 Interim Agreement (Jakarta); 1995 Interim Agreement (Jakarta), 1996 Davao	Mediation/Facilitation by OIC	GRP / MN LF	Series of formal peace talks resulting in several agreements; Consensus Points in the following areas: (1) National Defense and Security; (2) Education; (3) Economic and Financial System, Mines and Minerals; (4) Administrative System,	Detail-bargaining	The 1995 failed assassination attempt on Pope John Paul II by Middle Eastern Muslim terrorists	1996 Senate Resolution No. 50 – Philippine Congress; the MNLF chair Nur Misuari was elected governor of ARMM

	Accord (Philippines)			Right of Representation and Participation in the National Government, and in all Organs of the State; (5) Shariah and the Judiciary			
	1996 Final Agreement for the Implementation of the 1976 Tripoli Agreement	Mediation/Facilitation by OIC with Indonesian chairmanship	GRP / MNLF	Implementation of the 1976 Tripoli Agreement; inclusion of those portions of the 1976 Tripoli Agreement left for further discussion and the transitional implementing structure and mechanism	Final Agreement and Post-Negotiation	The emergence of the Abu Sayaff extremist group conducting kidnap-for-ransom activities, which was responded to with force by the military; the armed resistance of the MILF, conducting bombings in public areas in Mindanao	Executive Order No. 371, which proclaims a Special Zone of Peace and Development in the Southern Philippines (SZOPAD), establishment of the Southern Philippines Council for Peace and Development (SPCPD) and the Consultative Assembly (CA)
	1997 General Cessation of Hostilities Agreement (Cagayan de Oro City, Philippines); 1997 Supplemental Agreement on Repositioning Troops and the Display of Firearms	Mediation/ Facilitation by Malaysia with support of OIC	GRP / MILF	ceasefire	initiation		

1998-2001 (Joseph "Erap" Ejercito Estrada)	1998 General Framework of Agreement of Intent	Mediation/ Facilitation by Malaysia with support of OIC	GRP / MILF	Resumption of peace talks	Initiation; Norm-setting	Continued violence in Mindanao	
	1999 (Feb.) Agreement on Joint Acknowledgement of MILF camps	Mediation/ Facilitation by Malaysia with support of OIC	GRP / MILF		Initiation; Norm-setting	Continued violence in Mindanao	
	1999 Agreement to Reaffirm Pursuit of Peace	Mediation/ Facilitation by Malaysia with support of OIC	GRP / MILF		Initiation; Norm-setting	Continued violence in Mindanao	
	2000 Agreement on Safety and Security Guarantees	Mediation/ Facilitation by Malaysia with support of OIC	GRP / MILF	Ceasefire, security guarantees	Initiation	Declaration of "All-Out-War" against MILF through Estrada; the emergence of the Abu Sayaff and other kidnap-for-ransom gangs in Mindanao	2000 MILF suspension of peace talks; Continuation of Fighting after collapse of ceasefire, Breakdown of Negotiations; OIC Resolution No. 56/9-P (IS) on 12 November 2000 in Doha urging GRP and MILF to end armed hostilities and

							resume peace talks
2001-2010 (Gloria "GMA" Macapagal Arroyo)	2001 General Framework on the Resumption of Peace Talks (Malaysia); 2001 Tripoli Agreement on Peace	Mediation/ Facilitation by Malaysia with support of OIC	GRP / MILF	Ceasefire	Agenda-setting; Issue-clarification, Norm-setting, which served as a framework for future agreements)	Series of bombings and attacks through the MILF; Allegations of ties between MILF and Jemaah Islamiyah and between MILF and Al-Qaeda, Sept. 11, 2001 attacks in the United States; the US-RP joint military exercises	Escalation of violence, displacement of more than 600,000 local residents, continuation of fighting, breakdown of negotiations, 2007 recognition of human rights for the Moro people through the GRP
	2003 Joint Statement (Kuala Lumpur)	Mediation/Facilitation by Malaysia with support of OIC	GRP / MILF	Resumption of talks, improvement of the existing mechanisms for monitoring and the cessation of hostilities, consensus on (1) security and (2) rehabilitation	Detail-bargaining;	Military offensive against the MILF	Establishment of a International Monitoring Team (IMT); Displacement of 400,000 local residents; 14 exploratory talks between January and March 2003,
	2008 Memorandum of Agreement on Ancestral Domains (MOA-AD)	Mediation/Facilitation by Malaysia with the support of OIC	GRP / MILF	Consensus on (3) ancestral domains; Conclusion of all disputes and beginning of formal talks, which	Issue-clarification, Detail-bargaining	Declaration of the unconstitutionality of the MOA-AD by the Philippine Supreme Court on the grounds of lack of a per-	Escalation of violence, resumed fighting, dissolving of the GRP negotiating panel, withdrawal of the Malaysia-led Interna-

				would lead to the drafting and eventual signing of a Final Comprehensive Compact		tinent consultation process; 2009 Massacre in Maguindanao prompted fighting between the Ampatuans (government allies) and the MILF	tional Monitoring Team (IMT) in 2004; MILF attacking troops and villages; breakdown of negotiations (deadlock); displacement of 703,949 local residents (NDCC 2009)
2010 – present (Benigno "Noynoy" Aquino III)	Oct 2012 Framework Agreement on Bangsamoro	Mediation/Facilitation by Malaysia, with support of the IMT and ICG	GRP / MILF	Creation of an autonomous political entity named "Bangsamoro" superseding the ARMM	Initiation, agenda-setting	Breaking away of the Bangsamoro Islamic Freedom led by Ameril Umbra Kato from the MILF; Followers of Sultan Jamalul Kiram III landed in Sabah, Malaysia leading to deaths of 68 Filipinos and 10 Malaysians	Resumption of formal peace negotiations over the implementation of the Framework Agreement on Bangsamoro

The intervention of the OIC by the invitation of the MNLF and the Philippine government signaled the international community has recognized MNLF as the (sole) representative of the Bangsamoro. The acceptance of the OIC Committee of Four to mediate/facilitate made it easier for the Philippine government to politically acknowledge the MNLF as the legitimate negotiating partner. The 1976 Tripoli Agreement serves as a framework for subsequent negotiation rounds for both the Government of the Philippines (GRP) and MNLF negotiation process and the GRP-MILF negotiation process.

A significant characteristic of a long-term process outlook is not only the forward- and backward, but also the horizontal and vertical linkages between agreements. The 1976 Tripoli Agreement resulted in a ceasefire and paved the way for the initiation of the negotiation process. The agreement answered the question, how the game should be conducted – through non-violent means. The OIC was in this part to a significant extent actively convincing the MNLF to drop its claim of independence in order to enable the initiation of talks.

Although the 1976 ceasefire agreement collapsed in 1977, the agreement resulted in the unilateral declaration of autonomy in several regions in Mindanao by the GRP through the 1977 Presidential Decree 1628. This declaration was determined from the knowledge achieved by the government during the talks about the structural causes of the insurgency. The re-establishment of democratic rule in the Philippines through the administration of President Corazon Aquino favored the peace process. She eventually established the ARMM. A further side-effect of this political momentum is the establishment of the Cordillera Autonomous Region (CAR), which was in reaction to the increased claim for self-determination of the indigenous Cordillera community. The 1987 Jeddah Accord was reached through the mediation/facilitation of the OIC in Saudi Arabia. The accord accommodated the question, how exactly the agenda and issues were to be addressed.

However, the accord enhanced the intra-group conflict within the MNLF leading to its division along tribal lines: *MNLF, MNLF-Reformist* and *MILF*. The hardliner MILF's refusal to accept the accord led to the continuation of fighting. The government unilaterally pushed for the adoption of the Autonomous Region in Muslim Mindanao without the cooperation of the MNLF in 1988, which signaled good intentions to the Muslim population. It was not part of any agreement, but is a result of the failure to reach an agreement in previous negotiation round. This development shows lessons may be taken from the knowledge aquired from previous negotiations.

The administration of President Fidel Ramos witnessed series of agreements eventually leading to the 1996 Final Peace Agreement on the Implementation of the 1976 Tripoli Agreement. This agreement paved the way to a ceasefire agreement with the MILF, which has continually used previous agreements between the GRP and MNLF as framework to its own peace talks with the GRP. This pattern confirms the horizontal linkages of agreements.

Following several set-backs brought on by the Sept. 11, 2001 attacks in the United States, as well as the escalation periods, minor agreements were reached. The negotiation collapsed immediately after the intervention of the Philippine Supreme Court in 2008; however, exploratory and back-channel talks were conducted since then with the support of the Malaysian government. The prospect of the continuation of talks is more likely because the GRP and the MILF have already reached a consensus on the goal and procedure. The impasses are more or less related to the last items of the desired Final Comprehensive Compact. However, the "hurdle of re-negotiation" has been increased due to the distrust on the administration of President Gloria Macapagal Arroyo through the MILF. With the election of President Benigno Aquino III, optimism about the peace process has returned.

The collapsed MOA-AD (agreement) led to the re-structuring of the International Monitoring Team (IMT), which now includes new members Japan and Norway. The IMT received a major face lift through the expansion of its responsibilities, which now includes humanitarian assistance instead of merely monitoring the ceasefire agreements. The collapsed MOA-AD furthermore led to the re-organization of the NGO landscape in the Southern Philippines. NGOs are now given more access to the negotiation process through the invitation of several local and international NGOs being part of the IMT and ICG.

8.5 The Implementation of Agreements – Dilemmas in the Operationalization

The agreement is as an output of a decision-making process. The concretization of the solutions brought up to the table requires further negotiations particularly, when determining concrete numbers. For example, the 1976 Tripoli Peace Agreement was followed by several agreements dealing with its implementation until the 1996 Final Peace Agreement, which constituted the full implementation of the 1976 Tripoli Agreement, was signed.

In the 1976 Tripoli Agreement, Article 3 – Paragraph 2 states, "the National Defense Affairs shall be the concern of the Central Authority provided the arrangements for the joining of the Moro National Liberation Front forces with the Philippine Armed Forces be discussed later." The implementation of this item in the agreement is accommodated by Article 19 (The Joining of the MNLF elements in the Philippine National Police (PNP)…) and Article 20 (The Joining of the MNLF forces with the Armed Forces of the Philippines (AFP). The 1996 Final Peace Agreement includes the concretization of this implementation, such as the number of MNLF members to be integrated to the AFP (5,750). This concretization itself is the product of a separate series of difficult negotiations between the government and the MNLF conducted following the 1976 Tripoli Agreement.

The final stage of the mediation involves the formalization of the agreement. It either involves the immediate implementation of the design and monitoring procedure. In most agreements to resolve identity conflicts, an agreement is followed by series of new agreements on the implementation. Implementation refer to the procedural steps disputants or mediators take in order to operationalize an agreement and to terminate a dispute (Coser 1967).

The success of a substantive agreement depends on the effectiveness of the implementation plan. Christopher Moore (Moore 1996, p.301) argues insufficient consideration of the implementation may result in settlements, which create devastating precedents, and these precedents may create a reluctance to negotiate in the future. Moore (1996, p.303) suggests mediators and negotiators should consider eight factors, which are important for the successful implementation of a settlement:

1. A consensual agreement about the criteria used to measure successful compliance
2. The general and specific steps required to implement the decision
3. Identification of the people, who have the power to influence the necessary changes, if changes are even possible in the first place
4. An organizational structure,if applicable, to implement the agreement
5. Provisions, which will accommodate both future changes in the terms of the agreement and changes in disputing parties themselves
6. Procedures to manage unintended or unexpected problems, or violations of the settlement, which may arise during implementation.
7. Methods to monitor compliance, as well as the identity of the monitor(s)
8. Determination of the monitor's role (for example, whistleblower or enforcer).

These eight factors for the successful implementation of an agreement involve the identification of actors (role of monitors and the people, who have the power the influence the necessary changes), issues (steps required to implement), structures (procedures of managing violation), process (methods to monitor compliance), and outcomes (criteria to be used to measure compliance).

8.6 Monitoring Agreements

Agreements require external assistance to ensure the implementation of peace agreements and measure compliance. For example, while timelines and deadlines are usually defined in agreements, parties still need to define standards and schedules of performance, which involve concrete steps to implement the decision. For example, the government should schedule plebiscites or initiate proposed resolutions in the legislation to implement some provisions of the agreement. Furthermore, the government should have already initiated necessary structural changes to address the rehabilitation of former rebel combatants. The rebel group leaders need to prepare for the re-integration of combatants and their immediate family members in the society. In addition, periodic meetings are needed to review compliance (Moore 1996, p.304) or to renegotiate minor implementation provisions without threatening the whole agreement. Verification procedures are necessary components of any agreement. It should be noted mediated settlements are often more susceptible to violation than conflict resolution approaches with strictly defined implementation procedures, such as judicial or legislative decision (Moore 1996, p.304).

The implementation of agreements may be monitored by the parties themselves, by a joint committee composed of party representatives, or by a third party, who is usually not the mediator, for example a governmental agency, a respected third party, a court, an independent monitoring committee, a regional or an international organization, as well as NGOs themselves. The degree of responsibility given to monitoring groups, who are assigned to oversee the implementation, varies from one case to another. It varies because of its character as an outcome of the negotiation between conflicting parties. Monitors may merely review and document progress. They may confirm or deny compliance has occurred, or they may actually oversee implementation of the agreement (Moore 1996, p.305) by giving concrete suggestions. Monitors may establish a mechanism of addressing grievances. A grievance mechanism is a process through which the disputants consult, when disagreements arise in the implementation of an agreement.

Some monitoring measures were included in the 1996 Peace Agreement between the Philippine government and the MNLF. In Article 8, the Southern Philippine Council for Peace and Development (SPCPD) is mandated to monitor, promote and coordinate the development efforts in the ARMM. Most importantly, in Article 13, a Joint Monitoring Committee is formed with the help of the OIC, which is composed of members from the Philippine government and the MNLF. It shall continue to meet, to review, and identify agreements, which can be immediately implemented, and monitor the implementation of the agreement particularly in the so-called Phase I or the transition period.

While the 1996 Peace Agreement between the Philippine government and the MNLF is monitored by a joint monitoring team with members from both conflicting parties and assistance being given by the OIC, the ceasefire agreements between the Philippine government and the MILF are monitored by the so-called "International Monitoring Team" (IMT), which is led by Malaysia. After the 2003 Cessation of Violence Agreement, the IMT was established in 2004 to monitor the ceasefire and to provide a conducive environment for peace negotiations. Since 2004, the presence of the IMT has been said to be a major factor in significantly reducing clashes in Mindanao (Abu Bakar 2010). However, the 60 man-strong IMT was dissolved in 2008, when violence escalated following the declaration of the MOA-AD as unconstitutional through the Philippine Supreme Court. A group of MILF rebels led by Commander Robot raided towns in Lanao del Sur, which resulted in the displacement of hundreds of thousands and the retaliation of the

Armed Forces of the Philippines (AFP). More than 12,000 combatants of the MILF responded to this retaliation prompting the escalation of the armed confrontation to a full-scale war, which led to more displacement and destruction of infrastructures.

Exploratory talks resumed in 2009. Malaysia eventually resumed its heading of the International Monitoring Team (IMT), which now formally includes Brunei, Indonesia, Japan, Norway and the European Union. The IMT is assisted by various local and international governmental and non-governmental organizations. Based on the revised terms of reference for the IMT, which was upon agreed in December 2009, the IMT includes four components: security, socio-economic assistance, and civilian protection; as well as the humanitarian, rehabilitation, and development component. The European Union leads the Humanitarian, Rehabilitation and Development component of the IMT (Balana 2010; Fabe 2010). Since the end of 2008, EU and its member states have already provided more than 14.5 million Euro in humanitarian assistance (Uy 2010).

A feature of the newly established IMT is the official invitation of local and international civil society organizations, such as the Nonviolent Peaceforce, which is an international civilian peacekeeping NGO working hand in hand with representatives of the IMT member countries. NGOs are part of the Civilian Protection Component (CPC) of the IMT, which oversees the civilian protection issues of the peace process between the Philippine government and MILF. The International Civilian Protection Monitor (ICPM) works along with other members of the CPC and the IMT to monitor, verify, and report non-compliance by the Parties in their basic undertaking to protect civilians and civilian communities.

Furthermore, the new IMT is complemented by the so-called International Contact Group (ICG), which was established in September 2009. The group is composed of Japan, Turkey, the United Kingdom, and Saudi Arabia (Uy 2010). Furthermore, four international NGOs – *Muhammadiyah, the Asia Foundation, Conciliation Resources and the Centre for Humanitarian Dialogue (CHR)* (see Herbolzheimer & Leslie 2013) are part of the ICG. The ICG is envisioned to provide support for the negotiations between the Philippine government and the MILF (People's Daily Online, 2009).

8.7 Interim Conclusion - Managing Process Complexity

Relating agreements to the peace process, which inevitably calls for a long-term process outlook on how outcomes are reached through (mediated) negotiations and how single agreements promote or inhibit the process. Negotiation outcomes

– agreement, no agreement, or collapsed agreement – are ambivalent in their implications and are highly dependent on the conditions of the context. Therefore, outcomes should be managed in a systematic and comprehensive way to limit negative externalities and to maximize synergies and co-benefits. As it will be discussed in the next chapter, interdependency partly defines the complexity of the negotiation process. In many cases, the failure to cope with this complexity promotes intractability of the conflict.

The agreement is related to the peace process by designating it as an integral part of the negotiation system. An agreement following negotiations rounds is an output of a decision-making process and codifies how to constitute future interactions between conflicting parties. Nevertheless, linking what actors desire as outcomes and what are contextually viable may be contributing to the intractability of the conflict, as expectations are not met and caveats for future outcomes are intensified.

Finally, it remains a huge challenge how single agreements can actually resolve identity conflicts. As identity conflicts require the achievement of a new social contract, which would structure future social interactions, actors may not always have the general outlook on the meaning of negotiation outcomes to the whole peace process. As no single agreement can take the role of a social contract and it remains unclear, how a social contract is to be codified (in what form or scope), a process outlook is needed.

References:

Adebajo, A. ed., 2006. *United Nations Mediation Experience in Africa*, Cape Town: Centre for Conflict Resolution.

Anstey, M., 2006. *Managing Change: Negotiating Conflict*, Lanadowne: Juta Legal and Academic Publishing.

Abu Bakar, A.-H., 2010. Brunei to join Mindanao Peace Monitors. *Brunei FM*. Available at: http://news.brunei.fm/2010/03/02/brunei-to-join-mindanao-peace-monitors/ [Accessed September 20, 2013].

Balana, C., 2010. EU to Monitor Mindanao Peace Process. *Philippine Daily Inquirer*. Available at: http://newsinfo.inquirer.net/inquirerheadlines/nation/view/20100520-271049/EU-to-monitor-Mindanao-peace-process [Accessed September 20, 2013].

Bercovitch, J., 1997. Mediation in International Conflict: An Overview of Theory, A Review of Practice. In I. W. Zartman & J. L. Rasmussen, eds.

Peacemaking in International Conflict: Methods and Techniques. Washington D.C.: United States Institute for Peace, pp. 125–154.
Bercovitch, J. & Gartner, S.S., 2006. Empirical Studies in International Mediation: Introduction. *International Interactions*, 32(4), pp.319–357.
Coser, L., 1967. *Continuities in the Study of Social Conflict*, New York: The Free Press.
Easton, D., 1965. *A Framework for Polical Analysis*, Englewood Cliffs, NJ: Prentice Hall.
Fabe, B., 2010. EU joins IMT in peace process in Mindanao. *The Mindanao Daily Mirror*. Available at: http://www.dailymirror.ph/May-2010/May2010/front4.html.
Gartner, S.S. & Melin, M., 2009. Assessing Outcomes: Conflict Management and the Durability of Peace. In J. Bercovitch, V. Kremenyuk, & I. W. Zartman, eds. *The SAGE Handbook of Conflict Resolution*. Los Angeles & London: SAGE Publications, pp. 564–579.
Herbolzheimer, K. & Leslie, E., 2013. *Innovation in Mediation Support: The International Contact Group in Mindanao*, London: Conciliation Resources. Available at: http://www.c-r.org/sites/c-r.org/files/PracticePaper_MindanaoICG_ConciliationResources_0.pdf [Accessed September 9, 2013].
Iklé, F.C., 1964. *How Nations Negotiate: Written under the Auspices of the Center for International Affairs, Harvard University*, New York: Harper & Row.
Merriam-Webster, 2013. Comprehensive. Available at: http://www.merriam-webster.com/netdict/comprehensive [Accessed September 21, 2013].
Meyer, A., 1960. Functions of the Mediator in Collective Bargaining. *Industrial and Labour Relations Review*, 13, pp.159–165.
Moore, C., 1996. *The Mediation Process. Practical Strategies for Resolving Conflict* Second Edition., San Francisco: Jossey-Bass Publishers.
People' s Daily Online, 2009. UK agrees to joining International Contact Group in S Philippines. *People's Daily Online*. Available at: http://english.peopledaily.com.cn/90001/90777/90851/6829282.html [Accessed September 21, 2013].
Rumsfeld, D., 2002. DoD News Briefing - Secretary Rumsfeld and Gen. Myers. Available at: http://www.defense.gov/transcripts/transcript.aspx?transcriptid=2636 [Accessed September 23, 2013].
Sharkansky, I., 1970. Environment, Policy, Output, and Impact: Problems of Theory and Method in the Analysis of Public Policy. In I. Sharkansky, ed. *Policy Analysis in Political Science*. Chicago: Markham Publishing Co., pp. 61–79.

Simkin, W., 1971. *Mediation and the Dynamics of Collective Bargaining*, Washington D.C.: Bureau of National Affairs.

Underdahl, A., 2002. The Outcomes of Negotiation. In V. Kremenyuk, ed. *International Negotiation. Analysis, Approaches, Issues*. San Francisco: Jossey-Bass.

Uy, V., 2010. EU to send experts for Mindanao Peace Process. *Philippine Daily Inquirer*. Available at: http://newsinfo.inquirer.net/breakingnews/regions/view/20100519-270905/EU-to-send-experts-for-Mindanao-peace-process.

Winham, G.R., 1977. Complexity in International Negotiations. In D. Druckman, ed. *Complexity in International Negotiations*. Beverly Hills: Sage, pp. 347–366.

Young, O., 1967. *The Intermediaries: Third Parties in International Crisis*, Princeton, NJ: Princeton University Press.

Zartman, I.W., 2000. Ripeness: The Hurting Stalemate and Beyond. In P. Stern & D. Druckman, eds. *International Conflict Resolution after the Cold War*. Washington D.C.: National Academy Press, pp. 225–250.

Zartman, I.W., 2001. The Timing of Peace Initiatives: Hurting Stalemate and Ripe Moments. *Th Global Review of Ethnopolitics*, 1(1), pp.8–18.

9 Stumbling Blocks - Reasons for Collapse of Agreements

A stumbling block is an impediment, which has a structural character, and hence, is not tied exclusively to one single event or situation (see Sjöstedt & Penetrante 2013). Stumbling blocks may lead to the interaction between parties unnecessarily becoming ineffective, time-consuming and costly. The analysis of stumbling blocks enables the drawing of lessons from negotiations. For example, by analyzing and noting the problems of biased mediation, it may be possible to cope with it through measures, which would provide biased mediators incentives to be impartial. The critical approach on analyzing structures may lead to the identification of underlying structural problems, which should be confronted. At the end, such lessons may become the basis for long-term approaches to push forward the peace process, namely, *strategic facilitation.*

Factors, which contribute to the intractability of identity conflicts, can be classified through a taxonomy of complexity categories: *actors, issues, structures, processes* and *outcomes*, which provides an analytical framework for the assessment of the reasons for the intractability of identity conflicts. Behind these categories are dilemmas, which impede the desirable flow of the negotiation process and the peace process as a whole. Stumbling blocks may relate directly to the complex problem area of identities such as security, development and justice, which have been framed for negotiation purposes (issues). They may relate to the motivation and performance of individuals at the bargaining table (actors). Some problems are related to the how the negotiation has been designed and how it unfolds (process), as well as certain features of the environment, where the negotiation takes place (structure), which determine, whether sets of decisions are possible or not. Similarly important are the effects of single agreements as outcomes of negotiation rounds and how a specific the agreement is to be related to the negotiation process. Unanticipated outcomes or "side-effects" of agreements may similarly represent stumbling blocks.

The critical criterion for the detection of stumbling blocks is simply their negative impact on the peace process. A stumbling block can generate four main types of obstruction. It can 1) prevent or delay the attainment of satisfactory agreements 2) hamper the quality of agreements (outcome effects), 3) create impasses in the negotiation process, and 4) prevent the sustainable implementation of agreements (see Sjöstedt & Penetrante 2013).

9.1 Actor-related Stumbling Blocks – Dealing with Humans

One of the key factors in the analysis of any conflict is the identity of the parties involved at the negotiation. As Bercovitch, Kremenyuk & Zartman (2009) state, "parties to a conflict" may refer to an entire scale of entities ranging from the individual to national and international organizations, with different parties to the conflict and different levels of analysis occurring at different aggregation levels. Nevertheless, some of the participants at the bargaining table represent governments and organizations, it should be noted in the end, negotiators are all humans. Humans are deferred to different logics of rationality depending on the priorities of each individual. What sounds rational for one is entirely irrational for the other.

9.1.1 Diversity of Actors, Professional Cultures and Communication Skills

Indeed, the diversity of actors is in itself a source of complexity. Actors may have contradictory interests or opposing objectives, which may be perceived irreconcilable. The diversity of actors in a multi-party setting does not only pertain to the quantity of actors, but more importantly to the quality of actors. Negotiating parties have diverging "professional cultures" (Sjöstedt 2003) formed by their education, training, professional practice and routine. Moreover, actors may have several preferences, when negotiating. Some actors have very competent rhetoric skills, while some prefer to listen first. Some have competitive negotiation style, while some may opt to avoid confrontations at the bargaining table.

9.1.2 Lack of Information and Lack of Institutional Memory

Two years after the signing of the 1996 Final Peace Agreement, the peace process in Mindanao was expected to profit from the momentum. However, by 1998, a new president was elected to office, who was never involved in the peace process and who had a different view of Mindanao's complexities (Vitug & Gloria 2000, p.97). President Joseph "Erap" Estrada was seen as a "clueless executive" (Vitug & Gloria 2000, p.240). The new president was short in institutional memory on how the peace process had developed in the last 30 years. The Office of the President in Mindanao, which was established by his predecessor was kept vacant.[7] In addition, the negotiating panel, which would negotiate peace with the MILF, was non-existent. Eventually, the government lost its institutional link to Mindanao and re-established the division of Mindanao, which the Ramos government had sought to unify. In 2000, he suspended the peace talks and conducted the so-called "All-Out-War" against the MILF. Without understanding the difference between insurgency and terrorism, he equated his war to the "global war against terror."

President Estrada named his friend Li Peng Wee, a businessman from Zamboange, as presidential consultant on Mindanao economic issues to thank him for the financial support. Mindanao became a prey to the "compadre system." Although Li Peng Wee is from Mindanao, he is seen as not knowledgeable with the underlying issues of the conflict in Mindanao. Misleading policies towards Mindanao followed the appointments of Estrada's friends to political offices in Mindanao (Vitug & Gloria 2000, pp.257–258).

This experience in the Philippines summarizes a stumbling block, which refers to changing profile of actors at the negotiation table, particularly when actors who do not have the institutional memory to understand the complexities of the issues, which are involved. In addition, when actors at the negotiation table do not share the common norms, which were previously established, the negotiation process is impeded.

9.1.3 Spoilers and Negotiators for "Side-Effects"

Another actor-related stumbling block refers to actors, who use negotiation as a strategy to reach goals other than reaching an agreement. The complexity of the negotiation is aggravated by diverging motivations, why negotiation is sought. Negotiating "side-effect" refers to the practice of engaging in negotiation, not with the intention of reaching an agreement but for instance, to buy time to mobilize combatants. Spoilers may be participating at the negotiation table not for the sake of reaching an agreement, which is the goal of negotiation, but rather to prevent the achievement of any agreement, which contradicts their vested interests. Other spoilers may be non-participants at the negotiation table, who are still successful in influencing the negotiating parties.

---

[7] The Office of the President in Mindanao was eventually dismantled in October 1, 1998. This decision led to the loss of an effective point of person who would coordinate island-wide programs and implement policy.

In 1995, the Abu Sayaff raided Ipil, Zamboanga del Sur. After separate investigations ovenseen by the government and the MNLF, they came to the same conclusion the raid was conducted by a coalition of all anti-Misuari forces – the Abu Sayaff and the National Islamic Command Council (NICC). Corrupt elements of the Philippine military were identified as having supported in the escape of the raiding group members in exchange for payments. Some members of the MNLF considered negotiation as only a means to attain power. Misuari, however, looks at the peace negotiation as the "be all and end all" of the MNLF (Vitug & Gloria 2000, p.193).

Melham Alam, the chief critic of Misuari and sacked chief of the MNLF, founded the NICC. He says, "Peace is a very deceptive term. Everybody wants it. But if it becomes the ultimate objective of a rebel organization, the organization loses sight of why, it's waging a revolution in the first place. The MNLF (leadership) declared victory after the signing of the 1996 peace agreement... that bothered me so much" (Vitug & Gloria 2000, p.193). This experience confirms rebel groups are usually not homogenous. Several factions within the group may have different perceptions about what the outcome of the negotiation should be.

Vitug & Gloria (2000, p.240) identify the media as spoilers in the peace process in the Philippines. They argue, the (almost only private) Philippine media, has not been helpful in clarifying important issues. For instance, they reported the arrest of Arab and Muslim terrorists between 2001 and 2004 without critical judgement. They assumed the versions supplied by intelligence reports without investigating, whether or not these reports were true or not. The weak culture of investigative journalism in the country spoils the peace process by reproducing hegemonial structures of social domination.

9.2 Issue-related Stumbling Blocks – Issue Complexity

Issue complexity involves real issues hidden behind other issues. In several cases, the conflicting parties are themselves not aware of the real issues, which should be discussed at the bargaining table. Furthermore, issue complexity may refer to events, which took place in the past and may have partially lost validity, but their relevance remains significant.

9.2.1 Problem of Ranges – Framing Problems and Issues

As Bercovitch et al (2009) argue, parties in conflict differ so widely in terms of their values, beliefs, and goals. In addition, they may differ with respect to their perception of what the problem is all about. For instance, many Christian Filipinos perceive the problem in Mindanao as a problem of the religious incompatibility between Christianity and Islam. Some link the problem of Mindanao to terrorism. The Muslim groups perceive the problem as a problem of structural imbalances. It is also a problem of the forceful incorporation of two Muslim sultanates in the Philippine state with the decolonization process.

Differing perception of issues prevent conflicting parties from finding common goals, which are needed to initiate cooperation. Differing perceptions of the problem, lead parties to pursue different solutions to the same problem depending on their understanding of what the problem is. In many cases, the pursued solutions are aggravating the conflict because they do not accommodate the diversity of the perspectives of the problem. For example, groups, which perceive the Mindanao problem as a problem of security, tend to form vigilante groups and armed citizen groups to counter perceived security deficits. This solution, however, further promotes an environment of violence and fails to address the underlying causes of the conflict. For one party, this measure is the solution and for the other, this solution is the problem.

The complexity of issues involved in identity conflicts is further aggravated by the enormous dynamics involved. As issues constantly evolve, as the negotiation process unfolds, new solutions other than the ones initially envisaged become necessary. The conflict in Mindanao has created new conflict cleavages in the last 40 years. Adaptability of the negotiation process is however almost impossible, if negotiations are too slow to follow the evolution of the conflict. A stumbling block in this regard is the lack of opportunities to exchange information between parties and the incapacity to manage an overview of the conflicts.

9.2.2 Multi-causality and Diffusion - Horizontal and Vertical Linkages of Issues

Another stumbling block in addressing identity conflicts refers to issues consisting of a multitude of different components representing causes, manifestations and effects. Multiple causality refers to the understanding there could be various possible causes for a given event or an effect occurs due to the aggregation of various factors. The conflict in Mindanao involves multiple issues, which are horizontally and vertically interlinked. For example, the proliferation of private armies and private security firms employed by clans in Mindanao is a direct implication of security deficiencies in the area brought by the security vacuum, which the state fails to fill. The poverty in Mindanao is brought by lack of investment in the area due to the 40 year old history of violence. Furthermore, vertical inter-linkages of issues refers to the inter-linkages of several negotiation systems. For instance, the negotiation issues between the government and the MILF will affect the status of the Christian majority and other indigenous groups in Mindanao.

Theodorson and Theodorson (1979) explain, in the case of multiple causation, the given effect may occur with the absence of all but one possible sufficient but not necessary all causes and conversely, the given effect would follow the occurrence of some, but not all of the various necessary sufficient causes. In short, these inter-linkages may further complicate agenda-setting, and may require a different coordination of a larger number of stakeholders. Problems involved in identity conflicts are never strictly linear, even though some cause-and-effect relationships can be shown, they are to be considered as part of a complex web of interactions (Malabed 2001).

Identity conflicts involve numerous linkages to other established issue areas of international and national politics – migration, human rights, small arms and light weapons, regional integration, etc. Hence, the political requirements of addressing identity conflicts in the context of these international and national politics require the management of horizontal and vertical linkages of issues. The coordination of actions across governmental agencies (environment, energy, trade, economics, and finance) is of an importance, which blurs institutional boundaries and needs integration of different interests on the national level.

9.2.3 Low Politics vs. High Politics – Problematization of Rewards and Costs

Another way of analyzing issues is to calculate the reward, or cost, each party can accrue from the issues defining the conflict. The allocation of costs and rewards depends on how the problem is politically prioritized. For example, when a specific problem has a high audience rating in the media and when this problem is prioritized by policy-makers, this problem is to be regarded as "high politics." On the other hand, "low politics" involves less media coverage as well as less priority by policy-makers. The conflict in Mindanao has experienced variation of prioritization by different administrations as well as diverging types of prioritization. While President Ramos prioritized the negotiations with the MNLF, other presidents such as President Estrada pushed for the military defeat of the MILF.

Two weeks into the presidency, President Ramos opened the Office of the President in Mindanao, the first ever to be established since the start of the Republic to decentralize government. He established a direct link to a "unified Mindanao." Ramos visited the island on 66 different occasions in 133 different locations during his six years in office. No other president gave such consistent priority to

Mindanao (Vitug & Gloria 2000, p.255). On the other hand, President Estrada declared an "all-out-war" against the MILF on March 21, 2000. With the fall of Camp Abubakar, thousands of MILF combatants surrendered to President Estrada. The newly installed President Arroyo prioritized the upgrade of the military capability (Leupp 2002; Burgess 2002) by tapping military aid from the United States. Nevertheless, it can be argued the Arroyo government has contributed a very important aspect in the peace process by convincing the MILF to drop its demand for independence (GMA News 2010).

Furthermore, after 40 years, a pattern of customization can be observed. Customization defines prioritization. The highlight of the media coverage can be seen in the 1990s due to the Abu Sayaff as well as the international terrorist ring, which was supposed to have entered the country in order to conduct a failed assassination attempt to Pope John Paul II. The Ramos government reacted to the high public attention towards terrorism, which took the failed assassination as a definite sign that Middle Eastern terrorists had converted the Philippines into one of their bases in Asia for their operations. President Ramos proposed the crafting of new laws and the creation of new agencies. The anti-terrorism law was adopted to bestow the right of security agencies to tap phones, pry into bank accounts, and arrest suspected terrorists with relaxed legal impediments.

Extensive media coverage of the Mindanao conflict had occurred again in 2001 with the peak of Abu Sayaff's kidnapping activities. The Abu Sayaff's occupation of the Malaysian dive resort island Sipadan, where foreign 21 hostages were taken (GMA News 2007), received extensive international media coverage. A series of kidnappings of foreigners by Abu Sayaff from 2002 to 2004 further increased international media coverage to the conflict in Mindanao. In 2001, the Abu Sayaff kidnapped 20 foreigners from Palawan and demanded ransom. Foreign reporters rushed to Mindanao to cover the stories and in most occasions, they were kidnapped themselves. ABS CBN Newsbreak reports Abu Sayaff abducted at least 20 journalists since 2000 and all of them were eventually released upon payment of ransom.

The increased media coverage has led to the consolidation of common perception of the link between terrorism and separatism. Vitug and Gloria (2000, p.222) observe terrorism has often been confused with guerrilla warfare. Even the government has found terrorism as a practical and convenient tool to describe all anti-government units. To conclude, the cycle of transformation of the Mindanao conflict from "low politics" to "high politics" and vice-versa has inevitable increased the complexity of the conflict.

9.2.4 The Zero-Sum Trap – Violence and Security

As Bercovitch et al. (2009, p.6) note, if the only possible outcome to each party is either victory or defeat, then the conflict is a "zero-sum game" (one party gains, what the other party loses). Zero-sum refers a situation, in which a participant's gain or loss is exactly balanced by the losses or gains of the other participant(s). If the total gains of the participants are added up, and the total losses are subtracted, they will sum to zero. In short, zero-sum involves one party gaining at the expense of the other actor.

Violence is a major contested issue to negotiations, because it supposes to involve a zero-sum framing. An increase in violence by one party increases the pain of the other. The other face of violence is security. The increase in security is usually perceived as a decrease in security for the other actor. Bloomfield (1998) points out, the renunciation of violence is usually demanded as a precondition for negotiation. Rebel groups, for instance, fear disarmament or even a ceasefire may lead to the loss of leverage they have in the absence of effective formal political structures. Once a cycle of violence has been established over a period of time, violence may either energize change or block any change. As Anstey (2006, p.298) argues, violence as an issue proves both an imperative to negotiate and an obstacle to getting to the table at first.

The 1996 Peace Agreement between the GRP and MNLF does not foresee the demilitarization of the conflict through the demobilization and disarmament of the MNLF. Instead Article 19 and 20 of the agreement pertain to the integration of the MNLF combatants in the Philippine army and police. This solution is an implication of the zero-sum framing of violence and security by the conflicting parties. It does not reduce the potentiality of violence, but just suspends it by assigning it an artificial label. The agreement does not, for example, intend to conduct a gradual reduction of the number of MNLF combatants in the long run.

9.3 Structure-related Stumbling Blocks

The social interactions between actors in the decision-making process influence the dynamics of the process and can also influence the subject matter of the conflict itself. Interactions require an environment or a space, where exchanges can take place. The act of negotiating represents specific codes, procedures and rules for behavior.

9.3.1 Power Structures and Asymmetries

Power relations and power structure may influence the negotiation performance of actors. Such structural power conditions represent stumbling blocks, if they impede the parties from reaching an agreement through the negotiation process. For example, actors who perceive themselves as the more powerful actor, who believe they can pursue the total military defeat with the belief their military success is enough to resolve identity conflicts, negotiation will not be effective and beneficial. It is only when both parties perceive negotiation is much more effective than military operations that negotiation can be successful.

The negotiation process tends to be confronted by different types of asymmetries. The negotiation process, which involves states and sub-state actors such as rebel groups, relates to diverging bargaining strength of actors due to asymmetries in resources and capacity, which are at the end, translated into perception of power. Asymmetries in bargaining strength imply stronger parties having greater influence on the procedures and on the outcome. Coercion may be applied in the bargaining process through economic, political and military resources. However, it should be noted not only "having more than the others", but also "having less than the others" can also be a source of bargaining strength particularly in identity conflicts, where rebels pursue guerrilla warfare. The so-called "negative power" pertains to the capacity to delay the process by having fewer resources than the others (Larson 2003).

In the case of the Philippines, the rebel groups were able to find powerful patronage states such as Libya, Iran and other OIC member states to match the military and financial resources of the perceived stronger party (the Philippine government). The sub-state status of the MILF spares the group from problems, which state actors are usually experiencing, such as impasses during election periods and the establishment of a new administration, constraints through the check and balancing of the judicative and legislative bodies, among others.

The incapacity of a specific negotiating party to make accurate power assessments is in itself a stumbling block, because it prevents the actor from developing an appropriate long-term policy. Such a difficulty may exacerbate the implication of constant change occurring in the power structure or merely by the lack of information. Furthermore, when the government believes its military is indeed capable of military victory against the rebel group, this government will tend to delay the negotiation process. On the other side, a rebel group may just intend to pose resistance without actually expecting to topple the government.

Asymmetries in negotiation capacity, as Carraro and Sgobbi (Carraro & Sgobbi 2008, p.1490) argue, may lead to differing preferences over the negotiation setting and design. A weak player prefers to negotiate simultaneously, a strong player bargains sequentially to signal his bargaining strength. A weak party may seek separating issues, while a stronger party may seek negotiating packages. While the government represents the Philippine state, both the MNLF and the MILF represent communities, which are striving for recognition. Sovereign states are usually reluctant in negotiating with rebel groups, because negotiation is politically seen to bestow legitimacy to the rebel groups as belligerents.

President Marcos was more or less coerced to negotiate after series of oil embargos from oil-producing OIC member states such as Iran, Saudi Arabia and Libya in the 70s and 80s. Furthermore, the OIC has diplomatically recognized the MNLF by declaring it the "sole representative of the Bangsamoro people." When the MNLF became a full member of the OIC, the rebel group was elevated to a rank, which convinced the Philippine government it was negotiating with an equal partner. The Philippine government interestingly had no objection to having the OIC as mediator perhaps because it perceived itself in a powerful position.

9.3.2 Lack of Information and Immeasurability of Stakes

The lack of information about the actors and issues represents a major stumbling block. For instance, the Philippine police and military could not seem to agree, whether the Abu Sayaff, was indeed an insurgent group, who manifest Islamic extremism. Some military intelligence officers said they have always considered Abu Sayaff as no more than a lawless armed group (Vitug & Gloria 2000, p.193). However, the practices of the military and the police reveal these security agencies have successfully framed terrorism within the framework of separatism (Vitug & Gloria 2000, p.229). This is then reenforced by the weak culture of investigative journalism in the country (Vitug & Gloria 2000, p.240).

Another stumbling block refers to the immeasurability of extreme values such as power, violence and security. The impossibility to assess power with exactitude and certainty such as the degree of destruction of the 40 year old insurgency contributes to the high degree of uncertainties in negotiation outcomes. This "critical immeasurability" impedes cost-benefit calculations of a potential negotiation outcome. Decision-makers require certainty or at least structured uncertainty to reach decisions. Information is needed to serve as a basis for decisions. This necessity leads to the vulnerability of decision-makers, who prefer "may-be-correct" than no information at all. Decision-makers tend to reject solutions merely because they feel they do not have enough information as a basis for decisions.

9.3.3 Constituency Accountability

The parties at the negotiation table are usually not participating on their own behalf. They are accountable to their constituents they are representing. A major stumbling block represents the situation, where the negotiating actors are not accountable to anybody but themselves. How can accountability be internalized by armed rebel groups, which also pursue vested interests? Both the MNLF and MILF have rather "autocratic" and patriarchal structures, where regular consultations with the Muslim population are seen as limited. Former budget secretary Enriquez says, "Nur is a poor bureaucrat. He's like a sultan, (he's) autocratic. He has no notion of a republican form of government, democratic and representative in nature" (Vitug & Gloria 2000, p.90).

Representatives are mandated by their constituents and therefore require regular consultation. Constituents maintain schemes of sanctions, when their representatives fail to pursue their interests. However, as Anstey (2006, p.177) notes, these constituents may often be somewhat unfamiliar with the process of negotiation. Furthermore, they may not be aware of the existing political conditions and other complexities, which make "absolute" victory impossible. The act of negotiation may be seen as an act of betrayal or surrender. Some of them may have unrealistic or inflexible expectations of the outcome and therefore place serious constraints on their bargaining team.

Constituency accountability is an important aspect of negotiations to resolve identity conflicts. If not properly addressed, the negotiating team may be seen as "selling out" to the other team and the reached agreement be rejected by the constituents. On the other hand, the negotiating panel should be given some flexibility to enable creativity. This requires constant consultation with the constituents. However, it should be noted the higher the degree of consultation is, the lower the degree of efficiency, which may become of the agreement. In short, a healthy balance between "democratic" participation and efficiency should be found. The dilemma of constituency accountability was clearly shown in the 2008 voiding of the MOA-AD, when the Philippine Supreme Court declared the MOA-AD unconstitutional because it lacks the appropriate consultation process. Local (mainly Christian) NGOs and local government officials conveyed their opposition to the agreement and have sought arraignment.

9.3.4 Multi-Party Setting

Bargaining in identity conflicts is bargaining in a multi-party setting. Identity conflict negotiations confirm no single actor or institution has a monopoly of ideas, issues, agendas, or bargaining power (Susskind & Crump 2008; see Hampson & Hart 1995; Zartman 1997; Crump & Zartman 2003). The aspirations of other stakeholders including neighboring countries, military, churches, citizen groups and NGOs need to be adequately addressed. Partnerships between the government, the NGOs and other civic society groups, research institutions and policy-think tanks enhance bargaining positions of parties. Institutional links between institutions and organizations operating in different areas such as agriculture, justice, human rights, security and livelihood may provide additional opportunities to resolve various conflict cleavages, which aggregately define the underlying causes of conflictual relationships. The multi-party setting becomes a stumbling block, when there is diffusion on the stakeholders. Some NGOs are used by governments to pursue their own interests. Scientific reports of research institutes may be manipulated to meet the demand of donors. The lack of transparency may lead to unnoticed conflict of interests.

9.4 Process-related Stumbling Blocks

In negotiation terms, the process is the course of how different stages of negotiation are experienced leading to a specific outcome. The process represents the patterns of interaction between relevant actors, particularly how actors strive to change the status quo. Negotiations equate decision-making processes, whose function is to communicate and establish instruments to empower actors to cope with existing conflict cleavages to prevent further outburst of coercion. Such instruments are codified in formal and informal agreements as well as through norms established as the process unfolds. The critical analysis of process-related dynamics leads to the identification of stumbling blocks: the *"time frame paradox" (short-term vs. long term approaches) and sectoral arrangements.*

9.4.1 Time Frame Paradox – Between Short-term and Long-Term Approaches

The gaps, on how problems and issues are framed, are to be considered as stumbling blocks. Gaps may be caused, for example, by diverging perceptions of time. State negotiators may address issues within a short-term frame, because of domestic constraints such as national elections and limited legislation periods. Policies are usually framed by the Philippine government to fit in the 6 year-term it has been mandated to govern. Policy-makers then expect results of their policies and strategies within this time frame. However, identity conflicts involve processes, which take place within a long-term perspective. Gaps between expectations and realities follow.

Abdul Sahrin, one of the MNLF commanders was quoted by Vitug & Gloria (2000: 59) to have recognized this gap. He says, "*we have short memories. We always get so noisy demanding for autonomy without consulting his people. No president can grant us autonomy without consulting his people. He has to be a dictator to be doing that, and even then, he will have to confront himself later on, perhaps his conscience, if he has any left*." Sahrin has made a good point regarding the expectation on the side of the government, if it is to ignore the needs of acting in a long-term process. Framing long-term issues through the short-term perspective may prove detrimental to the whole negotiation process.

For example, to save time, the government negotiators did not adequately consult relevant stakeholders in the MOA-AD. The issue of ancestral domains is one of, if not the most, contested issues in the GRP-MILF talks. This poor process management is blamed to have caused the current impasse following the latest escalation of violence. Furthermore, policies are expected to show results in a short-term perspective to enable the administration to harvest the positive results of its policies. However, identity conflicts involve complexities and the introduction of new policies may lead to observable results only in the long-term perspective. The formulation of "objective" criteria to measure the success of policies requires identity conflicts involve a linear process. The peace process is, however, never linear as it will equally involve set-backs and breakthroughs.

Rebels such as the MNLF and MILF are not confronted by rigid time constraints. Therefore, they tend to address issues through a long-term perspective. Nevertheless, rebel groups are confronted by limited resources. Therefore, they are also motivated to frame long term issues in a short-term perspective. While they do not need to consider election periods in their own positioning, they are more or less forced to consider such events, because the prospect of having a new administration means new policies may follow, which may endanger agreements that have been already reached.

Each new government administration constitutes different sets of policies and appoints different sets of people to be members of the government negotiating panel. The first months or year of the new administration is usually spent carefully assessing the positions of the actors involved. The rebel group has to spend some time trusting the government representatives particularly, if new government representatives lack institutional memory. Transition periods are usually problematic, because the negotiating parties are once again entrapped to repeat again certain stages (e.g., agenda-setting) of the negotiation process. The transition period conventionally starts with position-taking and identification of issues, which may be frustrating for rebel groups, because they have to repeat the same procedure all over again to adapt to the new administration.

9.4.2 Sectoral Arrangements

The problem of sectoral arrangements refers to the subdivision of complicated issues to various sub-issues aiming to simplify negotiations. Issue inter-linkages are generally so dense in the peace negotiations sectoral agreements may be ineffective to resolve identity conflicts. Different issues such as security, homelands and development are usually discussed separately in the GRP-MILF negotiations. Several agreements were reached between 2000 and 2008 such as the 2000 Agreement on Safety and Security Guarantees and the collapsed 2008 Memorandum of Agreement on Ancestral Domains (MOA-AD) following several rounds of negotiation. These agreements attempt to subdivide inter-linked issues.

While it may be necessary to subdivide issues, it remains necessary to address the complexity brought by the horizontal and vertical inter-linkages of issues. Each issue may require the participation of certain actors. For example, the issue on the introduction of Sharia law in the ARMM requires the participation of legal and religious experts. On the other hand, the issue of cultural autonomy requires the participation of other experts such as philanthropists and social scientists. Each issue has different sets of priorities and solutions. Therefore, sectoral arrangements are necessary; however, this separation of issues leaves some process-related problems unaddressed.

Sectoral arrangements have several disadvantages, which may impede the negotiation process. Some agreements on certain sectors may be against other agreements or are mutually exclusive. Because a sectoral arrangement is negotiated by different sets of actors, this arrangement may be unacceptable for the other actors negotiating on a separate sector. For example, an agreement, which intends to pursue good governance negotiated by the civilian representatives of the Bangsamoro, may imply the decrease of power of the rebel group. Without appropriate consultation the negotiated sectoral arrangement may then be resisted by the armed group. Furthermore, a sectoral approach to the peace process requires more coordination efforts, as well as, more resources and time to link the different arrangements with each other. Failing to coordinate the different sectors may actually prolong the conflict.

9.5 Outcome-related Stumbling Blocks

Outcome uncertainty refers to the lack of information about, what can be achieved and how the outcome will eventually change the status of the conflicting parties. When the negotiation itself has become the "end" to the process, agreements may fail to address the real issues needed to be confronted to resolve identity conflicts. Negotiation itself should not be the goal of negotiation. Furthermore, the difficulty in predicting directions (uncertainty) influences the course of negotiation. Predicting direction is required by negotiators to see, whether negotiation will bear the desired results or not. However, expectations, which are either too high or too low, may impede the negotiation process.

9.5.1 Varying Expectations

Expectations are tricky elements of the negotiation process. They may impede reaching an agreement, because expectations may function as a limiting framework for what the agreement should look like at the end. They may impede flexibility and may decrease the scope of the potential outcome by engraving "anchors" to the table. Too high of expectations may lower the threshold of frustration. The peace agreement was the much-coveted prize at the end of the negotiations between the Philippine government and the MNLF. Because of this high expectation, it was observed to be much more difficult to look beyond the document, which was going to put an end to the protracted armed conflict in the Southern Philippines (Vitug & Gloria 2000, p.264). Former security adviser Alexander Aguirre recalls, "We were too engrossed in the political settlement." He continues, "We didn't engage in any development effort side by side with the peace process." Agreements accompanied by too high expectations face much more public scrutiny, where minor deficiencies may invite disproportional frustration.

On the other side of the coin, too low of expectations may impede the negotiation process by underestimating the effects of the agreement so much less energy and resources are allotted to the negotiation process. The dilemma refers to the "self-fulfilling prophecy", whereas an ineffective agreement is already expected to result from the negotiation process before the actual negotiation starts. While the MNLF leadership had high expectations on the outcome of the negotiation, the Islamist faction of the MNLF (the MILF) had very low expectations, primarily because they question the appropriateness of negotiating with the government. The result was this group may have been taken by surprise, when the

1996 Final Peace Agreement was reached and signed. The MILF members eventually refused to recognize the agreement and decided to launch a separate insurgency.

9.5.2 Post-settlement Dilemma

The evaluation of the negotiation process should not end, when an agreement has been reached. Negotiation experts such as Kalhauge, Sjöstedt & Correll (2005) and Hampson and Hart (1995) refer to the concept of recursive negotiation or post-negotiations, where things which are not part of the agreement are clarified. For example, in international trade negotiations, the ratification of an international treaty remains problematic and in some cases such as the ratification of the Kyoto Protocol, the agreement may not be ratified by several major stakeholders preventing its effective implementation. In identity conflicts, the implementation of the agreement requires similar constitutional and legislative processes, which will be confronted by political opposition groups. The constitutional process will eventually mean delays due to the need to change structural conditions. Furthermore, there should be evaluative discussions about the post-agreement societal interactions, for instance whether reconciliation is actually taking place. Identity conflicts involve more than pacifying armed combatants.

The negotiation process should be assessed by looking at the sustainability of the outcome. Because of the tendency to subdivide issues as well as to reflect only the known power conditions, there can be no comprehensive agreement, which could cover all the aspects of identity conflicts. The failure to acknowledge reality cannot be reproduced on a sheet of paper, which may lead to disappointment on the negotiation outcome. This may lead to the collapse of agreement and impede re-negotiations.

As the Mindanao case shows, there are some aspects of the conflict no agreement can address, such as good governance and leadership. The ARMM under the MNLF is increasingly seen as a "failed experiment" (Vitug & Gloria 2000, p.82). This perception reduces the resources for the negotiations between the government and the MILF. The weakness of the ARMM is often cited by the MILF as a reason for pursuing other negotiation outcomes. This tendency is misleading. The weakness of the ARMM should not be blamed on the 1996 Final Peace Agreement, but rather the failure to adapt to reality.

The MNLF chair Nur Misuari easily won the ARMM election for governorship in September 1996, because President Ramos arranged his candidacy to have no real opposition. He was adjusting to his new role as politician. He spent most of his life waging a secessionist revolution against the Philippine government. Former rebels, local warlords and the established Muslim elite became part of the ARMM's constituency. The new ARMM government was able to avoid auditing and public bidding regulations particularly in the transition period. In December 1996, the office of the ARMM governor approved the 70 million Pesos school textbook publishing contract with White Orchids Printing and Publishing House. As Vitug & Gloria (2000, p.74) reiterates, public bidding was waived. However, to date, it is still unclear to whom the 68.2 million Pesos (1 million Euro) went. Such a case shows a lack of transparency and accountability in the ARMM (Vitug & Gloria 2000, p.77).

The ARMM remained tainted by charges of corruption and inefficiency. It is an administrative unit with an oversized and inept bureaucracy of more than 19,000 employees (Vitug & Gloria 2000, p.78). To conclude, good governance was not covered by the 1996 Final Agreement and more than 10 years after the signing of the agreement, the well-being of Muslim communities in Mindanao has not significantly improved. The ARMM still has the lowest functional literacy, per capita income, and life expectancy in the whole country.

Former Muslim rebels are unable to find jobs in the ARMM, now run by the MNLF and as Vitug and Gloria (2000, p.264) note, between 20,000 and 40,000 MNLF rebels, who could not be integrated into the military or absorbed by the ARMM bureaucracy are increasingly becoming frustrated with the incapability of their leaders to provide employment. As a result, despite the existence of the 1996 Final Peace Agreement, they remain unable to participate in the society as peers.

9.6 Interim Conclusion – When Means Become Ends

The identification of stumbling blocks in using negotiation as an instrument to resolve identity conflicts is necessary in the analysis of the intractability of identity conflicts. When the means to reach the ends impedes the resolution, a comprehensive assessment of the dynamics involved in the negotiation is inevitable. The introduction of the actors-issues-structures-process-outcome taxonomy offers a more focused analysis, which distinguishes existing analytical levels.

Actor-related stumbling blocks refer to the complexity brought by negotiators being humans. The asymmetry of information and institutional memory among actors present at the negotiation table is a source of complexity. The necessity to engage spoilers and hard-liners to negotiate is a major source of impasses in negotiations.

Issue-related stumbling blocks pertain to the complexity of issues. The historicity of issues complicates the identification of issues, which should be negotiated about. Furthermore, the negotiating parties may have different perceptions of the problems, which hinder reaching a common goal and common strategies. The multi-causality of issues implies the horizontal and vertical linkages of issues and limits the effectiveness of solutions.

Structure related stumbling blocks refer to the environment or space, which determines the decisions and actions of actors. The existing power structures may decrease the effectiveness of negotiations by increasing the benefit of seeking military alternatives. Other sources of impediments are the immeasurability of stakes and the lack of information about the actors and issues. This condition frames the behavior and decision of negotiating parties. The accountability of negotiating parties to their constituents represents mechanisms, which pressure the parties to reach specific outcomes. Finally, the multi-lateral setting of the negotiations produces difficulties, for example, by coalition-building.

Process-related stumbling blocks refer to difficulties faced by the negotiation parties in the different stages of negotiation. The diverging time perceptions of the actors lead to the diverging preferences on approaches. The perception of the complexity of identity conflicts leads to the separation of sectors to save resources. However, such a strategy produces other difficulties, which should be addressed.

Finally, outcome-related stumbling blocks refer to the uncertainty of the implications of the outcome and the expectations confronting the negotiation outcome. Too high and too low expectations may influence the negotiation. Furthermore, an outcome faces challenges, whether this outcome is comprehensive enough to include everything relevant to finally resolve the conflict.

References:

Anstey, M., 2006. *Managing Change: Negotiating Conflict*, Lanadowne: Juta Legal and Academic Publishing.

Bercovitch, J., Kremenyuk, V. & William, I.W. eds., 2009. *The SAGE Handbook of Conflict Resolution*, Los Angeles, London, New Delhi: SAGE Publications.

Bercovitch, J., Kremenyuk, V. & Zartman, I.W., 2009. *The SAGE Handbook of Conflict Resolution*, Los Angeles, London, New Delhi: SAGE Publications.

Bloomfield, D., 1998. Northern Ireland. In P. Harris & B. Reilly, eds. *Democracy and Deep-rooted Conflict: Options for Negotiators*. Stockholm: International Institute for Democracy and Electoral Assistance, pp. 121–132.

Burgess, M., 2002. *US Deployment to the Philippines: A Sensible and Timely Quid Pro Quo*, Center for Defense Information. Available at: http://www.cdi.org/terrorism/philippines.cfm [Accessed September 23, 2013].

Carraro, C. & Sgobbi, A., 2008. Modelling negotiated decision-making in environmental and natural resource management: A multilateral, multiple issues, non-cooperative bargaining model with uncertainty. *Automatica*, 44(6), pp.1488–1503.

Crump, L. & Zartman, I.W., 2003. Multilateral negotiation and the management of complexity. *International Negotiation*, 8(1), pp.1–5.

GMA News, 2007. Abu Sayaff Kidnappings, Bombings and other Attacks. *GMA News Online*. Available at: http://www.gmanews.tv/story/154797/abu-sayaff-kidnappings-bombings-and-other-attacks [Accessed September 20, 2013].

GMA News, 2010. Govt negotiator: MILF dropping independence option our biggest achievement. *GMA News Online*. Available at: http://www.gmanews.tv/story/194633/govt-negotiator-milf-dropping-independence-option-our-biggest-achievement [Accessed September 20, 2013].

Hampson, F.O. & Hart, M., 1995. *Multilateral Negotiations: Lessons from arms control, trade, and the environment*, Baltimore: John Hopkins University Press.

Kalhauge, A.C., Sjöstedt, G. & Correll, E. eds., 2005. *Global Challenges: Furthering the Multilateral Process for Sustainable Development*, Sheffield: Greenleaf Publishing.

Larson, M.J., 2003. Low-Power Contributions in Multilateral Negotiations: A Framework Analysis. *Negotiation Journal*, 19(2), pp.133–149.

Leupp, G., 2002. *The Philippines: "Second Front" in the U.S.'s Global War*, Available at: http://www.counterpunch.org/leupp2.html [Accessed September 21, 2013].

Malabed, R., 2001. *Ecosystem Approach and Interlinkages: A Socio-Ecological Approach to Natural and Human Ecosystems*, Tokyo: United Nations University.

Sjöstedt, G. ed., 2003. *Professional Cultures in International Negotiation: Bridge or Rift?*, Lanham, MD: Lexington Books.

Sjöstedt, G. & Penetrante, A.M. eds., 2013. *Climate Change Negotiations. A Guide to Resolving Disputes and Facilitating Multilateral Cooperation*, London and New York: Routledge.

Susskind, L. & Crump, L., 2008. *Multilateral Negotiation*, New York: SAGE Publications.

Theodorson, G. & Theodorson, A., 1979. *A Modern Dictionary of Sociology*, New York: Barnes and Noble Books.

Vitug, M. & Gloria, G., 2000. *Under the Crescent Moon : Rebellion in Mindanao*, Quezon City: Ateneo Center for Social Policy & Public Affairs : Institute for Popular Democracy.

Zartman, I.W., 1997. *Peacemaking in International Conflict*, Washington D.C.: USIP Press.

10 Strategic Facilitation of the Mindanao Peace Process – Dealing with Stumbling Blocks

The ultimate goal of this book project is to propose measures for the strategic facilitation of the negotiation process. *Facilitation* is external intervention in the negotiation process to support the parties involved in the process to reach a satisfactory agreement, or to move the talks in a constructive direction (see Sjöstedt & Penetrante 2013). Facilitation occurs in terms of preparing negotiators to empower them to cope with various dilemmas at the negotiation table. It relates to the interventions on the process and procedure of reaching an agreement, and not to the content or substance of the conflict. Facilitation is not limited to actors assuming the role of mediators at the negotiation table. Other facilitators may include NGOs or even the conflicting parties themselves, when they introduce changes in the structure to enhance communication. In the context of multiplicity of issues and status involved in identity conflicts, there can be no single facilitator, but rather a concert of several actors and structures which should be coordinated to maximize synergies.

Strategic facilitation aims to create conditions, which are "conducive to reaching agreement" (Hopmann 1996, p.231) in future peace talks. Strategic means a long-term oriented mind-set through the application of certain instruments. Many successful facilitation measures being carried out presently will possibly not yield a positive results in the near future. It involves looking at different negotiation rounds and the resulting outputs,in form of an agreement or norm, as part of a long-term process. Furthermore, strategic facilitation involves the anticipation of the effects of several factors created by negotiation in the whole peace process and the (critical) argument such effects may be both helpful and detrimental to the resolution of the conflict in general.

After conceptualizing, what strategic facilitation means and how it relates to stumbling blocks, to elevate it as a conceptual framework to allow prescriptions, for which there is a necessity to clarify how the criteria for successful facilitation should be understood. Strategic facilitation measures are to be classified as successful, if they contribute directly or indirectly to attain goals of the parties, who are commonly drafted for the negotiations. Coming from the rational perspective, the emphasis of goal attainment leads to the focus on output variables such as quality, productivity and effectiveness. Relating goal attainment as a criteria for a success negotiation, where a negotiation is successful, when it ends up with the desired output of negotiation. Nevertheless, this "goal achievement approach" in assessing strategic facilitation is a necessary, but not a sufficient criteria.

The long-term nature of strategic facilitation undermines the using of goals as criteria for evaluation. The determination of goals requires full access to information and its measurability to enable cost-benefit calculations, which is not always the case in negotiations. Goals are rather static entities, which limit the flexibility of the process. Goals promote the "fixed-pie" perception (see Thompson & Hastie 1990; Bazerman & Neale 1992), which pertains to the belief outcomes other than what was envisaged are completely in opposition. Once the parties have expressed approval of the goal, the pie stops expanding. The zones for possible agreement (ZOPA) are identified and marked.

Furthermore, goals may be based on consensual knowledge, which has become outdated in the course of time due to changing conditions at the bargaining table. For example, new parties may have emerged. New power structures may motivate parties to redefine goals in the course of negotiation or to reject agreements they have reached in the past. Hence, the consensual nature of goals, which refer to a mutual collaborative understanding, may decrease over time. Some parties may start to doubt the previously attained goals. Others may later refer to a newly formulated goal.

This chapter suggests another criterion for assessment pertains to the capability of facilitation measures to assist parties to break out of conventional cognitive and normative constraints through strategic facilitation. Looking at the listed stumbling blocks (see chapter 9), there seems to be the need to re-frame mind-sets and perceptions. Once measures of strategic facilitation allow such "breaking-out" of normal and normative constraints, then these efforts can be classified as successful.

The next step after the identification of stumbling blocks is to recommend strategies to enable mediators and negotiating parties to cope with them. A common pattern of the following prescriptions is the attempt to provide techniques to empower conflicting parties to shift cognitive paradigms.

10.1 Actor-related Prescriptions

Coping with actor-related stumbling blocks does not foresee the removal of specific actors from the negotiating table. Spoilers, although they regularly and deliberately sabotage the negotiation process, are legitimate stakeholders. They hold stakes in the process, because an agreement may reduce their resources, for example when they draw revenues from the civil war economy. Spoilers are usually those actors, who profit from the status quo. As it will be discussed below, launching military offensives to hardliners, who spoil the process cannot be a viable solution.

10.1.1 Problem-Solving Mode – Separating Persons (Relationships) from Problems (Issues)

Zartman (1989) has noted, some groups are structured solely for the purpose of fighting. Adjustment of goals is not possible without the group collapsing. It can be argued such groups are not machines, but humans. These individuals may have the sole disposition of fighting; however, looking through a long-term process outlook, these individuals experienced a radicalization process, when violent paths were chosen in the past. Extremism is a product of the learning process. Although some may be born in the situation, where they could not think otherwise, these persons are not the problem, but rather the conditions, which transformed them to "fighting machines." This approach involves the separation of the people from problems and requires careful considerations of the factors and structures promoting trajectories of violence.

At the negotiation table, the negotiation takes place between people with differing views, emotions, perceptions and backgrounds. Fisher & Ury (1981) suggests difficulties arise, when relationships and issues become entangled. A working relationship does not require parties approve the positions of the others nor that they share values. Fisher & Brown (1989) propose the disentangling of relationships from substantive issues. Simply put, the people should be separated from problematic issues. A problem-solving mode requires conflicting parties realize they need each other to solve the common problem. Cooperation requires interdependent relationships. The recognition parties have common problems leads to a mind-set, where cooperation is imperative.

10.1.2 Management of Professional Cultures and Group Cohesion in Negotiation

As Sjöstedt (2003, p.258) notes, awareness and knowledge are prerequisites for the management of the role of professional culture in negotiation, which may pertain to either problem-solving or creative facilitation. He continues problem-solving means measures are taken in order to cope with the negative consequences, which may arise from the confrontation of different professional cultures. The motivation and behavior as influenced by training, education and professional practice and routine refer to profession cultures (Sjöstedt 2003). At the bargaining table between the GRP and the MILF, negotiators have different professional backgrounds. Some are military personnel, academes, scientists, clergymen, NGO advocates, politicians and lawyers. In the course of the negotiation, experts coming from different background may be invited to either advise the negotiators or to actually act as negotiators themselves. They must be trained systematically to participate in international negotiations (Sjöstedt 2003, p.259).

For example, Nur Misuari's leadership was questioned by several Muslim conservatives claiming he is a communist and a dictator. This style of leadership may be accounted to his professional background as a university professor (communist) and a military man (dictator). However, there was no effective attempt to coordinate the internal positions of the MNLF members, which may have led to the fragmentation of the group. As Sjöstedt (Sjöstedt 2003, p.260) argues, the ability of the head of delegation to handle the positive and negative effects of professional culture in negotiation may sometimes be a significant condition for a skillful performance at the table. He claims the internal coherence of the negotiating team is an important condition, when negotiating with other parties.

The same coordinating mechanism can be applied in addressing other positions within the group. Not only are professional cultures the source of different views within the group, but age, religiosity and ethnicity also need to be considered. Without any legitimate formal space for interactions between group members, contradicting positions are not heard and may eventually lead to fragmentation. Again, a problem-solving mode may be applied to facilitate negotiation between members of the group.

10.1.3 Capacity Building

Successful negotiation requires resources, which ensure participation at the decision making process. Furthermore, many negotiating parties have great difficulties in defending or even understanding their positions and interests in the negotiations, because they lack the necessary resources and capabilities (Gupta 2007). Rebel groups usually have limited financial budgets, which prevent them from preparing for the negotiations, sponsoring large scale consultation meetings with experts on various issues, coordinating positions between different fields on a deliberative manner, sending qualified delegations to several (parallel) meetings, assessing provisions proposed by other parties and communicating or consulting with constituents to find out their responses to proposed provisions. Because preparing for negotiations is subjected to a learning process, the rebel group should have the capacity to manage knowledge.

Powerful parties should realize it is to their interest to enhance the negotiating skills of weaker parties. Empowering rebel groups, by building their negotiation capabilities, is an approach, which ensures their integration in the negotiation system. Exchange of concessions is particularly difficult for weak parties, which do not fully understand the technical issues and how they should be framed for the negotiation (e.g. horizontal and vertical linkages of issues).

Programs of capacity building in the Southern Philippines should not only focus on technical assistance and human resources development such as livelihood programs, the construction of roads and other infrastructures, and schools in Mindanao, but as well as programs and training to enhance the negotiation skills of all parties. With no background in negotiation, delegates may be easily overwhelmed by the complexity. Delegates should have a clearer focus on the difficulties with respect to negotiation. Training sessions may review the prerequisites for successful negotiation, analyze power asymmetries at the negotiating table, and suggest how to deal with incomplete information.

To cope with the lack of institutional memory, the establishment of negotiating panels should not be totally dependent on the government. In the Philippines, every newly elected government has to establish a new government negotiation panel. It has been a common practice by a new government to dismantle the whole negotiation panel. This practice impedes continuity and a long-term process outlook of the problem issues. The newly appointed panel members need to spend some time getting used to the actual negotiation. In some cases, like in the Philippines, the first months of the administration involve the repetition of negotiation episodes, such as the initiation of talks, which involves the re-identification of panel members, re-setting of agenda and the re-clarification of issues for the purpose of clearance with the policies of the new government (Dacpano 2010).

Particularly with the concern of the MILF, the new government of Noynoy Aquino may not honor the agreements made between the Arroyo government and the MILF, which causes the MILF to engage in "rhetoric wars." All of these difficulties may be avoided, when there is continuity of the negotiating panel. There should be at least a norm, if not formal rules, to promote the continuation of the negotiating panel beyond the term of a government administration unless the new President can prove the incompetence of the panel, which his or her predecessor has established.

Furthermore, formal and informal preparation rounds should be regularly conducted before the actual negotiation. Such preparation rounds may be conducted by the panel members themselves or by back channels would ensure the parties are aware of the positions and interests of the other party before the official negotiation starts. They will have enough time to familiarize themselves with the problem issues. Such preparation rounds are of course already conducted by the negotiating panels through exploratory talks. However, such preparation rounds may be conducted in a more systematic way. Such preparatory rounds may be used as a formal space of interactions with other stakeholders, who are not represented at the negotiation table, such as local government units, scientists and experts, churches, NGOs and other civic organizations. For example, NGOs and universities may organize preparatory rounds, which involve the discussion of technical aspects of the conflict.

10.1.4 Dealing with Spoilers – Identifying Structural Weaknesses

The Abu Sayaff Group (ASG) is indeed a major spoiler of the peace process in the Philippines (Frake 1998; Gomez 2009). This group has never joined the negotiation table with the government. Nevertheless, the "spoiling capacity" of the ASG should not be referred to the persons, who are members of the group but rather to the conditions, which enable Abu Sayaff to have impact in the process. Spoilers may only spoil the process, when the process allows them to do so. The founder of the ASG, Khadaffy Janjalani, had been associated with the MNLF since his youth. He began questioning Nur Misuari's leadership in 1986, when the MNLF started negotiating with the Aquino government and he was sent to Libya, where he consolidated his extremist view. While in Libya, Janjalani would tell his fellow students how Misuari's remote-control and dictatorial style of leadership was damaging the MNLF (Vitug & Gloria 2000, p.211).

Khadaffy Janjalani was successful in forming the ASG with the assistance of nothing more than corrupt military officials, who were reported to have provided Abu Sayaff with firearms and money (see Vitug und Gloria 2000). In the April 1995 raid of Ipil town by 650 members of the ASG, the aim was to disrupt negotiations and to gain resources from looting. Since 2000, the main sources of income for the ASG have been ransom and extortion (Banlaoi 2008). On one occasion, Libya paid 20 million US to the ASG (Niksch 2002) in exchange for kidnapped foreigners from Sidapan, Malaysia, without calculating this amount would be used to buy more powerful firearms. The international community could easily be extorted because of the extensive media coverage. Furthermore, although the ASG was known to kidnap foreigners specifically, journalists from abroad flocked to Mindanao to have an interview with the Abu Sayaff. More than 20 journalists were kidnapped and eventually released after more than 25 million US were paid to Abu Sayaff(BBC 2000). The search for sensation by journalists contributed to the increase in the military strength of the ASG, which used the ransom money to buy firearms and bribe both military and police officials.

An important question refers to the source of firearms. As mentioned above, the 1996 Final Peace Agreement between the GRP and MNLF did not lead to the demilitarization of the MNLF. With the situation of fragmentation within the MNLF, some uncontrolled "rogue" elements or the so-called "lost command" engage in firearms trade with impunity. In addition, there were some reports, where known ASG men could go to the cities without being arrested. Those who were arrested were released later. There are suspicions of a military's link with the ASG as many residents and members of the MNLF would claim (Vitug & Gloria 2000, p.218). The MILF notes "in the past, the ASG had procured their firearms including big guns from unscrupulous members of the Armed Forces of the Philippines (AFP)" (GMA News 2010). A former kidnap victim, Gracia Burnham, has caused controversy since returning to the US in 2002 by claiming Philippine military officials were colluding with her captors. She made the claim in her book, *In the Presence of My Enemies* (2003).

Following the approach of separating the problem from the persons, the example of the ASG shows spoilers gain strength through structural weaknesses, which promote conditions for the spoilers to actually act as spoilers. The Philippine Army and the Philippine National Police are vulnerable to its own corrupt officers, which strengthen spoilers such as the ASG. A prescription in this regard is thinking about the relationship of the structural weaknesses in the military and police and how these weaknesses relate to the whole peace process. The Philippine military and police must undergo reforms, which would prevent corruption, impunity and increase accountability.

10.1.5 Dealing with "Side-Effects" and Hardliners through Engagement

Conflicting parties, who negotiate to benefit from "side-effects" of the negotiation to win time to regain military strength, are themselves spoilers at the negotiation table. Without the genuine intention to resolve conflicts, when they have gained the anticipated side-effect, they would eventually leave the negotiation table. However, it can be argued it is a more effective approach to have these "side-effect benefactors" at the negotiating table than having them outside. Such negotiating parties are not yet convinced the potential outcome of the negotiation is much more attractive than these "side-effects." Having these parties at the negotiating table may persuade them of otherwise. A strategy to deal with parties negotiating for side-effects includes the discussion with these parties about the reasons, why an agreement should be rejected. The mediator may engage these conflicting parties to formulate their Best Alternative to a Negotiated Settlement (BATNA) (Fisher & Ury 1981) and to clarify the advantages and disadvantages of engaging in negotiations.

The MILF's initial negotiations can be considered as negotiation for side-effects. In 1997, the MILF sought out Ruben Torres, the executive secretary of President Ramos, who was aiming for a general ceasefire agreement particularly after several successful military offensives. Torres later says that "the MILF wanted the military to give up control of Buldon." Some officers of the military interpreted the MILF motive in negotiating as a way of shielding themselves. Torres relayed to the government the willingness of the MILF to negotiate. Several government officials such as Defense Secretary Renato de Villa and Abat, who was then chief negotiator with the MILF, objected and called the act as "surrender." As a compromise, President Ramos later suggested to turn over the MILF camp in Buldon to civilian authority. Eventually the MILF agreed (Vitug & Gloria 2000, p.144). Nevertheless, this negotiating for a specific side-effect eventually led to more negotiations, particularly when communication channels were successfully identified and maintained. In this case, Abat and De Villa, who objected negotiating with the MILF for the reason they were negotiating for "side-effects", were successful preventing negotiation, then there would have been no chance to provide the MILF the experience, in which negotiation is the appropriate channel to pursue interests.

The Buldon ceasefire agreement eventually became a general cessation of hostilities, which was signed in July 1997 in Cagayan de Oro. Although it can be observed several ceasefire agreements were only reached following several military defeats of the MILF, the rebel group eventually started negotiating on substance, when the MILF introduced the so-called "nine-point agenda", which identifies negotiation issues. These issues include ancestral domain, displaced and landless Bangsamoro, destruction of properties and war victims, human rights issues, social and cultural discrimination, corruption of mind and moral fiber, economic inequities and widespread poverty, exploration of natural resources, and agrarian related issues. The MILF started moving away from negotiating for side-effects and in the end they were actually negotiating "outcomes."

The same approach may be applied to hard-liners of both sides. Engaging hardliners as early as possible in the negotiation process may be better than marginalizing them from the negotiation process. Hardliners, when they become parts of the negotiation process, may realize their interests may be reached more effectively through talks. Involving hardliners equally requires their empowerment as negotiators, enabling them to participate in setting up the agenda. This would eventually enable them to formulate agendas. In addition, through their involvement, they may familiarize themselves with the history, context, and moderate extremist views. At the end, they may realize they could actually more effectively control the outcome yields through participation. Mediators and negotiating parties should not be afraid of hardliners at the negotiating table. It is only, when they are at the negotiation table, a transformation process may occur.

10.2 Issue-related Prescriptions

Coping with issue-related stumbling blocks does not foresee the elimination of issues, which are perceived as non-negotiable at the negotiation table. Instead, coping refers to how issues are related to the peace process in general. Issues cannot be taken as given and permanent conditions. Although issues involve concrete objects such as land, weapons and buildings, how these issues are interpreted to relate to the negotiation process remains a subjective and dynamic process, which should be adequately addressed. Issues are in the context of identity conflicts mere constructions by the conflicting parties and are accordingly neither given by nature as fixed. As Sjöstedt & Penetrante (2013) argue, the genuine intrinsic qualities of issues follow from how they have been framed, constructed, and developed for negotiations.

10.2.1 Knowledge Management – Truth Commissions and Early Warning Systems

Any formulation of strategy requires the drawing of information. The handling of knowledge and other complex information represents a critical factor in peace negotiations. Issues, which involve extreme values, immeasurable stakes as well as horizontal and vertical inter-linkages, are vulnerable to manipulation, because of their diffuse characteristics. Extremist group leaders may easily instrumentalize minor set-backs to escalate violence. For instance, the confusing information about the Ipil Town massacre leaves residents still guessing, who are to blame for the casualties hey have suffered. The lack of the systematic documentation of events leads to the more contestation between parties.

The system for knowledge management constructed by the peace process is a precondition for the talks. For instance, the media uses reports from the military or from the police for "objective" news casting. What follows are "objective" news reports, which do not encompass objective realities. Although the armed conflict in Mindanao is more than 40 years old and although the conflict has led to the death of hundreds of thousands and to the displacement of millions people, there is no single attempt to establish an independent truth commission in the Philippines to manage knowledge on the conflict in Mindanao. The establishment of a formal space for the interaction between scientists, historians, investigative journalists, NGOs and universities is required to manage critical knowledge of issues relevant to Mindanao.

10.2.1.1 Truth Commissions

Truth commissions are defined as "bodies set up to investigate a past history of violations of human rights in a particular country, which can include violations by the military, other government forces, or armed opposition forces" (Hayner 1994, p.558). Hayne notes that truth commissions focus on the past and are not intended to replace human rights commissions. Furthermore, truth commissions are temporary bodies,which investigate patterns of abuse over a set period of time rather than a specific event.

The 1996 Final Peace Agreement foresees the integration of MNLF combatants in the Philippine Army and Police without any process of coming to terms with the past. Former enemies are expected to start a working relationship, as if nothing has happened in the past. However, the agreement ignores the accommodation of facts, which combatants from all sides are human beings, who need mechanisms of "closure." Military personnel and MNLF combatants both experienced decades of fighting, where experiences of trauma are regularly collected. Truth commissions may be capable of addressing problems with the lack of a process of coming to terms with the past (*Vergangenheitsbewältigung*).

The truth commissions' main goal is to outline patterns of abuse in the past. Commissions do not have the power to prosecute and do not even have to "name names." Truth commissions are not an adversarial event, which court proceedings may be, thereby providing a more comfortable environment for victims (Brahm et al. 2004). The final report of the commission provides recommendations for rebuilding society. It highlights institutional factors facilitated from the abuse of human rights. Finally, a widespread dissemination of the report intends to assist the public in better understanding the trauma, which all groups have experienced. It is not unusual for the commission calls for symbolic reparations through public memorials or national remembrance days.

10.2.1.2 Early Warning Systems

The anticipation and identification of events, which could lead to the collapse of agreements and the peace process as a whole, offer resources to design and implement appropriate tools such as early warning systems and quick response tools, which would confront imminent changes, to contain damage. Early warning systems were initially developed to forecast natural disasters such as drought. In the context of identity conflicts, early warning is employed to predict or respond in an early manner to prevent large scale casualties. Early warning systems involve mechanisms of response to the development of conflict, which prevent the outburst and escalation of violence. Early warning systems refer to activities such as conflict analysis and monitoring, data analysis, risk assessment or advocacy (Mwaura & Schmeidl 2002; Austin 2003).

Nevertheless, any early warning system requires the management of knowledge. A national body can be established, which would constantly document events, may include events not related to human rights. Such a body may be similar to the Intergovernmental Panel of Climate Change (IPCC) in regards to the climate change negotiations. The main task of this body is to manage knowledge, which is relevant to Mindanao. It integrates information collected by several government bodies, research communities, universities, journalists, think tanks, NGOs, and expert networks to incorporate the latest state of the art knowledge. It intends to enable the exchange of best and worst practices as lessons from different societal groups intervening in the conflict.

To conclude, the transparent integration of several perspectives on the issues may reduce the degree of contestation. Knowledge management involves not only the collection of historical facts for "healing" purposes, but the systematic analysis of facts to enable early warning systems in order to prevent the collapse of agreements and future escalation of violence.

10.2.2 Sequential Agreements and Amendment Procedures – Flexibility of Agreements

Agreements are to a significant degree a static codification of a decision. It involves the drawing of a specific aggregation of conditions such as power structuring, which have determined hoe the decision are made. Agreements refer to boundaries and cuts, which have been made. Identity conflicts are, however, dynamic and in many cases agreements will be inevitably obsolete in a specific time period. This obsolete agreement will eventually collapse, because it fails to reflect the actual structural conditions and therefore loses legitimacy.

Agreements, which are intended to be resilient, must involve mechanisms of adaptability and flexibility. Not only are preparatory rounds needed before the start of the actual negotiation for a specific agreement, there is also the necessity to conduct post-negotiation activities, which would ensure the agreement will continuously reflect the changes of conditions. While major frameworks will no longer be subjects of re-negotiation, provisions on the implementation of the agreement should be regularly reviewed and should be reflected with additional amendments or protocols to the existing agreement. The post-negotiation phase may include amendment procedures in form of protocols. Similar to the Kyoto protocol of the United Nations Framework for Climate Change Convention, negotiating parties may meet regularly and discuss the changes, which have occurred and may undermine the agreement. If needed, amendments in form of protocols may be negotiated. Post-negotiations require knowledge to monitor, measure or verify, and estimate variables, which may be relevant to the agreement.

10.3 Structure-related Prescriptions

The characteristics of the multi-party, multi-level and muli-dimensional environment, which frame negotiations reflect potential stumbling blocks, should be addressed. The procedural rules of negotiations, the methods of consensus-building and the institutional design, which influences the flow of negotiation, contribute to the already complex dynamics of identity conflicts. The instrument of decision-building may become an impediment in the process. The first structural prescription refers to the building of a negotiation environment involving integrative bargaining. The second structural prescription refers to the establishment of more public spheres (Habermas 1989), which would complement the "negotiation space" established in the first track of negotiations.

10.3.1 Integrative Bargaining

Conflicting parties negotiating on a more "cooperative" level may realize joint problem-solving, which involves mutual respect on each other's legitimacy, needs and interests, is more effective than "subordinative" bargaining through which the conflicting parties seek to dominate and control the process to achieve their goals. Integrative bargaining requires a joint problem-solving approach, where the negotiating parties cooperate to solve a common problem. It is through integrative bargaining, where the parties cease to act as "conflicting parties" and are transformed to “problem-solving parties”, which look forward to a common problem as it affects both parties.

A negotiation environment, which is defined through integrative bargaining, requires a set of attitudes in order to promote cooperation. Filey (1975) suggests several key beliefs must be shared by the parties, if integrative decision-making is to occur:

1) A belief in which mutually acceptable solutions are available;
2) A belief in which such solutions are desirable;
3) A belief in which cooperative endeavor is better than competition;
4) A belief everyone is of equal value;
5) A belief the other’s views are legitimate statements of their positions;
6) A belief in differences of opinion are helpful;
7) A belief the other party could compete, but has chosen to cooperate.

The negotiations on Mindanao still lack an environment promoting integrative bargaining. Although the GRP and the MILF were successful in negotiating the dropping off of the claim for independence, the parties are still sometimes trapped in zero-sum issues such as the highly contested ancestral domains issue, which involve a possible redistribution of land in Mindanao. Some zero-sum issues are not yet re-framed and they could be accommodated in the negotiation process as this can be interpreted as the reason for the collapse of the Memorandum of Agreement on Ancestral Domains (MOA-AD). Zero-sum issues involve solutions, which cannot be mutually accepted. Furthermore, not all factions of the MILF are convinced dropping the claim for a separate state is desirable. However, as Mohaqer Iqbal reiterates in an interview by Felongco (2010), the MILF seems to have realized the difference between independence and self-determination.

While independence is a non-negotiable zero-sum issue, for the GRP, the right for self-determination refers to a non-negotiable positive-sum issue, for the MILF. The principle of national sovereignty and the right for self-determination, which is framed as claim for independence, of the Muslim communities are not per se mutually exclusive. Framing such “non-negotiable” solutions as positive-sum promotes a cooperative environment and reduces competition at the negotiation table. In addition, framing problems as problems of all parties preconditions everyone at the table is of equal value. Having a common problem reiterates equality among parties. While parties may have different views on how a common problem may be solved, these views will not be interpreted as threats to the other party, because in a cooperative setting, it is not possible to harm the other without harming oneself.

10.3.2 Dealing with Constituency Gaps – The Role of Public Spheres

Constituency gaps refer to the situation, where representatives of a minority follow vested interests and are not conducive to peace and reconciliation. For example, the lack of political parties representing Muslim communities in the overall political framework of the Philippines reduces the influence of the moderate Muslim elite members, who are not members of either the MNLF or MILF. The Bangsamoro struggle is perceived as an armed struggle, which is reduced to the security domain, and fails to address sociopolitical dimensions are equally important to address, if a new social contract is to be achieved. However, the claim for recognition through pure armed struggle fails to confront social issues due to structural reasons such as how exchanges of concessions are to be made.

The armed struggle should be complemented and balanced by a socio-political struggle, which aims to forge a new social contract. The Muslim insurgency in the Philippines shows armed groups seeking self-determination. These groups, however, are agents of violence, who may have an interest to maintain the status quo in order further legitimize their existence. Without any perspective, which a peaceful situation will make them better-off, negotiating for peace will fail to emerge as one of "entrenchment" (Felongco 2010). The 1996 Final Peace Agreement between the GRP and the MNLF failed to address the employment of former MNLF combatants, who were not integrated in the Philippine military or police. Having this outcome in the minds, the MILF combatants will remain reluctant to believe in a negotiated outcome.

The peace process in the Philippines should acknowledge Muslim communities are represented by armed groups such as the MNLF and MILF. The more appropriate step is to find mechanisms to complement the armed struggle with a social struggle. The establishment of more public spheres is needed. A public sphere is a space or an area in social life, where people can meet freely to discuss and identify societal problems (Hauser 1998) concerning the members of this sphere. The Philippines require the establishment of several public spheres to bridge constituency gaps. Psychological and structural factors should be found, which will bind the parties to the negotiated settlement (Moore 1996, p.307). Expanding the public spheres to less politically controversial issues such as culture, science and the preservation of the environment would involve actors other than armed groups. This may lead to more social interactions, which would eventually come up with a new social contract, thus reducing pressure on the armed groups.

Such public spheres may include religious forums between Christians and Muslims, which would enable more communication between the two sides to eliminate stereotypes and prejudice. A public oral exchange of good intentions between groups and other symbolic gestures of friendships between bishops and *ulamas* would demonstrate trust between the groups. Although such public spheres should be independent during the first track negotiations, these should be prepared to assist the government and the armed groups in reaching a negotiated settlement. Issues concerning religion can be best addressed by religious groups and not by armed groups.

Another example of a public sphere involves a forum of scientists from all communities dealing with environmental problems concerning all communities in Mindanao. By identifying common threats, environmental scientists may play an important role in convincing policy-makers such problems are of common concern and should be dealt with by combined resources. Such a scientific public sphere enables more interaction between Christians and Muslims through cooperation in order to solve non-political problems, which equally confront all communities, and may expand the zones of possible agreement (ZOPAs) in general as a learning process unfolds.

Complementing the GRP-MILF talks with non-political public spheres offers a counter-strategy to constituency gaps, because these public spheres enable the forwarding of interests through other channels in case the armed groups fail to address imminent issues, which are of concern to the Muslim communities. In addition, the introduction of more public spheres increases the degree of social interactions between groups; thus providing experiences of cooperation. Furthermore, Public spheres reduce pressure on armed groups in forwarding issues, which can better addressed by non-political actors such as religion and environmental protection. No armed group should have the monopoly of ideas, issues, agendas and bargaining power at the peace process.

10.4 Process-related Prescription – Process Management

Process-related prescriptions need to address the stumbling blocks pertaining to the time-frame paradox as well as the difficulties arising from sectoral arrangements. With the uncertainties over the implications of agreements, no agreements or collapsed agreements, the strategic facilitation of the peace process through process management is recommended.

Process management involves the recursive development of conditions as the negotiation process unfolds. All negotiations move along a similar sequence of process stages from pre- to post-negotiation. Certain functions are repeated in all phases of negotiations such as the establishment of consensual knowledge (e.g. negotiation is the best instrument to resolve conflict) and the use of a problem-solving approach (e.g. cooperation and interdependence). Drawing from these recurrent patterns and features, entry points to design the process can be found.

The first step for strategic facilitation involves the specification of goal structures. Through the assistance of mediators and/or facilitators, conflicting parties may formulate their intentions. Furthermore the mediator should attempt to reframe these intentions in a way it can be related to the negotiations. It may involve direct intervention through mediators allowing conflicting parties to realize they have a common problem. The consensual knowledge on the goals is a critical element of the negotiation process. Once consensus on common goal is found, the process may move to the next stage. Goal-setting is therefore the formal point of departure of the negotiation process. For the GRP-MNLF negotiation process, the 1976 Tripoli Peace Agreement has identified the goals of the parties and has summarized the issues that are on the agenda.

Process management requires the capacity to generate considerable synergy effects through the framing of the interactions of the parties as constructive and integrative. Furthermore, it involves the backward and forward linking of several elements such as negotiation rounds and outputs. Round 1 is a prerequisite of round 2. Round 2 in turn involves the implementation of the agreement reached in round 1. This linking intends to identify the types of interdependence between elements, which enables the anticipation of both positive and negative effects. While the government negotiates with the MILF, religious leaders from both sides do have their own negotiation processes to cover the aspects of the conflict, which could not be addressed by the first track negotiations.

In addition, process management requires the establishment and maintenance of trust and confidence. Lewicki & Litterer (1985) outline several factors, which may contribute to the development of trust. The most important factors they mention are the perceptions of similarity and the perception cooperation will generate more pay-offs than competition. Trust and confidence are important factors in the negotiation process. However, trust is not self-evident. Therefore, distrust should not be connoted in a negative way. Distrust is the starting point of the negotiation process. Trust-building is a process of entrenchment.

10.5 Outcome-related Prescriptions

Outcome-related stumbling blocks emerge either immediately after agreements have been signed or when anticipated outcomes serve as cognitive anchors influencing behavior of negotiation actors before any agreement has been reached. After the ceremonial signing of an agreement following difficult negotiation rounds, stakeholders, including spoilers, who were not participating at the table, will assess the items included in the agreement and will interpret, what this agreement would mean for them. Spoilers may find the agreement useable to mobilize various societal forces. New coalitions may be forged to adapt to the anticipated shifts of power configurations. Furthermore, the negotiating parties would need time to communicate the agreement to their constituents and discuss about the practical implementation of the agreement.

The whole government bureaucracy has to take necessary actions such as the holding of a plebiscite, or convincing the legislative and judicial bodies to create new laws, or to modify existing laws. Hence, the post-agreement process involves other sets of difficulties. For example, peace agreements between the Philippine government and Moro rebel groups would require amendments of the Philippine constitution. However, with the still fresh memories of the abuse by former President Marcos of the constitution in order to consolidate his power, the public is highly sensitive and usually apathetic to any move to amend the constitution.

The first Charter Change attempt on the 1987 Constitution was proposed under President Ramos, which included a shift to a parliamentary system and the lifting of term limits of public officials. On September 21, 1997, the Catholic Church was able to mobilize an estimated half a million people in Rizal park (Mydans 1997) to protest against the charter change (Cha-Cha) initiatives of President Ramos. President Estrada was similarly unsuccessful in pushing a similar attempt to change the constitution. The Constitutional Correction for Development (CONCORD) of President Estrada failed after objections from opposition politicians, religious groups and left wing organizations (Sprague & Lopez 2000). Under President Arroyo, there were more solid attempts to change the 1987 constitution. After winning the 2004 elections, by virtue of Executive Order No. 453, she created the Consultative Commission (Martin 2004). After consultations, the Consultative Commission came up with proposals includeding: a shift to a unicameral parliamentary form of government; economic liberalization; further decentralization of national government and a transition to a parliamentary-federal government system (Lyall 2004). However, all attempts by President Arroyo and her political allies in the Philippine Congress failed on grounds she intended to hold on power beyond her term limit (Lopez et al. 2008).

The MNLF and MILF face their own problems in the implementation of the agreements they have signed with the government. While the MNLF has difficulties running a huge bureaucracy without prior expertise and experience, the MILF has difficulties in preventing fragmentation of its own ranks. Some "uncontrollable" elements of the MILF are held responsible for violent attacks on Christian communities, which undermine the efforts of MILF to implement signed agreements.

10.5.1 Expectation Management

Expectations may lead to the collapse of agreements. Expectations play a crucial role in assessing agreements, because they may lead to frustrations, when expectations are not fulfilled. Furthermore, too low of expectations may similarly generate frustration, because an agreement may confirm their concerns. Similarly, when low expectations were confronted with too high outcomes, the agreement may be as well rejected for the reason the time is deemed not yet ripe. In addition, an agreement reflects a specific moment of time. Conditions will usually change after the signing and parties may realize that the agreement is no longer useful.

The strategic facilitation of the peace process requires a mechanism for dealing with varying expectations. It should be understood expectations reflect the perceived needs of the parties. Expectations may be out of reality. Expectations may either be too high or too low. Parties may find themselves adjusting their efforts to meet the expectation of the other as opposed to, what was specifically agreed upon. In adjusting efforts, the direction of the process may change and this may lead to further confusion particularly on situation of rigid goal structures. Therefore, facilitators and negotiating parties should manage expectations and bring them to a reasonable level. The fulfillment and management of expectations is the responsibility of all parties. Expectation management involves a formal process to continuously capture, document, and clarify the content of expectations for negotiating parties and other stakeholders by providing objective information.

Expectations are legitimate concerns of parties. Expectations are reflections of motivations and intentions of parties and how they see the negotiation process relates to the realization of the goals they previously formulated. When expectations are too high or too low, the parties may not have been able to understand completely the situation due to a lack of information, which includes either a lack of access to or obsolete information.

When managing expectations, it is necessary to establish and structure clear goals. The facilitators should explain to the parties goals may be compromised in the course of negotiations and goals may be modified anytime. Expectations will accompany the negotiation process. Managing expectations preconditions transparency of the process to allow evaluation of information could lead to the modification of expectations. Furthermore, it requires constant communication between parties and other stakeholders. Therefore, the facilitators should establish communication lines between parties. In case of miscommunications or failure to communicate, the facilitators should propose procedures to re-establish communication. If the formal channel is in impasse, the facilitators may provide informal back-channels to initiate informal communication. In addition, managing expectation requires mutual access to information, which would be used in evaluating, what is and what is not working. Hence, expectation management requires a systematic documentation of information.

Prof. Abhoud Syed Lingga of the Institute of Bangsamoro Studies states after the signing of the 1996 Final Peace Agreement between the MNLF and the GRP, there was a prevailing high expectation peace will immediately reign in Mindanao (Guiam 2008). But the agreement failed to meet the high expectations of Muslim stakeholders, who believed this agreement will deliver peace. The frustration of the ineffectiveness of the 1996 agreement is the product of unmanaged expectations. This frustration is furthermore reflected in the negotiations between the GRP and MILF. Lingga adds the MILF-GRP peace talks should move several notches higher to enable a more comprehensive peace agreement (Guiam 2008) and to prevent another unsatisfactory agreement. This implies the current peace negotiations between the MILF and GRP are confronted with too low expectations and the issues negotiated may follow the same path of the 1996 Final Peace Agreement. Nevertheless, no agreement can be comprehensive enough to deal with the complex issues of identity conflicts. Such frustrations brought by too high, in this case the GRP-MNLF, or too low, in the case of the GRP-MILF, expectations can be prevented by regularly providing transparent assessments of the situations. Furthermore, measures for amending agreements should be possible, when an agreement fails to meet expectations.

10.5.2 Dealing with Insufficient Outcomes – Evaluation and Selection of Alternatives

No agreement can be comprehensive enough to include all complex aspects of identity conflicts. Emialiano Bolongaita, an academic scholar formerly affiliated with the Asian Institute of Management (AIM), recalls a conversation he had with Misuari soon after the signing of the 1996 Peace Agreement. Bolongaita realizes Misuari needed new navigational tools in the changed arena he has found himself in (Vitug & Gloria 2000, p.83). Technical aspects and political competence are required to relate the peace agreement to the whole peace process in Mindanao. These technical and political competences are aspects, which cannot be addressed by agreements. The agreement is not capable of adjusting the Bangsamoro struggle for self-determination from armed insurgency to self-government.

The agreement intends to generate solutions for problems. However, the signed agreement may be trapped in a static condition. The agreement may find it at one time obsolete and ineffective to resolve problems. Therefore, peace agreements should include mechanisms of evaluation and monitoring. With the use of knowledge management, facilitators and parties should regularly meet and identify new problems. Parties should be able to identify their changing needs and develop alternatives to meet those needs. A procedure may be introduced to add amendments or "protocols" to the current agreement, which will be subject to further negotiations in the post-negotiation stage. Such a procedure adds flexibility and adaptability to the agreement.

For instance, the 1996 Final Peace Agreement (FPA) should have included mechanisms of evaluating new problems. Without undermining the 1996 FPA, post-negotiation rounds may be initiated to discuss reasons for the ineffectiveness of this agreement. The absence of such mechanisms to allow post-negotiation rounds without questioning the credibility of the agreement creates more frustration among both parties. During the signing of the 1996 FPA, President Ramos articulated the end of the peace process in the Southern Philippines. According to him, the FPA "brings to a close almost 30 years of conflict, at the cost of more than 120,000 Filipino lives." He hailed the agreement as "a new era of peace and development in the Southern Philippines, and for the Philippines as a whole" (Mercado 2006). Nevertheless, 17 years after the signing of the agreement, peace still seems to be unreachable. Despite billions of pesos spent by multi-donor interventions and bilateral assistance for reconstruction and capacity-building, Mindanao remains the poorest region in the country.

Mercado (2006) enumerates the reasons for the failure of implementing the agreement. However, his enumeration fails to recognize there is a difference between implementation and the actual achievement of goals. Implementation does not guarantee poverty alleviation. He mentioned the failure of coordination between government offices, specifically with the Local Government Units (LGU) as the cause of the delays in implementation. The Southern Philippines Council for Peace and Development (SPCPD) and the Consultative Assembly (CA) were tasked to promote, coordinate and accelerate development initiatives. Yet, there was little coordination between or among government agencies, departments and instrumentalities including government-owned and controlled corporations (Mercado 2006, p.5).

This failure occurred, however, not because of structural deficiencies in the 1996 Final Peace Agreement, but rather because not all aspects of reality can be reflected in the agreement. Implementation requires a detailed concretization, which cannot be included in any agreement. The real problem in this case is the absence of mechanisms to re-evaluate agreements and to introduce amendments when necessary. Hence, mechanisms of verification, monitoring and evaluation are as important as agreements themselves.

10.6 Interim Conclusion – Bridging the Gaps

An alternative approach in resolving identity conflicts involves providing preparations for parties to enable them to cope with negotiation-related stumbling blocks. The long-term process outlook on negotiation introduces a criterion on how to assess strategies chosen to facilitate complexity. The convention approach of using goals as criterion for standards is argued as necessary but insufficient as quality indicator. The goal-approach limits the flexibility of the process. The goal may be based on consensual knowledge, which has become outdated and obsolete in the course of time due to changing conditions at the bargaining table. A goal-approach implies the goal is determined in the pre-negotiation stage. However, there is need to adapt to conditions. Hence, it is necessary to redefine goals. The goal-approach as standard criterion should be complemented by the capability of shifting frames, paradigms and mind-sets. The capability of facilitation measures in assisting parties to move out of their boxes and to break out from convention cognitive and normative constraints as an innovative approach in assessing measures intended to resolve identity conflicts.

Actor-related prescriptions involve the use of problem-solving mode, the management of professional cultures and group cohesion, capacity-building, dealing with spoilers by identifying structural weaknesses, and dealing with side-effects and hardliners by engagement. Issue-related prescriptions include the establishment of knowledge management, sequential agreements and amendment procedures ensuring the flexibility and resilience of agreements. Structure-related prescriptions include the use of integrative bargaining and the enhancement of public spheres to deal with constituency gaps. Process-related prescription involves the management of the process. Finally, outcome-related prescriptions refer to the management of expectations and measures to deal with insufficient outcomes.

References:

Austin, A., 2003. Early Warning and the Field. A Cargo Cult Science? In Berghof Research Centre for Constructive Conflict Management, ed. *Berghof Handbook for Conflict Transformation*. Berlin: Berghof Foundation.

Banlaoi, R., 2008. *The Abu Sayyaf Group and Terrorism in the Southern Philippines Seven Years After 9/11: Threat and Response*, Manila: Philippine Institute for Political Violence and Terrorism Research.

Bazerman, M.H. & Neale, M.A., 1992. *Negotiating Rationally*, New York: Free Press.

BBC, 2000. Philippine Hostages Head for Libya. *British Broadcasting Corporation*. Available at: http://news.bbc.co.uk/2/hi/asia-pacific/898190.stm [Accessed September 20, 2013].

Brahm, E., Burgess, G. & Burgess, H., 2004. Truth Commissions. In *Beyond Intractability*. Boulder, CO: Conflict Research Consortium, University of Colorado. Available at: http://www.beyondintractability.org/essay/truth_commissions/ [Accessed September 20, 2013].

Burnham, G., 2003. *In the Presence of My Enemies*, Wheaton, IL: Tyndale House Publishers, Inc.

Dacpano, F., 2010. UP Dean to Head Government Peace Panel. *Manila Times*. Available at: http://www.manilatimes.net/index.php/news/regions/21575-up-dean-to-head-government-peace-panel [Accessed September 20, 2013].

Felongco, G., 2010. Liberation Front hopes to finally settle the Moro question. *Gulf News*. Available at: http://gulfnews.com/news/world/philippines/liberation-front-hopes-to-finally-settle-the-moro-question-1.669681 [Accessed September 20, 2013].

Filey, A., 1975. *Interpersonal Conflict Resolution*, Glenview, IL: Scott Foresman.

Fisher, R. & Brown, S., 1989. *Getting Together: Building Relationships As We Negotiate*, New York: Penguin Books.

Fisher, R. & Ury, W., 1981. *Getting to yes: Negotiating agreement without giving in*, Boston: Houghton Mifflin.

Frake, C., 1998. Abu Sayaff: Displays of Violence and the Proliferation of Contested Identities among Philippine Muslims. *American Anthropologist*, 100(1), pp.41–54.

GMA News, 2010. MILF claims Abu Sayyaf got high-powered firearms. *GMA News Online*. Available at: http://www9.gmanews.tv/story/150723/milf-claims-abu-sayyaf-got-high-powered-firearms [Accessed September 20, 2013].

Gomez, J., 2009. Moro Rebel Talks Have Many Spoilers. *Philippine Daily Inquirer*. Available at: http://www.inquirer.net/specialfeatures/mindanaopeaceprocess/view.php?db=1&article=20090119-184 [Accessed September 20, 2013].

Guiam, R., 2008. GRP-MILF Peace Process at the Crossroads: Exploring Different Paths. *Policy Forum*, (Institute for Autonomy and Governance & Konrad-Adenauer-Stiftung). Available at: http://www.iag.org.ph/cgi-bin/publications/files/GRP%20-MILF%20Peace%20Process%20at%20the%20Crossroad.pdf [Accessed September 20, 2013].

Gupta, J., 2007. Legal Steps Outside the Climate Convention: Litigation as a Tool to Address Climate Change. *Review of European Community & International Environmental Law*, 16, pp.76–86.

Habermas, J., 1989. *The Structural Transformation of the Public Sphere: An Inquiry into a Category of Bourgeois Society*, Cambridge: Polity Press.

Hauser, G., 1998. Vernacular Dialogue and the Rhetoricality of Public Opinion. *Communication Monographs*, 65(2), pp.83–107.

Hayner, P., 1994. Fifteen Truth Commisions – 1974 to 1994: A Comparative Study. *Human Rights Quarterly*, 16(5), pp.597–665.

Hopmann, P.T., 1996. *The Negotiation Process and the Resolution of International Conflicts*, Columbia, SC: University of South Carolina Press.

Lewicki, R. & Litterer, J., 1985. *Negotiation*, Homewood, Ill.: RD Irwin.

Lopez, A. et al., 2008. Rage vs Arroyo, Charter Change, Makati protest draws 7,000 from left to right. *Philippine Daily Inquirer*. Available at: http://newsinfo.inquirer.net/inquirerheadlines/nation/view/20081213-177739/Rage-vs-Arroyo-Charter-change [Accessed September 21, 2013].

Lyall, K., 2004. Arroyo's Radical Solution. *The Australian*. Available at: www.aph.gov.au/library/pubs/rn/2004-05/05rn13.pdf [Accessed September 21, 2013].

Martin, S., 2004. Senate Not Too Upbeat on Cha-Cha. *Manila Times*. Available at: www.aph.gov.au/library/pubs/rn/2004-05/05rn13.pdf [Accessed September 21, 2013].

Mercado, E., 2006. GRP-MNLF Final Peace Agreement: 10 years later. *Minda News*.

Moore, C., 1996. *The Mediation Process. Practical Strategies for Resolving Conflict* Second Edition., San Francisco: Jossey-Bass Publishers.

Mwaura, C. & Schmeidl, S. eds., 2002. *Early Warning and Conflict Management in the Horn of Africa*, Asmara, Eritrea: The Red Sea Press.

Mydans, S., 1997. Manila Journal: People Power 2: A Sleeping Giant Is Awakened. *The New York Times*. Available at: http://www.nytimes.com/1997/09/20/world/manila-journal-people-power-2-a-sleeping-giant-is-awakened.html?sec=&spon=&pagewanted=all [Accessed September 23, 2013].

Niksch, L., 2002. *Abu Sayyaf: Target of Philippine-U.S. Anti-Terrorism Cooperation*, Washington D.C.: Federation of American Scientists. Available at: http://www.fas.org/irp/crs/RL31265.pdf [Accessed September 21, 2013].

Sjöstedt, G. ed., 2003. *Professional Cultures in International Negotiation: Bridge or Rift?*, Lanham, MD: Lexington Books.

Sjöstedt, G. & Penetrante, A.M. eds., 2013. *Climate Change Negotiations. A Guide to Resolving Disputes and Facilitating Multilateral Cooperation*, London and New York: Routledge.

Sprague, J. & Lopez, A., 2000. Act II for Estrada, The president strives to turn the page on his struggling administration,. *Asia Week*, 26(2). Available at: http://edition.cnn.com/ASIANOW/asiaweek/magazine/2000/0121/nat.phil.estrada.html [Accessed September 21, 2013].

Thompson, L. & Hastie, R., 1990. Social Perception in Negotiation. *Organizational Behavior and Human Decision Processes*, 47, pp.92–123.

Vitug, M. & Gloria, G., 2000. *Under the Crescent Moon : Rebellion in Mindanao*, Quezon City: Ateneo Center for Social Policy & Public Affairs : Institute for Popular Democracy.

Zartman, I.W., 1989. *Ripe for Resolution* 2nd ed., Oxford: Oxford University Press.

11 Conclusion – Lessons for Theory and for Action to Resolve Identity Conflicts

Mediation is the intervention of choice to resolve the intractable identity conflict in the Southern Philippines. The resolution of this 40-year old conflict was long overdue, when the earliest attempt in 1976, the Tripoli Agreement, was achieved. It was due in March 25, 1977, when President Ferdinand Edralin Marcos initiated the "Presidential Proclamation Nr. 1628", which formed the "Autonomous Region in Southern Philippines." It was due in 1986, when the regime of the dictator Ferdinand Edralin Marcos was toppled through a popular revolt. It was due in August 1, 1989, when President Corazon Cojuanco Aquino created the Autonomous Region of Muslim Mindanao (ARMM) by virtue of Republic Act No, 6734. It was due in September 2, 1996, when the government under President Fidel Valdez Ramos and the Moro National Liberation Front signed the Final Peace Agreement. It is due, when the 2012 Framework Agreement on the Bangsamoro was signed between the MILF and the Philippine government. However, history shows the contrary. For more than 40 years now, peace still seems to be unattainable. It seems the time will never be ripe for peace in the Philippines.

This book started with a clear conviction – to find the reasons, why a peaceful settlement is never enough. Why is it almost impossible to close mediated agreements to resolve the identity conflict once and for all? The Southern Philippines has been a witness of several negotiation rounds, which did not end with an agreement, of several peace agreements, which collapsed immediately after signing, of highly applauded peace agreements, which did not bring peace, reconciliation and development, of a conflict, which has resisted several non-coercive intervention efforts, and of a conflict, which has mutated in various forms so agreements reached may be both conducive and detrimental to peace, reconciliation and development.

The intellectual challenge posed by this book project involves the formulation of a set of ideas, which are not just abstract in terms of theoretical value, but more importantly, which are of immediate and practical value. Concrete prescriptions were formulated to deal with identified stumbling blocks. These stumbling blocks do not refer to concrete issues, which are not universal, hence not comparable, but they practically refer to the dilemmas and paradoxes found in the negotiation process, which impede any positive outcome of the process.

11.1 Lessons for Theory and for Action – Dealing with Complexity

It is the intention of this book project to draw from the Southern Philippines lessons for theory and lessons for action. This intention is motivated by the disposition, which dispute resolution procedures are needed to assist conflicting parties in meeting their needs, satisfying their interests, and empowering them to reach sustainable settlements, which promise to end violence. However, any chosen intervention measure such as mediation inevitably adds to the complexity of identity conflicts. Mediators may follow vested interests prolonging the conflict. Mediation may shift existing power configurations by bestowing legitimacy to one actor. Negotiation may divert the attention and resources of conflicting parties as they are entrapped in procedural issues. In various cases, negotiation itself has become its "ends"; therefore, distracting the parties away from the real underlying issues involved.

11.1.1 Conflict is an inevitable and omnipresent phenomenon in social life.

No matter how similar humans are, they will always find ways to distinguish themselves from the others. There will always be differences between humans and these differences determine membership to specific groups. Paradoxically, humans realize their similarities with some through the evaluation of their differences with the others. At one point, a person becomes a member of Group X, when he or she differentiates him or herself from those persons who become members of Group Y. Drawing lines are often coincidentally dictated by history or by the context. Nevertheless, the implication of the institutionalization of similarities and differences depends on the means, in which the participants are able to resolve their differences. Conflict may lead to increased productivity and structured cooperation. It may, however, lead to destruction of life and property. The implication of conflict depends on how the conflict is framed. If it is framed as an opportunity, it will lead to growth. If it is framed as a threat, it will lead to violence.

A significant challenge for theorists and policy-makers is how to deal with the negative connotation of conflict. A conflict is often linked with violence, threat, instability, and destruction. This book project defines conflict as a phenomenon, which "refers to the belief of actors on incompatibilities of goals (values, needs or interest) and behavior (actions to eliminate, defeat, or neutralize the other as expression of how incompatibilities are intended to be handled) within a social context." This definition leads to the assumption conflict does not automatically mean the outburst of violence. Conflict can be managed. Because conflict refers to beliefs and therefore perceptions, it can be argued conflict is merely constructed.

If it is constructed, then it can be constructed otherwise. The perception conflict can be managed enables a neutral conceptualization of conflict.

11.1.2 Violence is legitimized by a nationalistic term of reference of state-building.

Identity conflicts arise within the premise of the relations between groups and how these relations are addressed in the state-building process. The conceptualization of the practical meaning of misrecognition and how it is obviously and latently manifested in the relations between the society at large and minorities enabled the analysis of the link between violence and state-building. Violence is the implication of the nationalistic term of reference of state-building, where a hegemonic national group uses violence to maintain its hegemony. In the context of hegemonic nation-building, the nationalistic term of reference operates at every level of social interactions, which aggravates group relations. Identity does not anymore determine behavior. Identity becomes rather the product of these interactions. Nation-building legitimizes the use of violence to deter status quo altering elements within the state territory. The Southern Philippines provides an interesting example of how violence contributes to the development and maintenance of identity in a self-sustaining conflict cycle.

One of the main challenges for theorists and policy-makers is to find ways to re-frame the understanding of what a nation is. This book project introduced the concept of a non-competitive nation-building. This concept attempts to produce an understanding of nation-building, which intends to shift paradigm from the understanding of a nation as an identity based on primordial ties to the understanding of a nation as "an identity of solidarity." Referring to the nation as a community united by solidarity enables a more inclusive framing of nation-building. The understanding of what a nation means is constantly evolving and this evolution should be reified in state institutions. While it is impossible to eliminate a dominant national group in the state, it is possible for institutions to evolve independently from the hegemon through which biased political, normative and constitutional orders are alleviated. Furthermore, the separation of politics from economics, welfare and other spheres of social life ensures institutional pluralism, which at the end contains the bias of the hegemon.

11.1.3 Identity conflicts are about power and violence.

The identity conflict in the Philippines can be understood as the circumstance following the use of violence and opposition to the state violence through violence within the framework of eroding power and authority of the central government among the Muslim population. As Hannah Arendt (2009, p.55) says, "Violence comes, when power is lost." Identity conflicts are explainable in social context, through which a group assumed hegemony to establish normative orders at its own disposal. Through the equation of nation- and state-building, the hegemonic group expects political loyalty. Nevertheless, hegemonic domination is never sustainable. It is when specific members of the nation-state, who are marginalized and unable to participate as peers that identity labeling occur. The same categories, which the hegemonic group has used to legitimize marginalization, are used by the emerging nation to differentiate themselves from the society at large and to create a "new identity." With the lack of both international and state level channels to push for their claims, as well as the intensified use of violence by the hegemonic group to suppress any claim, which it sees to threaten the hegemonic stability, the emerging nation resorts to violence.

The main challenge for theorists and policy-makers in this regard is to find a way out of the cycle of violence. Mediation in the Philippines has failed to empower the conflicting parties to find an acceptable exit strategy. Violence has usually accompanied negotiated agreements. For instance, the 1996 Final Peace Agreement did not push for a genuine demilitarization of the MNLF. The integration of MNLF combatants into the Philippine Army and Philippine Police has just provided a new label for the combatants. On the contrary, the Final Peace Agreement paradoxically led to an increased militarization of Mindanao. For peace to return to Mindanao, there is a need to confront armed insurgents with demobilization and demilitarization. Surely, the MNLF and MILF will resist any measures to demilitarize their combatants for security reasons; however, there are strategies available to cover the security needs of insurgent groups, while demilitarizing. For instance, the weapon stocks of the MNLF and MILF can be deposited to the OIC, IMT or ICG. International peacekeeping forces can guarantee security for Moros. There can be a plan to gradually reduce the stockpiles of weapons of the rebel groups.

11.1.4 From Hawks to Doves – the Political Transformation of Armed Groups

A huge challenge for the insurgents is how to transform themselves from being combatants to political actors. Political transformation of armed groups should complement the peace process. Such a transformation involves several challenges. The MNLF leadership was overwhelmed with the complexity of running a bureaucracy, where rules and regulation such as auditing mechanisms and public biddings are needed to ensure transparency and accountability. Self-determination requires the autonomous government can actually sustain itself without the help of the central government. The ARMM derives almost all of its budget from the central government. The main priority of the ARMM government must be to find a way out of this dependence, if it wants a genuine self-determination. Rights come along with responsibilities.

The MNLF-run government of the ARMM is seen as corrupt and inefficient as the authority mechanism it followed. The proposed autonomous political entity named Bangsamoro, as envisaged by the Framework Agreement on Bangsamoro, which supersedes the Autonomous Region of Muslim Mindanao (ARMM) may suffer the same fate as its predecessors, when it fails to advance human well-being in Mindanao. Good governance is something, which cannot be codified fully in any peace agreement. Any future final agreement between the GRP and the MILF will be confronted with this difficulty. Any agreement will be vulnerable to attacks by spoilers, because it cannot fully address all relevant issues such as good governance. Furthermore, the MNLF should find ways to transform itself from a rebel group to an inclusive political party. While the MILF started with an armed struggle, the group should have by now engage itself with a political struggle. The ARMM is increasingly seen as a "failed project." However, the author of this book project argues it is better to start with the current ARMM than to start from scratch. Efforts should be initiated to revive the ARMM by introducing reforms ensuring its sustainability, effectiveness and resilience. The Philippine government and the ARMM officials should conduct series of formal consultations with experts on how to support the ARMM to be self-sufficient.

The resolution of the identity conflict in Mindanao calls for a new social contract. The representation of the Bangsamoro should not be exclusive for the agents of violence such as MNLF and MILF. One of the reasons for the protraction of the armed conflict is the absence of an effective alternative to the MNLF and MILF. The Bangsamoro should be represented as well by "non-violent" political actors. The rebel groups should realize it should open the ARMM government or the Bangsamoro, or any political entity to non-rebel group members. Furthermore it should not feel threatened by the emergence of "competing" political groups, who similar to them claim to represent the sentiments of the Bangsamoro. The ARMM government should be a government of the Bangsamoro and not of the any rebel group. The MNLF as well as the MILF should engage into partnerships with Muslim political groups, which could push for political institutional reforms by guaranteeing physical protection. The political transformation of the armed rebel groups is however impeded by the political landscape in the Philippines, where political parties are de facto non-existent. Hence, structural reforms are needed.

11.1.5 Confronting Angst of Changes

The Philippine public must realize the constitution constantly needs reforms. These reforms do not always mean a threat to the state. The constitution cannot codify everything at one time and should therefore be dynamic. The constitution is not written to satisfy a single moment, but needs to remain relevant in perpetuity (Bednar 2009, p.1). The constitution is the aggregate of the experiences of the state. It should be possible for the constitution to evolve to accommodate claims of minority groups. While it is understandable the Philippine public resists any measures to change the Philippine constitution, because of the Marcos experience, this conviction is not sustainable. The constitution must maintain flexibility, while enforcing rules. The public must understand any resolution of the conflict in the Southern Philippines needs revisions of the constitution. The Filipinos must learn to trust again in the political processes of the country. Not all proposed measures to change the constitution are moved by the intention to install another military regime in the country. Nevertheless, this anxiety of the Philippine public of any change must be addressed as well. This anxiety is indeed well grounded and is therefore legitimate. Hence, the peace process in the Southern Philippines must be complemented by a rejuvenation of the political culture in the country.

A major challenge for the Philippine public is to form a new political culture hospitable to social justice and trust. However, such a new political culture can neither be achieved through the revival of traditional indigenous values nor through the imitation of Western practices. The Philippines needs to learn from its own experience and actually implement reforms based on lessons from its experiences. It needs a culture of "healthy public debate", which could empower the citizens to step out of the skin of the existing culture and mind-sets. The Filipino public needs to de-securitize critical views. The public needs new perspectives, which can be too advanced for the times. The Philippines need to live out of the "*zeitgeist*", spirit of time, if it wants to have a society, which can overcome the past and move on to a common future.

11.1.6 Managing Conflict Management – Negotiating for Negotiation

Mediation as the other form of negotiation is the intervention of choice in identity conflicts. Mediation is a process of conflict management involving strategic facilitation of contestation through acceptable actors or structures transforming contestation to a legitimate phenomenon. Nevertheless, mediation inevitably contributes to the complexity of the whole peace process and therefore can actually contribute more problems, which need to be addressed. Intervening actors become part of the conflict. In some cases, intervention efforts are actually prolonging the conflict. Therefore, interventions such as third-party mediation should be carefully designed bearing in mind the risks and opportunities. Mediation should be transparent and be held accountable.

Mediation may prolong the conflict, when states conduct mediation. The case of the Philippines shows states pursue historical, political or ideological interests in intervening. Biased mediation is inevitable, when states are involved. Nevertheless, the Mindanao case confirmed bias mediators such as Libya and Malaysia can still manifest impartiality, when they have stakes in being impartial. For instance, the historical and cultural bias of Malaysia for the benefit of the Muslim population was balanced by Malaysia's political interest to adhere to international norms on national sovereignty and territorial integrity. In the end, although Malaysia has a long record of military and diplomatic assistance to the MNLF and MILF, Malaysia is still a state and it prefers to resolve the Philippine conflict without hurting itself.

The probably biggest challenge to theorists and policy-makers is how to prevent intervention itself from being part of the conflict. Intervention can be counterproductive, if the wrong formula is introduced. Mediation can be counterproductive, when mediators pursue vested interests. It may prolong the conflict, if intervention offers an opportunity for conflicting parties to negotiate for "side-effects". Therefore, intervention requires a more comprehensive understanding of the context. Furthermore, intervention comes in concerto. In some cases, intervening groups such as NGOs are competing for limited resources to actually assist conflicting parties. There may be an environment of rigid competition between intervening actors brought by the pressure to come up with a concrete outcome. Therefore, a mechanism of coordination of all interventions should be established, which will promote exchange of best practices and promote cooperation between intervening actors.

11.1.7 A Process Outlook in Assessing Outcomes

The success of mediation is not to be evaluated through the mere act of achieving an agreement. Mediation is to be evaluated by referring to its outputs (agreement or norm) and how these outputs relate to the whole peace process. Mediation (negotiation) rounds may produce an agreement, which is detrimental to the whole peace process. Negotiation rounds may end up without any agreement; however, consensual knowledge (norms) may have been reached, which enables future talks. The assessment of mediation should be conducted by analyzing the impact of its outputs on the peace process and relating these outputs to the desired outcome.

A major challenge for theorists and policy-makers in this regard refers to the ways a process outlook can be useable in formulating policies. The conflict in the Southern Philippines involves a high degree of complexity determining, which sets of decisions are viable. The horizontal and vertical inter-linkages of issues in identity conflicts impede a clear overview of the effects of policies. These inter-linkages may prevent seeing concrete results of specific policies. The search for the answers to these questions should be conducted through the analysis of the interdependencies of variables. This approach enables the structuring of complexity and uncertainty, which facilitates the decision-making process.

11.1.8 Moving Out of the Box through Mediation

Mediation is not only about reaching an agreement. It is about shifting paradigms. Mediation should aim to empower conflicting parties to move out of their skins. The mediators should assist conflicting parties to evaluate and, if needed, to re-frame their perceptions. For example, zero-sum issues can be re-framed as positive sums in order to facilitate the negotiation process. A major challenge for mediators and negotiating parties is to actually identify these paradigms, which are prolonging the conflict. Mediators may be themselves vindicating paradigms, which are counter-productive to the negotiation process. As the Mindanao case shows, state mediators are themselves entrapped in a paradigm of regulating the international system. The international system invokes bias against sub-state actors claiming independence. Malaysia is not prepared to undermine its own national sovereignty and territorial integrity by supporting the claim for independence of the MILF.

11.1.9 Rethinking Democracy

This study of the conflict in Mindanao initiated a discussion about rethinking democracy. The nature of democracy in the Philippines has significantly contributed to the intractability of the conflict. Democratization is often a context and source of conflict. As Bercovitch et al. (2009, p.672) argue, once attained, democracy should be both a procedure for handling conflict and a condition for reducing it. Nevertheless, the analysis of the conflict in the Philippines showed democracy alone is not a guarantee for the resolution of the conflict. Particularly, when democracy is based on majority ruling, democracy becomes an instrument of the majority group to follow its interest at the expense of minority groups.

An important challenge for theorists and policy-makers is to translate democracy in institutions, which hinder the notion of "winner-takes-it-all." Democracy in the Philippines fails to integrate minorities in the political system. Democracy consolidates structural imbalances; therefore, it aggravates identity conflicts. The political system in the country involves a huge burden on individuals in the context of highly personified politics. Politics become exclusive through, which family names are more important than skills and competence. The country is run by families (political clans) compensating for a lack of effective political parties, which indicate deliberations and public discourse related to socio-political cleavages. While it may be true, family members may have the experience to govern, when this recruitment system becomes exclusive, then it is time to rethink, whether this kind of democracy is actually obstructing peace and development.

11.2 Outlook for Further Research

The conflict in the Philippines has evolved in the last 40 years. As new dynamics have emerged, new actors came into the picture - private armies, international terrorist groups such as Al-Qaida, international mining corporations, with their own mercenary units, as well as Arab NGOs, which are perceived to contribute to the increased Islamist fundamentalism in Southern Philippines. With new actors, new issues such as terrorism, organized crime, and environmental deterioration. In addition, new political structures promise to influence the political processes in the Philippines – the increasing importance of the ASEAN and China as an emerging world power.

A particularly interesting research theme, which can be conducted in the future refers to comprehensive approach on analyzing the introduction of federalism in the country. While federalism may address claims for self-determination of several minority groups in the Philippines, it may also lead to more unaccountable power for local political warlords. Therefore, any attempt to introduce federalism must confront the problem of political warlords in local areas. Federalism may aggravate security problems of the country.

Furthermore, there is a need to introduce more "public spheres" in the Philippines to increase interactions between citizens of all ethno-linguistic groups. A future research may refer to the identification of existing public spheres in the country and to ask, why these are not enough to promote cooperation between different ethnic, religious and social groups. The next step is to introduce new public spheres, where Filipinos of all religions and ethnicity can exchange ideas and views.

References:

Arendt, H., 2009. *Macht und Gewalt*, München & Zürich: Piper Taschenbuch.

Bednar, J., 2009. *The Robust Federation: Principles of Design*, Cambridge: Cambridge University Press.

Bercovitch, J., Kremenyuk, V. & William, I.W. eds., 2009. *The SAGE Handbook of Conflict Resolution*, Los Angeles, London, New Delhi: SAGE Publications.

MIX
Papier aus verantwortungsvollen Quellen
Paper from responsible sources
FSC® C105338

FSC
www.fsc.org

If you have any concerns about our products,
you can contact us on
ProductSafety@springernature.com

In case Publisher is established outside the EU,
the EU authorized representative is:
Springer Nature Customer Service Center GmbH
Europaplatz 3, 69115 Heidelberg, Germany

Printed by Libri Plureos GmbH
in Hamburg, Germany